Business Maths
for bookkeeping and financial accounting courses

© Kaplan Financial Limited, 2008.

First edition in this series, 2017.

All rights reserved. No part of this publication may be reproduced, stored in a retrieval system, or transmitted, in any form or by any means, electronic, mechanical, photocopying, recording or otherwise, without the prior written permission of the publisher, or in accordance with the provisions of the Copyright, Designs and Patents Act 1988, or under the terms of any licence permitting limited copying issued by the Copyright Licensing Agency Limited, Barnard's Inn, 86 Fetter Lane, London, EC4A 1EN.

Published under licence by Osborne Books Limited
Unit 2
The Business Centre
Molly Millars Lane
Wokingham
Berkshire RG41 2QZ
Tel 01905 748071
Email books@osbornebooks.co.uk
Website www.osbornebooks.co.uk

Printed and bound in Great Britain.

British Library Cataloguing in Publication Data

A catalogue record for this book is available from the British Library

ISBN 978-1-911198-10-9

Acknowledgements

We are grateful to the Chartered Institute of Management Accountants, the Association of Chartered Certified Accountants and the Institute of Chartered Accountants in England and Wales for permission to reproduce past exam questions. Where answers are given to past exam questions they are the responsibility of the editorial team, not the examining board.

INTRODUCTION

Welcome to this Osborne Books edition of Business Maths which covers topics of relevance to courses and modules in bookkeeping and financial accounting. Throughout this book you will find plenty of relevant examples, activities, diagrams and charts. These will put Business Maths into context and help you to absorb the subject matter easily.

The following points explain some of the concepts we had in mind when developing the layout of this book:

DEFINITION

- **Definitions.** The book defines key words and concepts, placing them in the margin, with a clear heading, as on the left. The purpose of including these definitions is to focus your attention on the point being covered.

KEY POINT

- **Key points.** Also, in the margin, you will see key points at regular intervals. The purpose of these is to summarise concisely the key material being covered.

- **Activities.** The book involves you in the learning process with a series of activities designed to catch your attention and make you concentrate and respond. The feedback to activities is at the end of each chapter.

- **Self-test questions.** At the end of each chapter there is a series of self-test questions. The purpose of these is to help you revise some of the key elements of the chapter. All the answers to these questions can be found in the book.

- **End-of-chapter questions.** At the end of each chapter we include practice to test your understanding of what has been covered.

Osborne Books, February 2017

MATHEMATICAL TABLES AND FORMULAE

Logarithms

	0	1	2	3	4	5	6	7	8	9	1	2	3	4	5	6	7	8	9
10	0000	0043	0086	0128	0170						4	9	13	17	21	26	30	34	38
						0212	0253	0294	0334	0374	4	8	12	16	20	24	28	32	37
11	0414	0453	0492	0531	0569						4	8	12	15	19	23	27	31	35
						0607	0645	0682	0719	0755	4	7	11	15	19	22	26	30	33
12	0792	0828	0864	0899	0934	0969					3	7	11	14	18	21	25	28	32
							1004	1038	1072	1106	3	7	10	14	17	20	24	27	31
13	1139	1173	1206	1239	1271						3	7	10	13	16	20	23	26	30
						1303	1335	1367	1399	1430	3	7	10	12	16	19	22	25	29
14	1461	1492	1523	1553							3	6	9	12	15	18	21	24	28
					1584	1614	1644	1673	1703	1732	3	6	9	12	15	17	20	23	26
15	1761	1790	1818	1847	1875	1903					3	6	9	11	14	17	20	23	26
							1931	1959	1987	2014	3	5	8	11	14	16	19	22	25
16	2041	2068	2095	2122	2148						3	5	8	11	14	16	19	22	24
						2175	2201	2227	2253	2279	3	5	8	10	13	15	18	21	23
17	2304	2330	2355	2380	2405	2430					3	5	8	10	13	15	18	20	23
							2455	2480	2504	2529	2	5	7	10	12	15	17	19	22
18	2553	2577	2601	2625	2648						2	5	7	9	12	14	16	19	21
						2672	2695	2718	2742	2765	2	5	7	9	11	14	16	18	21
19	2788	2810	2833	2856	2878						2	4	7	9	11	13	16	18	20
						2900	2923	2945	2967	2989	2	4	6	8	11	13	15	17	19
20	3010	3032	3054	3075	3096	3118	3139	3160	3181	3201	2	4	6	8	11	13	15	17	19
21	3222	3243	3263	3284	3304	3324	3345	3365	3385	3404	2	4	6	8	10	12	14	16	18
22	3424	3444	3464	3483	3502	3522	3541	3560	3579	3598	2	4	6	8	10	12	14	15	17
23	3617	3636	3655	3674	3692	3711	3729	3747	3766	3784	2	4	6	7	9	11	13	15	17
24	3802	3820	3838	3856	3874	3892	3909	3927	3945	3962	2	4	5	7	9	11	12	14	16
25	3979	3997	4014	4031	4048	4065	4082	4099	4116	4133	2	3	5	7	9	10	12	14	15
26	4150	4166	4183	4200	4216	4232	4249	4265	4281	4298	2	3	5	7	8	10	11	13	15
27	4314	4330	4346	4362	4378	4393	4409	4425	4440	4456	2	3	5	6	8	9	11	13	14
28	4472	4487	4502	4518	4533	4548	4564	4579	4594	4609	2	3	5	6	8	9	11	12	14
29	4624	4639	4652	4669	4683	4698	4713	4728	4742	4757	1	3	4	6	7	9	10	12	13
30	4771	4786	4800	4814	4829	4843	4857	4871	4886	4900	1	3	4	6	7	9	10	11	13
31	4914	4928	4942	4955	4969	4983	4997	5011	5024	5038	1	3	4	6	7	8	10	11	12
32	5051	5065	5079	5092	5105	5119	5132	5145	5159	5172	1	3	4	5	7	8	9	11	12
33	5185	5198	5211	5224	5237	5250	5263	5276	5289	5302	1	3	4	5	6	8	9	10	12
34	5315	5328	5340	5353	5366	5378	5391	5403	5416	5428	1	3	4	5	6	8	9	10	11
35	5441	5453	5465	5478	5490	5502	5514	5527	5539	5551	1	2	4	5	6	7	9	10	11
36	5563	5575	5587	5599	5611	5623	5635	5647	5658	5670	1	2	4	5	6	7	8	10	11
37	5682	5694	5705	5717	5729	5740	5752	5763	5775	5786	1	2	3	5	6	7	8	9	10
38	5798	5809	5821	5932	5843	5855	5866	5877	5888	5899	1	2	3	5	6	7	8	9	10
39	5911	5922	5933	5944	5955	5966	5977	5988	5999	6010	1	2	3	4	5	7	8	9	10
40	6021	6031	6042	6053	6064	6075	6085	6096	6107	6117	1	2	3	4	5	6	8	9	10
41	6128	6138	6149	6160	6170	6180	6191	6201	6212	6222	1	2	3	4	5	6	7	8	9
42	6232	6243	6253	6263	6274	6284	6294	6304	6314	6325	1	2	3	4	5	6	7	8	9
43	6335	6345	6355	6365	6375	6385	6395	6405	6415	6425	1	2	3	4	5	6	7	8	9
44	6435	6444	6454	6464	6474	6484	6493	6503	6513	6522	1	2	3	4	5	6	7	8	9

CONTENTS

Mathematical tables and formulae

Chapters

1	The basics	
2	Percentages, ratios and proportions	25
3	Accuracy and rounding	35
4	Algebra, formulae, equations and graphs	41
5	Introduction to financial mathematics	71
6	Data collection	103
7	Presentation of data	115
8	Averages	131
9	Variation	145
10	Index numbers	159
11	Probability: basic rules	171
12	Expected value and decisions	193
13	Normal distribution	203
14	Correlation and regression	215
15	Time series	235
16	Spreadsheets	255
17	Answers to end of chapter questions	267

Index 299

Logarithms

	0	1	2	3	4	5	6	7	8	9	1	2	3	4	5	6	7	8	9
45	6532	6542	6551	6561	6571	6580	6590	9599	6609	6618	1	2	3	4	5	6	7	8	9
46	6628	6637	6646	6656	6665	6675	6684	6693	6702	6712	1	2	3	4	5	6	7	7	8
47	6721	6730	6739	6749	6758	6767	6776	6785	6794	6803	1	2	3	4	5	5	6	7	8
48	6812	6821	6830	6839	6848	6857	6866	6875	6884	6893	1	2	3	4	4	5	6	7	8
49	6902	6911	6920	6928	6937	6946	6955	6964	6972	6981	1	2	3	4	4	5	6	7	8
50	6990	6998	7007	7016	7024	7033	7042	7050	7059	7067	1	2	3	3	4	5	6	7	8
51	7076	7084	7093	7101	7110	7118	7126	7135	7143	7152	1	2	3	3	4	5	6	7	8
52	7160	7168	7177	7185	7193	7202	7210	7218	7226	7235	1	2	2	3	4	5	6	7	7
53	7243	7251	7259	7267	7275	7284	7292	7300	7308	7316	1	2	2	3	4	5	6	6	7
54	7324	7332	7340	7348	7356	7364	7372	7380	7388	7396	1	2	2	3	4	5	6	6	7
55	7404	7412	7419	7427	7435	7443	7451	7459	7466	7474	1	2	2	3	4	5	5	6	7
56	7482	7490	7497	7505	7513	7520	7528	7536	7543	7551	1	2	2	3	4	5	5	6	7
57	7559	7566	7574	7582	7589	7597	7604	7612	7619	7627	1	2	2	3	4	5	5	6	7
58	7634	7642	7649	7657	7664	7672	7679	7686	7694	7701	1	1	2	3	4	4	5	6	7
59	7709	7716	7723	7731	7738	7745	7752	7760	7767	7774	1	1	2	3	4	4	5	6	7
60	7782	7789	7796	7803	7810	7818	7825	7832	7839	7846	1	1	2	3	4	4	5	6	6
61	7853	7860	7868	7875	7882	7889	7896	7903	7910	7917	1	1	2	3	4	4	5	6	6
62	7924	7931	7938	7945	7952	7959	7966	7973	7980	7987	1	1	2	3	3	4	5	6	6
63	7993	8000	8007	8014	8021	8028	8035	8041	8048	8055	1	1	2	3	3	4	5	5	6
64	8062	8069	9075	8082	8089	8096	8102	8109	8116	8122	1	1	2	3	3	4	5	5	6
65	8129	8136	8142	8149	8156	8162	8169	8176	8182	8189	1	1	2	3	3	4	5	5	6
66	8195	8202	8209	8215	8222	8228	8235	8241	8248	8254	1	1	2	3	3	4	5	5	6
67	8261	8267	8274	8280	8287	8293	8299	8306	8312	8319	1	1	2	3	3	4	5	5	6
68	8325	8331	8338	8344	8351	8357	8363	8370	8376	8382	1	1	2	3	3	4	4	5	6
69	8388	8395	8401	8407	8414	8420	8426	8432	8439	8445	1	1	2	2	3	4	4	5	6
70	8451	8457	8463	8470	8476	8482	8488	8494	8500	8506	1	1	2	2	3	4	4	5	6
71	8513	8519	8525	8531	8537	8543	8549	8555	8561	8567	1	1	2	2	3	4	4	5	5
72	8573	8579	8585	8591	8597	8603	8609	8615	8621	8627	1	1	2	2	3	4	4	5	5
73	8633	8639	8645	8651	8657	8663	8669	8675	8681	8686	1	1	2	2	3	4	4	5	5
74	8692	8698	8704	8710	8716	8722	8727	8733	8739	8745	1	1	2	2	3	4	4	5	5
75	8751	8756	8762	8768	8774	8779	8785	8791	8797	8802	1	1	2	2	3	3	4	5	5
76	8808	8814	8820	8825	8831	8837	8842	8848	8854	8859	1	1	2	2	3	3	4	5	5
77	8865	8871	8876	8882	8887	8893	8899	8904	8910	8915	1	1	2	2	3	3	4	4	5
78	8921	8927	8932	8938	8943	8949	8954	8960	8965	8971	1	1	2	2	3	3	4	4	5
79	8976	8982	8987	8993	8998	9004	9009	9015	9020	9025	1	1	2	2	3	3	4	4	5
80	9031	9036	9042	9047	9053	9058	9063	9069	9074	9079	1	1	2	2	3	3	4	4	5
81	9085	9090	9096	9101	9106	9112	9117	9122	9128	9133	1	1	2	2	3	3	4	4	5
82	9138	9143	9149	9154	9159	9165	9170	9175	9180	9186	1	1	2	2	3	3	4	4	5
83	9191	9196	9201	9206	9212	9217	9222	9227	9232	9238	1	1	2	2	3	3	4	4	5
84	9243	9248	9253	9258	9263	9269	9274	9279	9284	9289	1	1	2	2	3	3	4	4	5
85	9294	9299	9304	9309	9315	9320	9325	9330	9335	9340	1	1	2	2	3	3	4	4	5
86	9345	9350	8355	9360	9365	9370	9375	9380	9385	9390	1	1	2	2	3	3	4	4	5
87	9395	9400	9405	9410	9415	9420	9425	9430	9435	9440	0	1	1	2	2	3	3	4	5
88	9445	9450	9455	9460	9465	9469	9474	9479	9484	9489	0	1	1	2	2	3	3	4	5
89	9494	9499	9504	9509	9513	9518	9523	9528	9533	9538	0	1	1	2	2	3	3	4	5
90	9542	9547	9552	9557	9562	9566	9571	9576	9581	9586	0	1	1	2	2	3	3	4	4
91	9590	9595	9600	9605	9609	9614	9619	9624	9628	9633	0	1	1	2	2	3	3	4	4
92	9638	9643	9647	9652	9657	9661	9666	9671	9675	9680	0	1	1	2	2	3	3	4	4
93	9685	9689	9594	9699	9703	9708	9713	9717	9722	9727	0	1	1	2	2	3	3	4	4
94	9731	9736	9741	9745	9750	9754	9759	9763	9768	9773	0	1	1	2	2	3	3	4	4
95	9777	9782	9786	9791	9795	9800	9805	9809	9814	9818	0	1	1	2	2	3	3	4	4
96	9823	9827	9832	9836	9841	9845	9850	9854	9859	9863	0	1	1	2	2	3	3	4	4
97	9868	9872	9877	9881	9886	9890	9894	9899	9903	9908	0	1	1	2	2	3	3	4	4
98	9911	9917	9921	9926	9930	9934	9939	9943	9948	9952	0	1	1	2	2	3	3	4	4
99	9956	9961	9965	9969	9974	9978	9983	9987	9991	9996	0	1	1	2	2	3	3	3	4

Area under the normal curve

This table gives the area under the normal curve between the mean and a point Z standard deviations above the mean. The corresponding area for deviations below the mean can be found by symmetry.

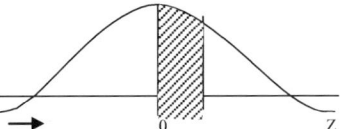

$Z = \dfrac{(x-\mu)}{\sigma}$	0.00	0.01	0.02	0.03	0.04	0.05	0.06	0.07	0.08	0.09
0.0	.0000	.0040	.0080	.0120	.0159	.0199	.0239	.0279	.0319	.0359
0.1	.0398	.0438	.0478	.0517	.0557	.0596	.0636	.0675	.0714	.0753
0.2	.0793	.0832	.0871	.0910	.0948	.0987	.1026	.1064	.1103	.1141
0.3	.1179	.1217	.1255	.1293	.1331	.1368	.1406	.1443	.1408	.1517
0.4	.1554	.1591	.1628	.1664	.1700	.1736	.1772	.1808	.1844	.1879
0.5	.1915	.1950	.1985	.2019	.2054	.2088	.2123	.2157	.2190	.2224
0.6	.2257	.2291	.2324	.2357	.2389	.2422	.2454	.2486	.2518	.2549
0.7	.2580	.2611	.2642	.2673	.2704	.2734	.2764	.2794	.2823	.2852
0.8	.2881	.2910	.2939	.2967	.2995	.3023	.3051	.3078	.3106	.3133
0.9	.3159	.3186	.3212	.3238	.3264	.3289	.3315	.3340	.3365	.3389
1.0	.3413	.3438	.3461	.3485	.3508	.3531	.3554	.3577	.3599	.3621
1.1	.3643	.3665	.3686	.3708	.3729	.3749	.3770	.3790	.3810	.3830
1.2	.3849	.3869	.3888	.3907	.3925	.3944	.3962	.3980	.3997	.4015
1.3	.4032	.4049	.4066	.4082	4099	.4115	.4131	.4147	.4162	.4177
1.4	.4192	.4207	.4222	.4236	.4251	.4265	.4279	.4292	.4306	.4319
1.5	.4332	.4345	.4357	.4370	.4382	.4394	.4406	.4418	.4430	.4441
1.6	.4452	.4463	.4474	.4485	.4495	.4505	.4515	.4525	.4535	.4545
1.7	.4554	.4564	.4573	.4582	.4591	.4599	.4608	.4616	.4625	.4633
1.8	.4641	.4649	.4656	.4664	.4671	.4678	.4686	.4693	.4699	.4706
1.9	.4713	.4719	.4726	.4732	.4738	.4744	.4750	.4756	.4762	.4767
2.0	.4772	.4778	.4783	.4788	.4793	.4798	.4803	.4808	.4812	.4817
2.1	.4821	.4826	.4830	.4834	.4838	.4842	.4846	.4850	.4854	.4857
2.2	.4861	.4865	.4868	.4871	.4875	.4878	.4881	.4884	.4887	.4890
2.3	.4893	.4896	.4898	.4901	.4904	.4906	.4909	.4911	.4913	.4916
2.4	.4918	.4920	.4922	.4925	.4927	.4929	.4931	.4932	.4934	.4936
2.5	.4938	.4940	.4941	.4943	.4945	.4946	.4948	.4949	.4951	.4952
2.6	.4953	.4955	.4956	.4957	.4959	.4960	.4961	.4962	4963	.4964
2.7	.4965	.4966	.4967	.4968	.4969	.4970	.4971	.4972	.4973	.4974
2.8	.4974	.4975	.4976	.4977	.4977	.4978	.4979	.4980	.4980	.4981
2.9	.4981	.4982	.4983	.4983	.4984	.4984	.4985	.4985	.4986	.4986
3.0	.49865	.4987	.4987	.4988	.4988	.4989	.4989	.4989	.4990	.4990
3.1	.49903	.4991	.4991	.4991	.4992	.4992	.4992	.4992	.4993	.4993
3.2	.49931	.4993	.4994	.4994	.4994	.4994	.4994	.4995	.4995	.4995
3.3	.49952	.4995	.4995	.4996	.4996	.4996	.4996	.4996	.4996	.4997
3.4	.49966	.4997	.4997	4997	.4997	.4997	.4997	.4997	.4997	.4998
3.5	.49977									

Present value table

Present value of £1 i.e. $(1+r)^{-n}$ where r = interest rate, n = number of periods until payment or receipt.

Periods (n)	1%	2%	3%	4%	5%	6%	7%	8%	9%	10%
1	.990	.980	.971	.962	.962	.943	.935	.926	.917	.909
2	.980	.961	.943	.925	.907	.890	.873	.857	.842	.826
3	.971	.942	.915	.889	.864	.840	.816	.794	.772	.751
4	.961	.924	.888	.855	.823	.792	.763	.735	.708	.683
5	.951	.906	.863	.822	.784	.747	.713	.681	.650	.621
6	.942	.888	.837	.790	.746	.705	.666	.630	.596	.564
7	.933	.871	.813	.760	.711	.665	.623	.583	.547	.513
8	.923	.853	.789	.731	.677	.627	.582	.540	.502	.467
9	.914	.837	.766	.703	.645	.592	.544	.500	.460	.424
10	.905	.820	.744	.676	.614	.558	.508	.463	.422	.386
11	.896	.804	.722	.650	.585	.527	.475	.429	.388	.350
12	.887	.788	.701	.625	.557	.497	.444	.397	.356	.319
13	.879	.773	.681	.601	.530	.469	.415	.368	.326	.290
14	.870	.758	.661	.577	.505	.442	.388	.340	.299	.263
15	.861	.743	.642	.555	.481	.417	.362	.315	.275	.239
16	.853	.728	.623	.534	.458	.394	.339	.292	.252	.218
17	.844	.714	.605	.513	.436	.371	.317	.270	.231	.198
18	.836	.700	.587	.494	.416	.350	.296	.250	.212	.180
19	.828	.686	.570	.475	.396	.331	.277	.232	.194	.164
20	.820	.673	.554	.456	.377	.312	.258	.215	.178	.149

Periods (n)	11%	12%	13%	14%	15%	16%	17%	18%	19%	20%
1	.901	.893	.885	.877	.870	.862	.855	.847	.840	.833
2	.812	.797	.783	.769	.756	.743	.731	.718	.706	.694
3	.731	.712	.693	.675	.658	.641	.624	.609	.593	.579
4	.659	.636	.613	.592	.572	.552	.534	.516	.499	.482
5	.593	.567	.543	.519	.497	.476	.456	.437	.419	.402
6	.535	.507	.480	.456	.432	.410	.390	.370	.352	.335
7	.482	.452	.425	.400	.376	.354	.333	.314	.296	.279
8	.434	.404	.376	.351	.327	.305	.285	.266	.249	.233
9	.391	.361	.333	.308	.284	.263	.243	.225	.209	.194
10	.352	.322	.295	.270	.247	.227	.208	.191	.176	.162
11	.317	.287	.261	.237	.215	.195	.178	.162	.148	.135
12	.286	.257	.231	.208	.187	.168	.152	.137	.124	.112
13	.258	.229	.204	.182	.163	.145	.130	.116	.104	.093
14	.232	.205	.181	.160	.141	.125	.111	.099	.088	.078
15	.209	.183	.160	.140	.123	.108	.095	.084	.074	.065
16	.188	.163	.141	.123	.107	.093	.081	.071	.062	.054
17	.170	.146	.125	.108	.093	.080	.069	.060	.052	.045
18	.153	.130	.111	.095	.081	.069	.059	.051	.044	.038
19	.138	.116	.098	.083	.070	.060	.051	.043	.037	.031
20	.124	.104	.087	.073	.061	.051	.043	.037	.031	.026

Cumulative present value of £1

This table shows the Present Value of £1 per annum, Receivable or Payable at the end of each year for n years $\frac{1-(1+r)^{-n}}{r}$.

Periods (n)	1%	2%	3%	4%	5%	6%	7%	8%	9%	10%
1	0.990	0.980	0.971	0.962	0.952	0.943	0.935	0.926	0.917	0.909
2	1.970	1.942	1.913	1.886	1.859	1.833	1.808	1.783	1.759	1.736
3	2.941	2.884	2.829	2.775	2.723	2.673	2.624	2.577	2.531	2.487
4	3.902	3.808	3.717	3.630	3.546	3.465	3.387	3.312	3.240	3.170
5	4.853	4.713	4.580	4.452	4.329	4.212	4.100	3.993	3.890	3.791
6	5.795	5.601	5.417	5.242	5.076	4.917	4.767	4.623	4.486	4.355
7	6.728	6.472	6.230	6.002	5.786	5.582	5.389	5.206	5.033	4.868
8	7.652	7.325	7.020	6.733	6.463	6.210	5.971	5.747	5.535	5.335
9	8.566	8.162	7.786	7.435	7.108	6.802	6.515	6.247	5.995	5.759
10	9.471	8.983	8.530	8.111	7.722	7.360	7.024	6.710	6.418	6.145
11	10.368	9.787	9.253	8.760	8.306	7.887	7.499	7.139	6.805	8.495
12	11.255	10.575	9.954	9.385	8.863	8.384	7.943	7.536	7.161	6.814
13	12.134	11.348	10.635	9.986	9.394	8.853	8.358	7.904	7.487	7.103
14	13.004	12.106	11.296	10.563	9.899	9.295	8.745	8.244	7.786	7.367
15	13.865	12.849	11.938	11.118	10.380	9.712	9.108	8.559	8.061	7.606
16	14.718	13.578	12.561	11.652	10.838	10.106	9.447	8.851	8.313	7.824
17	15.562	14.292	13.166	12.166	11.274	10.477	9.763	9.122	8.544	8.022
18	16.398	14.992	13.754	12.659	11.690	10.828	10.059	9.372	8.756	8.201
19	17.226	15.679	14.324	13.134	12.085	11.158	10.336	9.604	8.950	8.365
20	18.046	16.351	14.878	13.590	12.462	11.470	10.594	9.818	9.129	8.514

Periods (n)	11%	12%	13%	14%	15%	16%	17%	18%	19%	20%
1	0.901	0.893	0.885	0.877	0.870	0.862	0.855	0.847	0.840	0.833
2	1.713	1.690	1.668	1.647	1.626	1.605	1.585	1.566	1.547	1.528
3	2.444	2.402	2.361	2.322	2.283	2.246	2.210	2.174	2.140	2.106
4	3.102	3.037	2.974	2.914	2.855	2.798	2.743	2.690	2.639	2.589
5	3.696	3.605	3.517	3.433	3.352	3.274	3.199	3.127	3.058	2.991
6	4.231	4.111	3.998	3.889	3.784	3.685	3.589	3.498	3.410	3.326
7	4.712	4.564	4.423	4.288	4.160	4.039	3.922	3.812	3.706	3.605
8	5.146	4.968	4.799	4.639	4.487	4.344	4.207	4.078	3.954	3.837
9	5.537	5.328	5.132	4.946	4.772	4.607	4.451	4.303	4.163	4.031
10	5.889	5.650	5.426	5.216	5.019	4.833	4.659	4.494	4.339	4.192
11	6.207	5.938	5.687	5.453	5.234	5.029	4.836	4.656	4.486	4.327
12	6.492	6.194	5.918	5.660	5.421	5.197	4.968	4.793	4.611	4.439
13	6.750	6.424	6.122	5.842	5.583	5.342	5.118	4.910	4.715	4.533
14	6.982	6.628	6.302	6.002	5.724	5.468	5.229	5.008	4.802	4.611
15	7.191	6.811	6.462	6.142	5.847	5.575	5.324	5.092	4.876	4.675
16	7.379	6.974	6.604	6.265	5.954	5.668	5.405	5.162	4.938	4.730
17	7.549	7.120	6.729	6.373	6.047	5.749	5.475	5.222	4.990	4.775
18	7.702	7.250	6.840	6.467	6.128	5.818	5.534	5.273	5.033	4.812
19	7.839	7.366	6.938	6.550	6.198	5.877	5.584	5.316	5.070	4.843
20	7.963	7.469	7.025	6.623	6.259	5.929	5.628	5.353	5.101	4.870

Formulae

Probability

A∪B = A or B. A∩B = A and B (overlap)
P(B/A) = probability of B, given A.

Rules of Addition

If A and B are mutually exclusive: P(A∪B) = P(A) + P(B)
If A and B are **not** mutually exclusive: P(A∪B) = P(A) + P(B) − P(A∩B)

Rules of Multiplication

If A and B are *independent*: P(A∩B) = P(A)*P(B)
If A and B are **not** independent: P(A∩B) = P(A)*P(B/A)

E(X) = expected value = probability*payoff

Quadratic Equations

If $aX^2 + bX + c = 0$ is the general quadratic equation, then the two solutions (roots) are given by:

$$X = \frac{-b \pm \sqrt{b^2 - 4ac}}{2a}$$

Descriptive statistics

Arithmetic Mean

$$\bar{x} = \frac{\Sigma x}{n} \quad \text{or} \quad \bar{x} = \frac{\Sigma fx}{\Sigma f} \quad \text{(frequency distribution)}$$

Standard Deviation

$$SD = \sqrt{\frac{\Sigma(x - \bar{x})^2}{n}} \quad SD = \sqrt{\frac{\Sigma fx^2}{\Sigma f} - \bar{x}^2} \quad \text{(frequency distribution)}$$

Index numbers

Price relative = $100*P_1/P_0$ Quantity relative = $100*Q_1/Q_0$

Price: $\Sigma W*P_1/P_0 / \Sigma W * 100$, where W denotes weights

Quantity: $\Sigma W*Q_1/Q_0 / \Sigma W * 100$, where W denotes weights

Time series

Additive Model

Series = Trend + Seasonal + Random

Multiplicative Model

Series = Trend + Seasonal + Random

Linear regression and correlation

The linear regression equation of Y on X is given by:

$$Y = a + bX \text{ or } Y - \overline{Y} = b(X - \overline{X})$$

where

$$b = \frac{\text{Covariance}(XY)}{\text{Variance}(X)} = \frac{n\Sigma XY - (\Sigma X)(\Sigma Y)}{n\Sigma X^2 - (\Sigma X)^2}$$

and

$$a = \overline{Y} - b\overline{X}$$

Or solve

$$\Sigma Y = na + b\Sigma X$$
$$\Sigma XY = a\Sigma X + b\Sigma X^2$$

Coefficient of correlation

$$r = \frac{\text{Covariance }(XY)}{\sqrt{\text{Var}(X).\text{Var}(Y)}} = \frac{n\Sigma XY - (\Sigma X)(\Sigma Y)}{\sqrt{\{n\Sigma X^2 - (\Sigma X)^2\}\{n\Sigma Y^2 - (\Sigma Y)^2\}}}$$

$$R(\text{rank}) = 1 - \frac{6\Sigma\Sigma^2}{n(n^2 - 1)}$$

Financial mathematics

Compound Interest (Values and Sums)

Future value of S, of a sum X, inverted for n periods, compounded at r% interest

$$S = X[1 + r]^n$$

Annuity

Present value of an annuity of £1 per annum receivable or payable for n years, commencing in one year, discounted at r% per annum:

$$PV = \frac{1}{r}\left[1 - \frac{1}{[1+r]^n}\right]$$

Perpetuity

Present value of £1 per annum, payable or receivable in perpetuity, commencing in one year, discounted at r% per annum.

$$PV = \frac{1}{r}$$

1

THE BASICS

Contents

1 Basic mathematics
2 Fractions
3 Powers and roots
4 Log tables
5 Using a scientific calculator

1 Basic mathematics

1.1 Introduction

The basic tools of mathematics are addition, subtraction, multiplication, and division.

- The **addition** of two or more numbers results in an answer which is termed the **sum.**
- When two numbers are **multiplied** together the result is termed the **product.**
- When one number is **divided** by another the result is termed the **quotient.**

We won't insult you by teaching you how to add up and so on – you will use a calculator for the majority of calculations anyway and there are tips on getting the best use out of your calculator at the end of this chapter.

1.2 Negative numbers

When a negative number is **added** to another number, the net effect is to subtract the negative number from the other number.

- $10 + (-4) = 10 - 4 = 6$
- $-10 + (-6) = -10 - 6 = -16$

When a negative number is **subtracted** from another number, the net effect is to add the negative number to the other number.

- $15 - (-10) = 15 + 10 = 25$
- $(-15) - (-10) = -15 + 10 = -5$

When **two negative numbers are multiplied or divided**, the result is a **positive** number.

- $(-2) \times (-3) = +6$
- $(-12) \div (-4) = +3$

If there is **only one** negative number in a multiplication or division, the result is **negative**.

- $(-2) \times 3 = -6$
- $3 \times (-2) = -6$
- $15 \div (-3) = -5$
- $(-25) \div 5 = -5$

> **KEY POINT**
>
> For multiplication or division: two negatives make a positive; one negative makes a negative.

1.3 Table of operators and symbols

Here, for ready reference purposes, is a table of all the main symbols and operators used in this book. Some you don't need to be told, e.g. +, of course. Others, such as < often cause confusion amongst students. Still others, such as Σ, may be quite unfamiliar as yet, but don't worry, we'll introduce you to any you might need in the proper place.

+	Plus
−	Minus
±	Plus *or* minus (e.g. 'the answer is 18 ±2' is a shorthand way of saying 'the answer is between 16 and 20')
×	Multiply
*	Multiply (used, for example, in spreadsheet formulae)
÷	Divide
/	Divide (also used in spreadsheet formulae)
Σ	Sum of
=	Equals
≡	Exactly equals
≠	Does not equal
≈	Approximately equals
<	Less than (e.g. 2 < 3; if you can't remember which way round these go, just think that < looks like the L in 'Less than')
>	Greater than (e.g. 3 > 2)
≤	Less than or equal to
≥	Equal to or greater than
x^y	x to the power of y
x ^ y	x to the power of y (e.g. in a spreadsheet formula)
√	Square root
^{3}√	Cube root

1.4 Order of operations (BEDMAS)

When numbers are simply added together or multiplied together it does not matter what order you do things in. For instance 3 + 4 is the same as 4 + 3 (the answer is 7 in either case), and likewise both 3 × 4 and 4 × 3 give the answer 12.

When numbers are subtracted or divided, however, the order does matter. 4 − 3 gives 1, but 3 − 4 gives −1. And 3 ÷ 4 gives 0.75 while 4 ÷ 3 gives 1.33.

This possibly seems so obvious as to be not worth saying, but it is all too easy to forget to apply these fundamental rules when dealing with complicated algebraic formulae.

When there is a mixture of operations, for example 4 + 6 × 2 or 4 + 6 ÷ 2, the rule is that **multiplication and division** are done before addition and subtraction.

4 + 6 × 2 = 4 + 12 = 16 (NOT 10 × 2, which gives a different answer)

4 + 6 ÷ 2 = 4 + 3 = 7 (NOT 10 ÷ 2, which gives a different answer)

If you have both multiplication and division the operations are done from **left to right**.

6 ÷ 3 × 2 = 2 × 2 = 4 (NOT 6 ÷ 6, which gives a different answer)

When there is a **power or a root** (known as an 'exponent') involved, that calculation is done before multiplication, division, addition or subtraction.

8 ÷ 2^2 = 8 ÷ 4 = 2 (NOT 4^2, which gives a different answer)

> **KEY POINT**
>
> The order of operations can be remembered via the acronym BEDMAS. It is particularly important that you know how to multiply out brackets.

Brackets can be used however, to change the normal order of operations, because the numbers in the brackets must be evaluated **before anything else**.

$(4 + 6) \times 2 = 10 \times 2 = 20$

$6 \div (3 \times 2) = 6 \div 6 = 1$

$(8 \div 2)^2 = 4^2 = 16$

A useful mnemonic is **BEDMAS**.

Order of operations: BEDMAS	
1	**B**rackets
2	**E**xponents
3	**D**ivision and **M**ultiplication (left to right)
4	**A**ddition and **S**ubtraction (left to right)

1.5 Expanding brackets

If you want to get rid of brackets you can re-express a mathematical statement without them and follow the usual order of operations, but great care is needed.

- Numbers outside brackets multiply (or divide) **everything** within:

    $5(2 + 3 + 4) = 5 \times 2 + 5 \times 3 + 5 \times 4$

    $\dfrac{(2+3+4)}{5} = \dfrac{2}{5} + \dfrac{3}{5} + \dfrac{4}{5}$

- Signs outside brackets multiply (or divide) everything within:

    $-5(2 + 3 + 4) = (-5) \times 2 + (-5) \times 3 + (-5) \times 4$

- Each element within a bracket containing items linked by addition or subtraction signs multiplies each element in another such bracket, and then the elements are added together (but take great care with the signs).

    $(7 - 5) \times (2 + 3) = (7 \times 2) + (7 \times 3) + (-5 \times 2) + (-5 \times 3)$
    $= 14 + 21 + (-10) + (-15)$
    $= 10$

    Or $(7 - 5) \times (2 + 3) = (2 \times 7) + (2 \times -5) + (3 \times 7) + (3 \times -5)$
    $= 14 + (-10) + 21 + (-15)$
    $= 10$

    This may seem a very over-elaborate way of telling you that $2 \times 5 = 10$, but if you were faced with an algebraic expression such as $(a - b) \times (c + d)$ life would not be so straightforward, as we'll see in Chapter 4!

- The previous rule does not apply if the items within brackets are linked by multiplication or division signs.

    $(7 \times 5) \times (2 \times 3) = 7 \times 5 \times 2 \times 3 = 210$
    NOT $\neq (7 \times 2) + (7 \times 3) + (5 \times 2) + (5 \times 3) = 60$
    NOT $\neq (7 \times 2) \times (7 \times 3) \times (5 \times 2) \times (5 \times 3) = 44,100$

Activity 1

(a) What is -16×-11?

(b) What is $9 \div 3^3$?

(c) What is $(9 \times 3)^2$?

(d) What is $27 + 96 \times 4$?

(e) Expand and then solve $(6 + 8) \times (21 - 4)$.

(f) What does BEDMAS stand for?

Feedback to this activity is at the end of the chapter.

2 Fractions

2.1 Introduction

> **KEY POINT**
>
> It is essential to be able to understand simple fractions, so that you can manipulate equations and formulae properly.

If you think fractions are old hat you will be surprised how much you use them as you work through this book, especially when we reach the topic of probability in a later chapter.

It is also absolutely essential to understand fractions so that you can manipulate equations and formulae properly (see Chapter 4).

2.2 Terminology

In a fraction the number on the top is called the **numerator** and the number on the bottom is called the **denominator**.

$$\frac{\text{Numerator}}{\text{Denominato}}$$

You will mostly have to deal with fractions when they are part of an algebraic formula, but a few illustrations with very simple numbers (so that you can easily see that what we are saying is correct) may help to fix the rules in your mind.

2.3 Adding or subtracting fractions

If the fractions have the **same denominator** you can simply add (or subtract) the numerators.

$$\frac{1}{3} + \frac{1}{3} = \frac{1+1}{3} = \frac{2}{3}$$

If you need to add (or subtract) two fractions which have **different denominators** you need to find a common denominator, and the quickest way of doing this is to multiply the existing denominators together. Then, to find the new numerators multiply each fraction's existing numerator by the other fraction's denominator.

$$\frac{1}{4} + \frac{1}{2} = \frac{(1 \times 2) + (1 \times 4)}{(4 \times 2)} = \frac{2+4}{8} = \frac{6}{8}$$

2.4 Multiplying fractions

When multiplying fractions, numerators and denominators are dealt with separately:

$$\frac{1}{4} \times \frac{1}{2} = \frac{1 \times 1}{4 \times 2} = \frac{1}{8}$$

If you end up with the same number on the top and bottom of a fraction you can simplify the fraction by cancelling those numbers.

$$\frac{2}{4} \times \frac{1}{2} = \frac{2 \times 1}{4 \times 2} = \frac{1}{4}$$

(You can cancel because 2 divided by 2 = 1.)

2.5 Dividing fractions

When dividing fractions, **invert the one you are dividing by** (the 'divisor') and multiply them instead.

$$\frac{1}{2} \div \frac{1}{4} = \frac{1}{2} \times \frac{4}{1} = \frac{4}{2} = 2$$

2.6 Lowest common denominator

It is usually desirable to reduce fractions to their lowest common denominator because they are easier to understand and manipulate in that form.

For instance, if your calculations give you an answer of 147/1,617 it might be useful to know that this is the same as 1/11. The form 1/11 is more meaningful to most people, and one of your concerns in this text will be clear communication. It's also easier and quicker to tap 1/11 into your calculator without risk of error if you need to use the figure in subsequent calculations (it is **much** quicker and more accurate to tap in 1/11 than the decimal equivalent 0.0909090909 etc!).

You'll often recognise whether a fraction can be reduced and be able to do the maths in your head. For example 8/16 ≡ ½ and 63/81 ≡ 7/9. You're likely to spot these as being reducible because you learnt your multiplication tables (probably at least up to 12 × 12) at a very early age and that knowledge stays with you.

As for 147/1617:

- The denominator is clearly not exactly divisible by any even number, so don't test for those.

- If you add the digits 1 + 6 + 1 + 7 you get the answer 15 which is itself is divisible by 3; likewise 1 + 4 + 7 = 12 which is divisible by 3. The fraction can therefore be reduced to 49/539.

- The 49 may give you a further hint. To find out if a number is divisible by seven, take the last digit, double it, and subtract it from the rest of the number: for 539 this would give 53 – 18 = 35, which is divisible by 7. So 49/539 can be reduced to 7/77 (then obviously = 1/11).

- Alternatively, if you take 539 and add the first, third (etc) digits and subtract the sum of the second, fourth (etc) digits that's a more direct way of testing for divisibility by 11: (5 +9) – 3 = 11. (This trick also works directly with 1617: try it!)

You may not know tricks like this, of course. Failing simple recognition that a fraction can be reduced, there are various other methods of finding the lowest common denominator. Actually, however, you can reduce fractions at the touch of a button with a **scientific calculator** – we'll show you how at the end of this chapter. **Mental arithmetic** is quicker than fiddling with calculator buttons, of course, so we'll also give you some more hints and tricks that may help you improve your skills in that area.

Activity 2

(a) What is $\frac{7}{16} + \frac{5}{18}$?

(b) What is $\frac{7}{16} \times \frac{5}{18}$?

(c) What is $\frac{7/16}{5/18}$?

Feedback to this activity is at the end of the chapter.

3 Powers and roots

3.1 Introduction

When equal numbers are multiplied together the result is known as a **power** and is denoted by a superscript to the right of such a number, e.g.

$10^2 = 10 \times 10 = 100$ **(100 is the 'second power of' 10, or 10 to the power of two.)**

$10^3 = 10 \times 10 \times 10 = 1,000$ **(1,000 is the 'third power of' 10, or 10 to the power of three.)**

A number raised to the power of 2 is said to be **squared**, and if raised to the power of 3 is said to be **cubed**. These are the powers most commonly encountered in everyday life, of course, because they are relevant to the area and volume of the things around us.

However, a number can be raised to any power, and this is relevant to certain areas of accounting such as **financial mathematics** (as you will see later in this book). Therefore you need to learn some rules that will help you deal with powers.

In the examples below we have used the number ten because that makes it easy for you to see that what we are saying is correct, or to check it on your calculator using simple maths.

To make this even easier for you, note that when the number **ten** is expressed to a **power** the result is always **1 followed by a certain number of 0s**. The power tells us how many 0s to add, so $10^2 = 100$ (1 followed by two 0s), $10^3 = 1,000$ (1 followed by three 0s), and so on.

Terminology

A power (or root) is also called an **'exponent'**.

You may also come across the term 'index' (plural 'indices'), but that is not strictly correct and the word index has a more specific meaning which we will encounter in a later chapter.

3.2 Multiplying numbers expressed to powers [$(10^2 \times 10^3) = 10^{(2+3)}$]

When two or more powers of the same number are multiplied the individual exponents can be **added**.

For example: $10^2 \times 10^3 \quad = \quad (10 \times 10) \times (10 \times 10 \times 10) \quad = \quad 10^5$

But, more simply,

$$10^2 \times 10^3 \quad = \quad 10^{(2+3)} \quad = \quad 10^5$$

Note: For these rules to be correct (in both multiplication and division), both terms must have the **same base** – in this case 10.

For example $10^2 \times 2^3$ is **not** equal to $(10 \times 2)^{2+3}$ because the two bases, 10 and 2, are different.

KEY POINT

In general terms:

$a^m \times a^n = a^{(m+n)}$

3.3 Power of a product [$(10 \times 2)^2 = 10^2 \times 2^2$]

A product is the result of two numbers multiplied together. When taking a power of a product the exponent should be **applied to each factor** of the product.

For example: $(10 \times 2)^2 \quad = \quad (10 \times 2) \times (10 \times 2)$
$= \quad 10 \times 10 \times 2 \times 2$
$= \quad 10^2 \times 2^2$

KEY POINT

In general terms:

$(3ab)^m = 3^m a^m b^m$

3.4 Power of a quotient [$(10 \div 2)^2 = 10^2 \div 2^2$]

A quotient is the result of one number divided by another. When taking a power of a quotient the exponent should be **applied to both the numerator and the denominator**.

For example: $\left(\dfrac{10}{2}\right)^2 \quad = \quad (10 \div 2) \times (10 \div 2)$
$= \quad (10 \times 10) \div (2 \times 2)$
$= \quad 10^2 \div 2^2$

3.5 Power of a power [$(10^2)^3 = 10^{(2 \times 3)}$]

When a power is raised to a power the powers are **multiplied**.

For example: $(10^2)^3 = (10 \times 10) \times (10 \times 10) \times (10 \times 10) = 10^6$

Therefore $(10^2)^3 = 10^{(2 \times 3)} = 10^6$.

KEY POINT

In general terms:

$(a^m)^n = a^{m \times n}$

3.6 Division of powers [$(10^5 \div 10^2) = 10^{5-2}$]

When dividing a power of a number by another power of the same number the exponents are **subtracted**.

For example: $10^5 \div 10^2$ can be written out as a fraction and some of the 10s can be cancelled.

$$\dfrac{\cancel{10} \times \cancel{10} \times 10 \times 10 \times 10}{\cancel{10} \times \cancel{10}} = 10^3$$

But more simply:

$10^5 \div 10^2 \quad = \quad 10^{(5-2)} \quad = \quad 10^3$

KEY POINT

In general terms:

$a^m \div a^n = a^{(m-n)}$

3.7 Zero exponent ($10^0 = 1$)

> **KEY POINT**
>
> Any number to the power zero equals 1.

Any number to the power of 0 is **equal to 1**.

For example, we have proved that when dividing a power of a number by another power of the same number the exponents can be subtracted.

It follows that, for example, $10^3 \div 10^3 = 10^{(3-3)} = 10^0$.

But any number divided by itself is equal to 1 so $10^3 \div 10^3$ must $= 1$.

Therefore $10^0 = 1$.

3.8 Power of one ($10^1 = 10$)

Any number expressed to the power of one is equal to that number **not expressed to any power** – in other words itself only.

$10^3 \div 10^2 = 10^{(3-2)} = 10^1$

$10^3 \div 10^2 = 1{,}000/100 = 10$

Therefore $10^1 = 10$

3.9 Reciprocal exponents ($10^{1/2} = \sqrt{10}$)

The 'reciprocal' of a number is 1 divided by that number. For instance the reciprocal of 2 is ½.

> **KEY POINT**
>
> In general terms
> $a^{1/n} = \sqrt[n]{a}$

When a number is expressed to a reciprocal exponent that is the same as expressing the number to a root (indicated by the denominator of the power).

$$10^{1/2} = \sqrt{10}$$

because $10^{1/2} \times 10^{1/2} = 10^1$, hence $10^{1/2}$ is that quantity which when squared, gives 10, so by definition it is the **square root** of 10.

Likewise $10^{1/3} = \sqrt[3]{10}$ (the cube root) and so on for any other reciprocal.

3.10 Fractional exponents $\left[10^{2/3} = \sqrt[3]{10^2}\right]$

When a number is expressed to a fractional exponent, that is the same as expressing the number, to the power of the numerator, to the root indicated by the denominator. This is easier to understand in maths notation than in words:

For example $10^{2/3} = \sqrt[3]{10^2}$

This is actually just a further application of the previous rule if you think about it (because $10^{1/3} = \sqrt[3]{10^1}$).

3.11 Negative exponents [$10^{-2} = 1/10^2$]

> **KEY POINT**
>
> In general terms
> $a^{-n} = \dfrac{1}{a^n}$

A number expressed to a negative exponent is equal to one over that number to a positive exponent.

Consider $10^5 \div 10^7$

If we write this out in full and then simplify the fraction by cancelling where possible the result is as follows.

$$\frac{\cancel{10} \times \cancel{10} \times \cancel{10} \times \cancel{10} \times \cancel{10}}{\cancel{10} \times \cancel{10} \times \cancel{10} \times \cancel{10} \times \cancel{10} \times 10 \times 10} = \frac{1}{10^2}$$

But we also know that $10^5 \div 10^7 = 10^{(5-7)} = 10^{-2}$

$\therefore \quad 10^{-2} \quad = \quad 1/10^2$

This is a useful one to remember when you are doing **financial maths** because many of the formulae you use have powers in the denominators of fractions. For instance, later you will be told about the formula:

$$PV = \frac{1}{r} \times \left[1 - \frac{1}{[1+r]^n}\right]$$

This could be rewritten in a way that is easier to tap into a calculator as:

$PV = 1/r \times [1 - (1 + r)^{-n}]$

3.12 Summary of powers and roots

You don't really need to learn the 'proofs' above, they are only given so that you accept these basic rules. The letters a and b are used to represent any number and the letters x and y are used to represent any power.

- $a^x \times a^y = a^{(x+y)}$
- $(a \times b)^x = a^x \times b^x$
- $\left(\dfrac{a}{b}\right)^x = \dfrac{a^x}{b^x}$
- $(a^x)^y = a^{(x \times y)}$
- $a^x \div a^y = a^{x-y}$
- $a^0 = 1$
- $a^1 = a$
- $a^{1/2} = \sqrt{a}$
- $a^{1/3} = \sqrt[3]{a}$
- $a^{x/y} = \sqrt[y]{a^x}$
- $a^{-x} = 1/a^x$

Example

Calculate the following values (*Note*: these can all be done with an ordinary (non-scientific) calculator.)

(a) $3^{1/2}$

(b) $2^{0.5}$

(c) $4^{1.5}$

(d) 10^{-3}

(e) $36^{-0.5}$

Solution

(a) $3^{1/2} = \sqrt{3} = 1.732$

(b) $2^{0.5} = 2^{1/2} = \sqrt{2} = 1.414$

(c) $4^{1.5} = 4^{1\frac{1}{2}} = 4^{3/2}$

$4^{3/2} = \sqrt{4^3} = \sqrt{64} = 8$

or $4^{3/2} = (\sqrt{4})^3 = 2^3 = 8$

(d) $10^{-3} = \dfrac{1}{10^3} = \dfrac{1}{1,000} \ (= 0.001)$

(e) $36^{-0.5} = \dfrac{1}{36^{0.5}} = \dfrac{1}{36^{1/2}} = \dfrac{1}{\sqrt{36}} = \dfrac{1}{6}$

Activity 3

Calculate the following values:

(a) $9^{1/2}$

(b) 10^2

(c) $81^{-1/2}$

(d) $25^{5/2}$

Feedback to this activity is at the end of the chapter.

3.13 Decimal exponents [e.g. $10^{0.3010}$] and logarithms

It is, of course, possible to express a number to a decimal exponent (really this is exactly the same as expressing it to a fractional exponent), such as $10^{0.5}$, $10^{0.333}$, $10^{25.42}$ and so on.

This means that **any number** can be expressed as **10 to a power**. For instance the number 2 can be expressed as $10^{0.3010}$ (approximately). When used in this way (with the number 10) the exponent 0.3010 is known as a **logarithm**. We can look up the logarithm of any number in log tables (which we will explain a little later – just accept it for now).

All of the rules described above still apply, of course, so if we wanted to **multiply** two numbers such as 2 × 3, one way of doing it would be to find out what those numbers are when expressed as 10 to a power, add the powers, and then convert back.

$2 \times 3 = 10^{0.3010} \times 10^{0.4771}$

From the very first rule we learned above we know that

$10^{0.3010} \times 10^{0.4771} = 10^{(0.3010 + 0.4771)} = 10^{0.7781} = 6$

Obviously it would be sheer lunacy to work out 2 × 3 in this way, but before the advent of pocket calculators this was the quickest and easiest way to do difficult multiplication or division problems such as 127,583 × 29,861,974 or 87.213 ÷ 49.862 and so on.

12 BUSINESS MATHS

Using logarithms for powers and roots

You can also use this powerful idea to work out the value, of numbers that are tedious or impossible to work out on an ordinary calculator such as 5^{12} or $\sqrt[6]{56,257}$.

$$5^{12} = (10^{0.6990})^{12} = 10^{(0.6990 \times 12)} = 10^{8.388} = 244,140,625$$

$$\sqrt[6]{56,257} = (10^{4.7502})^{1/6} = 10^{(4.7502/6)} = 10^{0.7917} = 6.19$$

We'll use this technique in Chapter 5 on financial maths, where it helps to solve an otherwise unsolvable equation.

Very small numbers and 10^{-x}

You may have noticed that when your calculator returns a result that is a very small number it shows you the result in a form such as:

5.214×10^{-3}

The number is really 0.005214, but the calculator is avoiding displaying the leading zeros. The notation $\times 10^{-x}$ tells you to **move the decimal place x places to the left** (three places in the above example). This will make sense if you remember that 10^{-3} (for example) actually means $1/10^3$, in other words 1/1000.

This will also happen if you calculate a very large number (e.g. it might be shown as 5.6×10^{11}, which means move the decimal place eleven places to the right).

4 Log tables

4.1 Why bother?

If you have ever learnt about logarithms before there is a good chance that you think that using log tables is just a very tedious and old-fashioned way of doing calculations that can now be done in the blink of an eye with a calculator.

Frankly, that is pretty much true.

However, there are certain circumstances in management accounting where you still need to use logs – either because a log is **part of a formula** or because logs are needed to **solve an equation**. Because of this you should have a basic understanding of the format of logarithms, and this can best be explained by referring to log tables.

If you have a log button on your **calculator** that is fine – in fact we recommend it. We'll cover the use of calculators for this and other purposes in the last part of the chapter.

You will still need to know what the figure given to you by your calculator represents though, so please don't skip this section.

4.2 Use of log tables

(a) **Logs of numbers greater than 1, less than 10**

The log will be in the range 0 to 1.

Example

For example, suppose we want to find the log of 3.1623

Step 1

Here's an extract from the log tables, to save you flicking back and forth in the book.

	0	1	2	3	4	5	6	7	8	9	1	2	3	4	5	6	7	8	9
30	4771	4786	4800	4814	4829	4843	4857	4871	4886	4900	1	3	4	6	7	9	10	11	13
31	4914	4928	4942	4955	4969	4983	4997	5011	5024	5038	1	3	4	6	7	8	10	11	12
32	5051	5065	5079	5092	5105	5119	5132	5145	5159	5172	1	3	4	5	7	8	9	11	12
33	5185	5198	5211	5224	5237	5250	5263	5276	5289	5302	1	3	4	5	6	8	9	10	12
34	5315	5328	5340	5353	5366	5378	5391	5403	5416	5428	1	3	4	5	6	8	9	10	11
35	5441	5453	5465	5478	5490	5502	5514	5527	5539	5551	1	2	4	5	6	7	9	10	11

We are looking for log 3.1623. Take the first two digits (31) and read down the *far left hand* column to 31.

The figure in the column headed 0 in this line is 4914.

So log 3.1 is 0.4914

Step 2

Read across to the column headed 6: you will find the figure 4997

So log 3.16 is 0.4997

Step 3

Keeping a finger on 4997 read across again to the small columns to the column headed 2. This reads 3. **Add** this to 4997, giving 5000.

So log 3.162 is 0.5000

This agrees with our understanding of logs, since the number 3.162 happens to be the square root of 10, i.e. $10^{0.5000}$.

Note: the log tables at the front of the book are only constructed to four significant figures. Therefore we can only find the log of 3.162, not 3.1623. The figure is rounded down. This is sufficiently accurate for most purposes and indeed in this case does give us the correct answer.

(b) **Log of any number**

A log consists of two parts: the decimal part, called the **mantissa**, and a whole number, called the **characteristic**.

The **mantissa** is obtained from the log tables, as explained above. Ignore the decimal point in a number and any leading zeros, just look up the first four digits. For example for either 56,253.0 or 56.253 or 0.0056253 you would look up 5625.

The **characteristic** depends on the size of the original number.

		Example
0	if the number is greater than 1 but less than 10	**Log 2 = 0.3010**
1	if the number is greater than 10 but less than 100	**Log 20 = 1.3010**
2	if the number is greater than 100 but less than 1,000	**Log 200 = 2.3010**

and so on.

This applies to numbers less than 1 as follows.

		Example
–1	if the number is greater than 0.1 but less than 1	**Log 0.2 = –1 + 0.3010**
–2	if the number is greater than 0.01 but less than 0.1	**Log 0.02 = –2 + 0.3010**

The mantissa is still positive, only the characteristic being negative. The minus sign is sometimes written over the characteristic, for instance $\bar{1}$ (said as 'bar 1').

However, for Log 0.2, say, **calculators** will produce the result –0.6990, which = – 1 + 0.3010.

Activity 4

Using the tables in the beginning of this Book, find the logarithms of the following numbers.

(a) 48
(b) 2.463
(c) 0.84
(d) 0.0047

Feedback to this activity is at the end of the chapter.

4.3 Converting from logarithms back to ordinary numbers

There are antilog tables that can be used to convert back from the log to the number it represents. You can convert back by using the log tables backwards. For instance if a calculation gives you the answer (in logarithmic form) of 0.3564 find the nearest number to the mantissa (3564) in the body of the table. This is 3560 in the row for 22 and the column for 7. Then find the nearest number to 4 in the right-hand part of the table. This is in the 2 column. So the result is 2272.

The characteristic is 0 so the number must be in the range 1 to 10, i.e. it is 2.272

Activity 5

Using the tables at the front of this Book, find the antilogs of the following numbers.

(a) 2.6444
(b) 0.3395
(c) $-\bar{3}.8261$

Feedback to this activity is at the end of the chapter.

5 Using a scientific calculator

5.1 Introduction

You probably use a calculator every day in your job but if it is a calculator that does no more than add, subtract, multiply and divide it is **not** going to be adequate.

At the very least you will need a **scientific calculator** that can calculate 'unusual' powers (e.g. 5^{45}) and roots (e.g. $\sqrt[9]{256}$). A variety of other functions are highly desirable and if you learn to use them well it will make your studies easier.

The illustration below shows what we consider to be the minimum requirements in a calculator..

Study this carefully and look at the labels. Make sure you can find all the buttons mentioned on your own calculator, especially the SHIFT button and the button for powers and roots.

- The button labelled $a^{b/c}$ has nothing to do with powers and roots. You can press this to turn a decimal answer into a fraction. For example 0.75 is displayed as 3_4.
- The odd looking degrees button ° ' '' is useful when dealing with calculations involving **time**. For instance if you get an answer of 347 minutes you can divide by 60 (to get 5.783 hours) and then press this button to find that that means 5 hours and 47 minutes.

Your calculator may have differently labelled buttons or at least the buttons may be in a different position, so it is very important that you **read the instruction leaflet** that came with it.

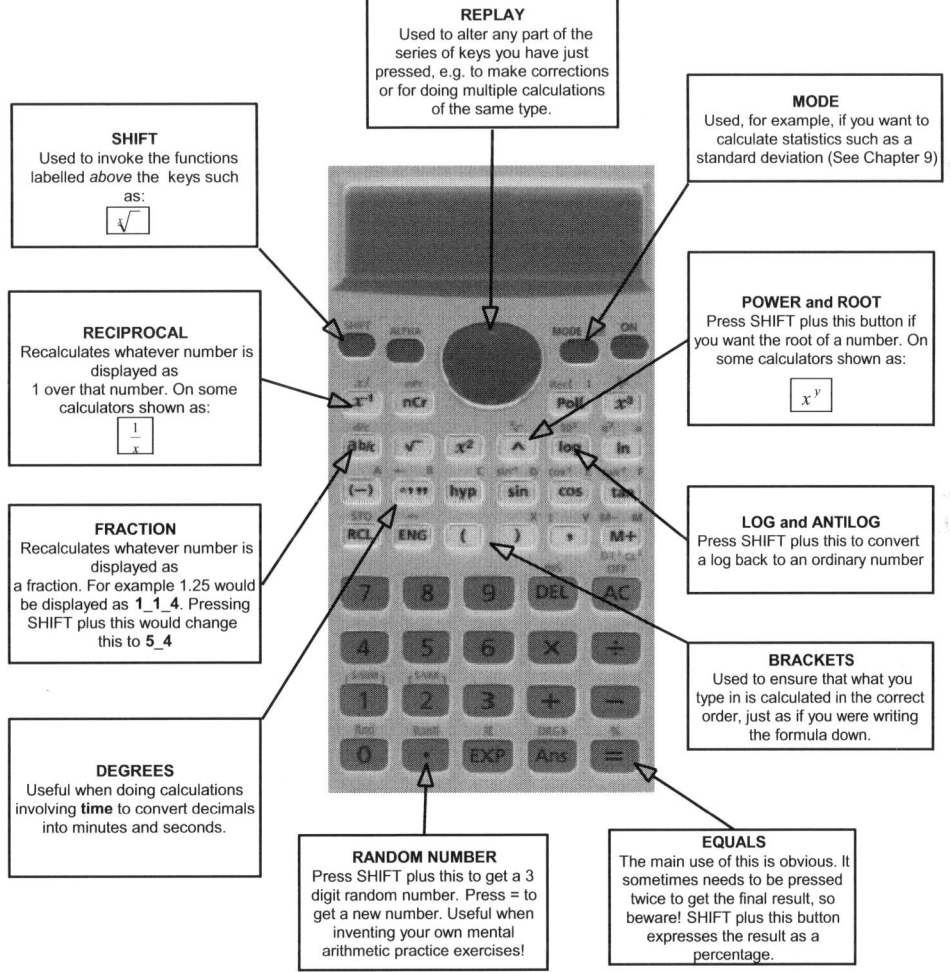

REPLAY
Used to alter any part of the series of keys you have just pressed, e.g. to make corrections or for doing multiple calculations of the same type.

MODE
Used, for example, if you want to calculate statistics such as a standard deviation (See Chapter 9)

SHIFT
Used to invoke the functions labelled *above* the keys such as:
$\sqrt[x]{}$

POWER and ROOT
Press SHIFT plus this button if you want the root of a number. On some calculators shown as:
x^y

RECIPROCAL
Recalculates whatever number is displayed as 1 over that number. On some calculators shown as:
$\frac{1}{x}$

LOG and ANTILOG
Press SHIFT plus this to convert a log back to an ordinary number

FRACTION
Recalculates whatever number is displayed as a fraction. For example 1.25 would be displayed as **1_1_4**. Pressing SHIFT plus this would change this to **5_4**

BRACKETS
Used to ensure that what you type in is calculated in the correct order, just as if you were writing the formula down.

DEGREES
Useful when doing calculations involving **time** to convert decimals into minutes and seconds.

RANDOM NUMBER
Press SHIFT plus this to get a 3 digit random number. Press = to get a new number. Useful when inventing your own mental arithmetic practice exercises!

EQUALS
The main use of this is obvious. It sometimes needs to be pressed twice to get the final result, so beware! SHIFT plus this button expresses the result as a percentage.

5.2 Upgrading your old scientific calculator

If you already have a scientific calculator, but it is more than a year or two old, then you are probably missing out. Modern scientific calculators have a number of **new features** that are **highly useful.**

If your calculator does not have some of the features illustrated above (especially the **replay** button) we strongly recommend that you invest in a new one.

- Modern calculators show not only the result of calculations but also the **interim figures and operators** you have entered. As a simple example, if you tap in 2 × 3 and press = you would see a display like this:

This is hugely helpful because it **allows you to double check** that you have entered the right figures.

- Modern calculators have a **'replay'** button which allows you to **alter anything** you enter (before or after you press =) and **correct any mistakes**. For instance, in the example above, if you had meant to enter 20 × 3.753 you can use the replay button to go back and put in a 0 after the 20 and add the extra numbers, without altering the other figures. That may not be a particular advantage in this simple example, but imagine you had tapped in '25,843,276 × 159,287 =' and only then realised that you should have tapped in '22,843,875' as the first number: the replay button would then save you a lot of retyping!

- You could also use replay to **alter the multiplication sign**, if that were an error and you meant to hit the plus sign, or perhaps to **insert** brackets, if you'd got the order of operations wrong.

- The replay is also a highly useful **time-saving device** if you have to **do similar calculations over and over** again, just changing one or two of the numbers each time: you can just edit the appropriate figures without changing any of the operators or constants involved.

- Modern calculators let you press the buttons in a **more logical and natural order**. For instance on an older scientific calculator to find $\sqrt[4]{81}$ (the fourth root of 81) you would type in 81 first, then the root button, then 4. In other words you have to think backwards! On a modern calculator you would type 4, then the root button, then 81, i.e. exactly as it is written. It is a small difference, but one that may save precious fractions of second if you are under time pressure.

We will mention calculator functions again at the appropriate places in this book, and by then we'll assume that you have successfully managed to get the correct answers to the next activity using your own calculator.

Activity 6

This activity will give you comprehensive practice at using your scientific calculator. The actual answers are less important than knowing how to get them with your calculator, so feel free to consult the feedback if you are not sure, then practise, hands on.

(a) Tap in the following key sequence exactly as written here

$2 + 4 \times 6\; \boxed{=}$

What answer do you get and what can you conclude about your calculator and the order of operations?

(b) Tap in the following (including the brackets) and make sure you get the answer 36.

$(2 + 4) \times 6$

(c) What is 3,432 ÷ 37,488 expressed as a fraction to the lowest common denominator?

(d) What is $5^{5.25}$?

(e) What is $\sqrt[9]{256}$?

(f) What is $1/0.1 \times [1 - (1 + 0.1)^{-5}]$?

(g) Using your calculator find the logarithms of the following numbers:

48
2.463
0.84
0.0047

(h) Why are some of the answers you found for (g) different from the answers you found from tables in Activity 4?

(i) Find the antilogs of:

2.6444
0.3395
−2.1739

(j) If a commuter spends 1 hour 17 minutes per day travelling, how long does he spend travelling in a working month of 23 days? Try to do this on your calculator without converting to decimals.

Feedback to this activity is at the end of the chapter.

5.3 Guidance on calculators

In most exams you will be required to show all your workings to numerical calculations. Examiners cannot award marks where your final answer is wrong if they can't see your workings and how you arrived at your answer.

Therefore tapping away for minutes at a time on a calculator without writing anything down except the final answer is an excellent way of **losing the credit** you might have got for knowing how to do a calculation, even if you accidentally tapped in the wrong figure at some stage!

Types of acceptable calculator

- Scientific calculator

  Scientific calculators will generally cover the requirements for most exams and are probably the best, as you can use them for powers and roots, logs, stats and regression modes. Several of these have programmable elements some of which exam boards accept.

- Programming functions

  Calculators with basic programming functions are now permitted and include:
  - standard memory functions and STO keys
  - formula memory calculators.

Unacceptable calculators

Invigilators will caution any candidate using models or equipment that contain:

- alphanumeric keyboards (an alphanumeric display of stored data – including text – equations or alphabetic formulae)
- personal organisers
- checklists and memo pads
- calculators that are capable of external programming (whether by detachable modules or the insertion of cards, tape, barcodes or cassettes, or any other means)
- calculators that feature graphical displays.

Summary

The order in which mathematical operations are performed is important in the solution of the more practical problems that you will encounter in later chapters, especially when dealing with formulae, so make sure that you learn the rules (BEDMAS) now.

If you don't learn the basics of dealing with fractions you will find the later material on algebra and equations very difficult to handle.

A good understanding of powers and roots is essential for financial mathematics..

Finally, get yourself a good scientific calculator and learn how to use it. Don't depend on it for very simple maths though – it will slow you down.

Self-test questions

1. What is a product? (1.1)
2. What do the following symbols mean: $\pm$, Σ, $<$? (1.3)
3. What is a denominator? (2.2)
4. How do you multiply two or more powers of the same number? (3.2)
5. What does any number to the power of zero equal? (3.7)
6. What is another way of writing $\sqrt{10}$? (3.9)
7. Show a^{-n} in the form of a fraction. (3.11)
8. How can a logarithm be converted back to an ordinary number? (4.3)

Practice questions

Question 1

The quantity 10^{-2} means:

A -100

B $-2/10$

C $1/100$

D $1/\sqrt{10}$

Question 2

There are two quantities, X and Y. X = –1 and Y = –2.

Therefore:

A $2X^2 > Y^2 < 0$

B $2X^2 < Y^2 < 0$

C $2X^2 < Y^2 > 0$

D $2X^2 > Y^2 > 0$

Question 3

The fraction X^{10}/X^5 equals:

A   2

B   5

C X^2

D X^5

Question 4

The expression $(x^3)^4$ equals:

A x^7

B x^{12}

C $7x$

D $x/7$

Question 5

The expression $\dfrac{(x^2)^3}{x^5}$ equals:

A   0

B   1

C x

D x^2

Question 6

The expression $\dfrac{x^5}{x^6}$ can also be expressed as:

A -1

B x^{-1}

C x

D $x^{5/6}$

Question 7

The numeric value of the expression $\dfrac{(x^3)^3}{x^7}$ when x = 5 is:

A   0
B   5
C   25
D   125

For the answers to these questions, see the 'Answers' section at the end of the book.

Feedback to activities

Activity 1

(a)   176

(b)   9 ÷ 27 = 1/3

(c) $27^2 = 729$

(d)   27 + 384 = 411

(e)   (6 × 21) + (6 × –4) + (8 × 21) + (8 × –4)
      = 126 – 24 + 168 – 32
      = 238

(f)   It indicates the order of operations: Brackets, Exponents, Division and Multiplication (left to right), Addition and Subtraction (left to right)

Activity 2

(a) $\dfrac{(7 \times 18) + (5 \times 16)}{16 \times 18} = \dfrac{126 + 80}{288} = \dfrac{206}{288} = \dfrac{103}{144}$

(b) $\dfrac{35}{288}$

(c) $\dfrac{7}{16} \times \dfrac{18}{5} = \dfrac{126}{80} = \dfrac{63}{40}$ or $1^{23/40}$

Activity 3

(a) $9^{½} = \sqrt{9} = 3$

(b) $10^2 = 10 \times 10 = 100$

(c) $81^{-½} = \dfrac{1}{\sqrt{81}} = \dfrac{1}{9}$

(d) $25^{5/2} = \sqrt{25^5} = 3{,}125$

22 BUSINESS MATHS

Activity 4

(a) 1.6812

(b) 0.3909 + 0.0005 = 0.3914

(c) $\bar{0}$.9243

(d) $\bar{3}$.6721

Activity 5

(a) 441

(b) 2.185

(c) 0.0067

Activity 6

We suggest you repeat any part of this activity you like, with numbers of your own choosing, as often as you need to know which buttons do what off by heart.

Our answer reflects the way the most up-to-date scientific calculators work: there may be slight differences in the way yours operates.

(a) You should get the answer 26 which confirms that your calculator understands the correct order of operations.

(b) The answer is in the question, but did you manage to get it on your calculator?

(c) Do the calculation as normal and press the = button to get an answer of around 0.091549295. Then simply press the $a^{b/c}$ button: this should give you the answer 13/142. To get the decimal answer back, just press the $a^{b/c}$ button again. You might like to experiment by dividing other simple numbers such as 4/3 and seeing the result. Try out SHIFT with this button too.

(d) Press 5 ^ 5.25 = to get the answer, which should be around 4,972.96. Practise this lots, using any examples of powers you can find in this chapter.

(e) Press 9 SHIFT ^ 256 = to get the answer, which should be around 1.8517. Again we advise you to practise using this button combination.

(f) Enter the keystrokes exactly as written in the question. For the negative power the buttons to press are ^ – 5 (there's no need to touch the reciprocal button). This should give 3.791.

(g) Just press log 48 (etc) to get the answers. Ours are rounded.

1.6812

0.3915

–0.0757

–2.3279

(h) The last two are different from the answers in Activity 4 because the calculator deals differently with the characteristic and the mantissa. Whereas the answer for 0.84 from tables is $\bar{1}$.9243, the calculator's answer is –1 + 0.9243 = -0.0757. Likewise for 0.0047 (–3 + 0.6721 = –2.3279).

This point was made in the body of the chapter, but you may have missed it. It is important that you are consistent – either use figures from log tables throughout a calculation, or use figures from your calculator throughout.

(i) Just press [SHIFT] [log] 2.644 (etc) to get the answers. Ours are rounded.

440.961

2.185

0.00670 (or you might see 6.7×10^{-3} on your display: it is the same thing)

(j) The buttons to press are as follows.

1 [° ' "] 17 [° ' "] × 23 =

This will give you an answer of 29°31°0, in other words 29 hours 31 minutes, 0 seconds. Try not to forget about this useful button: perhaps you could use it to work out how much overtime you'll be paid for each month!

2

PERCENTAGES, RATIOS AND PROPORTIONS

Contents

1   Percentages
2   Ratios
3   Proportions
4   The whole and the parts

1 Percentages

1.1 Percentages

DEFINITION

'Percent' means 'out of 100'.

'Percent' means 'out of 100'. The rule is: to convert a fraction into a percentage, multiply the fraction by 100; to convert a percentage into a fraction, divide by 100, e.g.:

$$40\% = \frac{40}{100}$$

$$= \frac{2}{5}$$

$$2\tfrac{1}{2}\% = \frac{2\tfrac{1}{2}}{100}$$

$$= \frac{1}{40}$$

We are well used to reading about percentages – wage increases may be, for example, restricted to 7%, in Britain VAT is levied at, for example, 17.5%. For example, to find the amount of VAT on £250, assuming a VAT rate of 17.5%.

$$17.5\% \text{ of } £250 = \frac{17.5}{100} \times £250 = £43.75$$

Percentages are usually very easy to deal with, and they are frequently used when handling business data.

The key thing in questions is to recognise **what represents 100%.** Any missing figures can then be worked out as **balancing figures**.

Example 1

Equipment is sold for £240 and makes a profit of 20% on cost. What is the cost price? What is the profit?

Solution 1

Whatever the percentage is **'on'** or **'of'** is 100%. In this case we are told that profit is 20% **on** cost.

If cost price	=	100%
and profit	=	20% (as we are told it is 20% of cost)
Selling price	=	120% of cost
120% of cost	=	£240
∴ 100% of cost	=	$\frac{£240}{120} \times 100$
Cost price	=	£200
∴ Profit	=	£240 – £200
	=	£40

The figure of 20% on cost is usually referred to as a 'mark-up'.

Example 2

Profit percentages are often expressed as a percentage of selling price.

If stock is bought for £210, what should the selling price be to achieve a profit of 30% of the selling price?

Solution 2

The clue in the question is the word **'of'**.

Selling price must	=	100%
because profit **of** the selling price	=	30%
Therefore cost	=	70%
70% of selling price	=	£210
∴ 100% of selling price	=	$\frac{£210}{70} \times 100$
Selling price	=	£300
(and profit	=	£300 − £210 = £90)

Example 3

A group of workers earn £120 per week. They want to negotiate an increase of £15 per week.

What percentage increase should they claim?

Solution 3

$$\frac{15}{120} \times 100\% = 12.5\%$$

A percentage increase (or decrease) uses the **original** figure as 100%. £15 is 12.5% of £120; it is not 12.5% of the new wage of £135.

Activity 1

A company buys a product from the manufacturer for £900. They feel that they need to make a profit of 35% on the selling price to cover overheads. At what price should the company sell the product?

Feedback to this activity is at the end of the chapter.

Example 4

A large machine costs £300 per hour to run. Non-productive time (for example when the machine is cooling or being reset) is typically 10%.

A batch of Product X takes exactly 2 hours of machine time to produce.

What is the cost of a batch of Product X in terms of machine time?

Solution 4

This needs a little care. It is tempting to say that the cost will be (2 × £300) × 110% = £660, but this is not quite correct.

For every 60 minutes that the machine is run, only 54 minutes (i.e. 60 × (100 − 10)% minutes) of output is obtained on average, due to cooling time, etc.

To get a full 60 minutes of output would take 60 **divided** by (100 - 10)% = 66.67 minutes. (You can check this: 66.67 × 0.90 = 60.)

Therefore, for 2 hours work the machine needs to run for 2 × 66.67 = 133.34 minutes.

Cost = £300/60 minutes × 133.34 = £666.70.

Example 5

This is another example like the previous one. The key point is that to get 100% of output you generally need **more than 100%** of input: if 5% of materials input are wasted, for instance, you need to input 100/95 = 105.2% to get 100%.

A shoe manufacturer is considering trying a new supplier for shoelaces. At present shoelaces bought in bulk cost £30 for 50, but the new supplier has offered them for £25 for 50. If the cheaper laces are used they are more likely to break while being threaded: early trials suggest that 5% of laces bought will have to be scrapped as compared with 3% at present.

If the company's output is 5,000 pairs of shoes per month what will be the financial effect of changing to the new supplier?

Solution 5

Don't forget that shoes come in pairs: 5,000 pairs will need 10,000 unbroken laces. We've also rounded up the number of laces needed, because a fraction of a lace is no good to anybody!

		£
Present inputs	10,000 ÷ 0.97 = 10,310 laces @ £30/50	6,186.00
Revised inputs	10,000 ÷ 0.95 = 10,527 laces @ £25/50	5,263.50
Savings		922.50

1.2 Discounts

> **KEY POINT**
>
> To get 100% of output you generally need more than 100% of input. For example if 5% of the materials that are input are wasted you need to input 100/95 = 105.2% to get 100%.

> **DEFINITION**
>
> A discount is a percentage or an amount deducted from the price, cost, etc.

A business may offer its customers benefits in the form of discounts; the bigger (financially) the customer to the business, the bigger the discount usually given.

The discount is normally deducted by calculating a fixed percentage of the total value of the goods, and then deducting this value from the original total. For example, a business offers its customer a 10% discount on all orders over £500.

Customer X orders goods to a value of £700. The discount is calculated as follows:

	£
Original order value	700
Less 10% discount (700 × 0.10)	70
Amount invoiced to customer	630

Example

Company Y offers its customers a 12% discount on all orders over £500 and 15% discount on orders over £1,000.

Customers A and B place orders for £1,010 and £620 respectively.

Calculate the value that company Y will invoice to both its customers.

Solution

Customer A:

Order value	1,010.00	
Less discount 15%	151.50	(1,010 × 0.15)
Value invoiced	858.50	

Customer B:

Order value	620.00	
Less discount 12%	74.40	(620 × 0.12)
Value invoiced	545.60	

2　Ratios

2.1　What is a ratio?

> **KEY POINT**
>
> A ratio shows how something should be divided up. The relative shares are usually (but not necessarily) expressed as whole numbers and they are separated by a colon, e.g. 2:5:7.

A ratio shows how something should be divided up or **shared**. The relative shares are usually (but not necessarily) expressed as whole numbers (integers) and they are separated by a colon.

For example, if you and your friend have a pizza delivered and it is cut into six slices, then an agreed ratio of 4:2, in your favour, indicates that you should get four slices and your friend should only get two slices.

In the interests of clear communication ratios can and should be **reduced** to the simplest numbers, in the same way as fractions are reduced. However, the **order** of items **does not matter**, so your pizza ratio of 4:2 could also be expressed as 1:2 (still in your favour). This would mean that for every one slice your friend eats, you eat two slices, and you carry on in this fashion until there are no more pizza slices left!

2.2　Dividing in a given ratio

> **KEY POINT**
>
> To divide a number into separate parts in a given ratio, the ratios are converted into fractions.

To divide a number into separate parts in a given ratio, the ratios must be **converted into fractions**.

To divide 275 into three parts in the ratio 2:4:5 proceed as follows.

- Add the three ratio numbers: 2 + 4 + 5 = 11.
- Express each as a fraction of the total: $\frac{2}{11}, \frac{4}{11}, \frac{5}{11}$
- Multiply the number you want to share out (275) by each fraction in turn.

The three parts are therefore:

(a) $\frac{2}{11} \times 275 = 50$

(b) $\frac{4}{11} \times 275 = 100$

(c) $\frac{5}{11} \times 275 = 125$

Thus 50, 100 and 125 are in the ratio 2:4:5 and add up to 275.

Example

Tom, Bill and Fred are in business together and one year make a profit of £39,000. They had previously agreed to share profits in the ratio 7:2:4 respectively. How much does each partner receive in money terms?

Solution

7 + 2 + 4 = 13

			£
Tom receives	$\frac{7}{13} \times 39{,}000$	=	21,000
Bill receives	$\frac{2}{13} \times 39{,}000$	=	6,000
Fred receives	$\frac{4}{13} \times 39{,}000$	=	12,000
			£39,000

How would it have been shared if the ratio was 4:3:3 respectively?

4 + 3 + 3 = 10

			£
Tom receives	$\frac{4}{10} \times 39{,}000$	=	15,600
Bill receives	$\frac{3}{10} \times 39{,}000$	=	11,700
Fred receives	$\frac{3}{10} \times 39{,}000$	=	11,700
			39,000

3 Proportions

3.1 What is a proportion?

DEFINITION

A proportion describes the relationship of some part of a whole to the **whole itself** and is usually given as a fraction.

In a class there are 20 girls and 10 boys. The ratio of girls to boys is 2:1, but the **proportion** of girls in the class is 20 out of 30, or 20/30, or (less usefully in this case) 2/3.

Activity 2

If the population in the town of Medton is 278,000, and 54,000 of these are old age pensioners (OAPs):

(a)   What is the ratio of OAPs to non-OAPs?

(b)   What is the percentage of OAPs in the population?

(c)   What proportion of the population are OAPs?

Feedback to this activity is at the end of the chapter.

4 The whole and the parts

4.1 Differences

The key difference between the measures studied in this chapter is in how they relate to whatever is the **whole**. This affects the information that can be communicated.

- A **percentage** (such as 5%) treats the whole in an abstract sense as 100%. You may have no idea what the actual number of the whole is. Because of this percentages are especially useful for **comparisons,** even if the actual numbers of the wholes are widely different.

- A **ratio** (such as 3:5:8) focuses on the **shares** that make up the whole. Again, it does not tell you the actual whole number. Ratios are particularly useful for describing **permanent relationships** between things.
- A **proportion** (e.g. 320 out of 1,600) is usually given as a fraction (sometimes, but not always, with the actual whole as the denominator). For instance you might read that '320 out of 1,600 people surveyed said that they prefer Brand X'. This gives more information than (the numerically equivalent) 'one-fifth of people surveyed said that they prefer Brand X', and it is more convincing (because in the latter case the surveyors may only have asked five people!).

4.2 Adding up to the whole

If you are told that 22% of people prefer Brand X then you can deduce that a total of (100 − 22) = 78% of people do **not** prefer Brand X. (If you find it easier you can use (1 − 0.22) in your calculations.)

Likewise if you are given a proportion in the form '320 out of 1,600 people surveyed prefer Brand X'. This information also (silently) tells you that (1,600 − 320) = 1,280 people **prefer other brands**.

However, if all you are told is that three partners share profits in the ratio 8:3:?, then there is absolutely no way of working out what the third ratio is without further information.

4.3 Decimal equivalents

Any of these measures can also be expressed in **decimal** form, of course.

- 5% is 0.05. (Watch out for traps like 0.2%, which = 0.002 in decimal form.) A percentage is just a decimal with the decimal point moved two places to the right.
- The ratio 3:5:8 could be rewritten as 0.1875:0.3125:0.5000
- 320/1600 (or 1/5) is 0.2.

For **calculation** purposes it is sometimes convenient to use decimals and sometimes not. For example if profits of £300,000 are divided between 3 people in the ratio 1:1:1 then it is better (and **quicker** on a calculator) to calculate each person's share as 1 ÷ 3 × £300,000 = £100,000 than to calculate it as 0.3333 × £300,000 = £99,990, and then have to deal with the rounding error.

Summary

The calculation and meaning of three important items – percentages, ratios, and proportions – were tackled. These basic techniques will be needed again and again in exam questions throughout your future studies, so make sure that you are very comfortable with them before moving on.

You have also seen that, although all of these measures can be expressed in terms of decimals, they may not be so because of their information value or to avoid rounding errors.

Self-test questions

1. What does 'percent' mean and what words are good clues when dealing with percentages? (1.1)

2. What figure is used as a basis when calculating a percentage increase? (1.1)

3. What is a ratio? (2.1)

4. How do you divide a number in a given ratio? (2.2)

5. What is a proportion? (3.1)

6. Why is it sometimes better to work in fractions than in decimals? (4.3)

Practice questions

Question 1

X% of 200 equals

A $\dfrac{X}{20,000}$

B $\dfrac{X}{200}$

C $\dfrac{X}{2}$

D $2X$

Question 2

A coat which was priced at £45.99 last year is now £53.99.

What is the percentage increase in price to 2 decimal places?

A 17.39%
B 17.40%
C 19.78%
D 20.09%

Question 3

At a value added tax (VAT) rate of 12½%, an article sells for 84p, including VAT. If VAT rate increases to 17.5%, the new selling price, to the nearest penny, will be:

A 87p
B 88p
C 94p
D 99p

Question 4

An article in a sales catalogue is priced at £298, including value added tax (VAT) at 17.5%. The price, excluding VAT, to the nearest penny, is:

A £247.34

B £253.62

C £255.00

D £280.50

Question 5

Three years ago a garden centre sold strimmers for £27.50 each. At the end of the first year they increased the price by 5% and at the end of the second year by a further 6%. At the end of the third year the selling price was £29.69 each. The percentage price change in year three was nearest to:

A −3%

B +3%

C −6%

D +9%

Question 6

An item priced at £90.68, including local sales tax at 19%, is reduced in a sale by 20%. The new price before sales tax is added is nearest to:

A £60.96

B £72.54

C £75.57

D £76.20

For the answers to these questions, see the 'Answers' section at the end of the book.

Feedback to activities

Activity 1

If selling price	=	100%
and profit	=	35%
Cost	=	65%
65% of selling price	=	£900
∴ 100% of selling price	=	$\frac{£900}{65} \times 100$
∴ Selling price	=	£1,384.62

Activity 2

(a) OAPs = 54,000
    Non-OAPs = 278,000 − 54,000
    = 224,000
    Ratio = 54,000:224,000
    = 27:112

(b) Percentage of OAPs = $\dfrac{54{,}000}{278{,}000} \times 100\%$
    = 19.4%

(c) Proportion of OAPs = 54 out of every 278 people
    Or you could say 27 out of every 139
    or just give the percentage figure of 19.4%.

3

ACCURACY AND ROUNDING

Contents

1. Rounding
2. Significant figures
3. Accuracy and approximation

1 Rounding

1.1 Introduction

You round numbers all the time. For instance if you are told that your holiday in the Bahamas will cost £799.99 you are not fooled by the sales trick of trying to make the holiday sound cheaper than it is: you round up to £800. Rounding makes numbers easier to understand: it sacrifices a little detail for the sake of clarity.

No doubt you know the usual rules of rounding.

- If the number you want to sacrifice is between 0 and 4 leave **the number to the left** as it is.

- If the number you want to sacrifice is between 5 and 9, round up (add 1 to) the number to the left.

Original number	Rounded to whole numbers
22.0	
22.1	
22.2	22
22.3	
22.4	
22.5	
22.6	
22.7	23
22.8	
22.9	

You should only look at one extra number when rounding. For instance if asked to round the number 1.3748 to two decimal places the answer is 1.37. You do **not** round to three decimal places (1.375) and then round that result to two decimal places (1.38).

Likewise 0.0499 rounded to one decimal place is 0.0 – a fact that distresses some people, but there is no cause for sentimentality in rounding! If reducing a figure like this to zero will cause an error in subsequent calculations (for instance a #DIV/0! error in a spreadsheet model) then it should not be rounded so much in the first place.

2 Significant figures

2.1 Size isn't important!

The term 'significant figure' (or 'significant digit') often causes confusion, partly because the word 'significant' is not used in its normal sense and partly because **size isn't important** when we are considering the 'significance' or otherwise of the figures that make up a number.

KEY POINT

In a mathematical context the word 'significant' means 'precise'; the number of significant figures is not an indication of how large or small the number is.

In a mathematical context the word 'significant' means **'precise'** and the number of significant figures is **not** an indication of how large or small the number is.

For example if we say 'it is 3 thousand miles from London to New York' there is only **one** significant figure – the figure 3. The remaining three zeros are not 'significant' – the actual other figures would not really be '000'.

If we say 'it is 3,415 miles from London to New York' there are four significant figures. And if we say 'it is 3,415.0 miles …' there are **five** significant figures because '3,415.0' implies that the number is not 3,415.2 or 3415.9 – it tells the reader what degree of precision is being used. (In fact, if you claimed 'it is 3,415.0 miles' you would probably add '…from Trafalgar Square in London to Times Square in New York City', to make your claim sound more credible.)

In general the number of significant digits in a measurement depends on **the ability of the measuring device**.

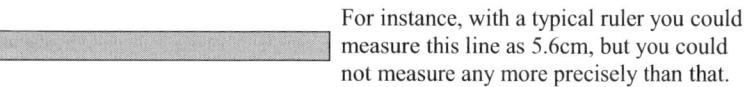

For instance, with a typical ruler you could measure this line as 5.6cm, but you could not measure any more precisely than that.

If you said this line was 5.623cm long you would be guessing the last two figures.

2.2 Rules

Remember, we are talking about **precision, not magnitude**, so (perhaps most confusingly of all) a number such as 0.005 is considered to have **one** significant figure.

Here are the rules more formally.

Rule	Examples	Significant figures.
All non-zero figures are significant.	127	3
	2.5	2
All zeros **between** non-zeros are significant.	10204	5
	10.03	4
Leading zeros in a decimal are **not** significant.	0.12	2
	0.034	2
Trailing zeros are not significant unless followed by, or to the right of, a decimal point	1540	3
	320	2
	320.	3
	320.00	5

KEY POINT

Don't confuse rounding to a certain number of significant figures with rounding to a certain number of decimal places.

2.3 Significant figures and rounding

Don't confuse rounding to a certain number of significant figures with rounding to a certain number of decimal places.

- 102.0304 to four decimal places is 102.0304

- 102.0304 to four significant figures is 102.0

If multiplying numbers the general principle is that if one of the numbers is only accurate to a certain number of significant digits, you can only trust that number of significant digits in the result, so you should round to that level of accuracy.

- If the numbers being multiplied are given in the form 48.20 and 4.90, there are 4 and 3 significant digits respectively, so the answer should have 3 digits: 236.
- If the numbers are given in the form 48.2 and 4.9, you should only keep 2 significant digits, so you round the answer up to 240.

This only applies, of course, if you are **specifically asked** to give an answer that is expressed to a certain number of significant figures. Otherwise all the usual more familiar rules apply, so don't get too het up about this topic.

Activity 1

How many significant figures are the following numbers expressed to?

70.0kg

4.32kg

0.0033g

4100g

40.007g

0.28m

0.010m

Feedback to this activity is at the end of the chapter.

3 Accuracy and approximation

3.1 Variables

Variables are the characteristics that are being measured. They can be classified in two different and distinct ways:

(a) Variables can be either **continuous** or **discrete**.

A **continuous** variable is one that can assume any value, including all **fractional or decimal values** (e.g. height, weight, temperature).

A **discrete** variable is one that can only assume certain specific values, usually **integer** (whole number) values (e.g. the number of children in a family, continental shoe sizes).

(b) Variables can alternatively be classified as **independent** or **dependent**.

An **independent variable** is a variable which is not affected by changes in another variable, whereas a **dependent variable** is affected by changes in another, e.g. changes in advertising expenditure in a year can be expected to affect sales, but a change in sales will not directly affect advertising expenditure. Hence, advertising is the independent variable and sales the dependent.

KEY POINT

A **continuous** variable is one that can assume any value, including all **fractional or decimal values** (e.g. height, weight, temperature).

KEY POINT

A **discrete** variable is one that can only assume certain specific values, usually **integer** (whole number) values (e.g. the number of children in a family, continental shoe sizes).

3.2 Measurement

> **KEY POINT**
>
> An **independent variable** is a variable which is not affected by changes in another variable, whereas a **dependent variable** is affected by changes in another, e.g. changes in advertising expenditure in a year can be expected to affect sales, but a change in sales will not directly affect advertising expenditure. Hence, advertising is the independent variable and sales the dependent.

As we've indicated, no measurement of a continuous variable is ever exact. If the length of a page of a book is measured, the result may be given as 21.6 cm when, in fact, the length could lie between 21.55 and 21.64 because 21.6 cm may have been rounded up or down to one decimal place. Measurements should not be quoted with greater accuracy than they merit; in this case the answer is said to be correct to three significant figures.

Another method of indicating the accuracy of a number is to quote the limits of possible error, e.g. to say that a person's height is 163 cm to the nearest cm means that their height lies between 162.5 and 163.5 cm and may be written as 163 ± 0.5 cm.

Even when a figure may be computed to, say, 4 significant figures it will sometimes be better to give the final answer to, say, 3 significant figures. This will depend upon the accuracy of the original data on which the computations are based. It is important not to mislead the reader of the final results by making them **spuriously accurate**.

An example of a particular area where it would be incorrect to be too accurate is the computation of price indices as an estimate for the rate of inflation.

Summary

This chapter looked at the level of precision in calculations and the presentation of results.

This should be taken into account in deciding to how many significant figures the result should be expressed. Conversely, if a result is required to, say, three significant figures, all values used in calculating that result must have **at least** four significant figures.

Self-test questions

1 What are the usual rules of rounding? (1.1)

2 What does the word significant mean in the term 'significant digit'? (2.1)

3 Are the leading zeros in a decimal such as 0.024 significant? (2.2)

4 What is the difference between a continuous and a discrete variable? (3.1)

5 What is the difference between an independent and a dependent variable? (3.1)

Practice question

Question 1

A radio which was priced at £56.99 has been reduced to £52.49. To two decimal places, the percentage reduction in price is:

A   7.89%

B   7.90%

C   8.57%

D   8.91%

For the answer to this question, see the 'Answers' section at the end of the book.

Feedback to activities

Activity 1

	Significant figures
70.0kg	3
4.32kg	3
0.0033g	2
4100g	2
40.007g	5
0.28m	2
0.010m	2

4
ALGEBRA, FORMULAE, EQUATIONS AND GRAPHS

Contents

1. Algebra and formulae
2. Equations
3. Simultaneous equations
4. Linear equations and graphs
5. Quadratic equations
6. Graphs of the quadratic function
7. Inequalities

1 Algebra and formulae

1.1 Algebra

Algebra is the branch of mathematics that uses letters and other general symbols to represent numbers and quantities in formulae and equations.

This is not done just to make life difficult for students – it has many practical applications. **Formulae** can be devised using algebra to describe general problems and then those formulae can be used with whatever actual values apply in specific situations. For example:

$$A = L \times B$$

This is a well-known formula for finding the area (A) of any rectangle of length (L) and breadth (B). Other letters could be used but these are obviously the most appropriate ones.

Whatever letters or symbols are used (and x and y are the most common) the following two points are important:

- It must be clearly stated what each letter or symbol represents.
- If any units of measurement are involved they must be clearly defined.

> **KEY POINT**
>
> Formulae can be devised using algebra to describe general problems and then those formulae can be used with whatever actual values apply in specific situations.

1.2 Illustration

There are two numbers; the first is multiplied by 3, and 5 is then added to the product. The sum is divided by 4 times the second number. This is expressed algebraically as follows.

Let x = first number
and y = second number

'The first is multiplied by 3 ..'. This gives $x \times 3$, usually written as $3x$

'.. and 5 is added to the product', i.e. $3x + 5$

'.. 4 times the second number' is $y \times 4$ or $4y$.

The first part divided by the second gives the following algebraic **'expression'** (so called simply because it 'expresses' the initial problem in algebra).

$$(3x + 5) \div 4y \quad \text{or} \quad \frac{(3x + 5)}{4y}$$

Note:

- The individual parts of an expression are called **terms**. For example the expression $100x + y$ contains two terms, $100x$ and y.
- 100 is called the **coefficient** of x. The coefficient of y is 1 (the term $1 \times y$ is conventionally written as just 'y' rather than '1y').

1.3 Like terms

If an expression contains terms which involve the **same letter** and differ only in the coefficients, then they are called **like terms**. The important point is that like terms can be added or subtracted by adding or subtracting the coefficients.

> **KEY POINT**
>
> If an expression contains terms which involve the **same letter** and differ only in the coefficients, then they are called **like terms**.
>
> The important point is that like terms can be added or subtracted by adding or subtracting the coefficients.

Example

Simplify the following expressions:

(a) $5a + 6b + 2a - 3b$

(b) $4x + 3x - 2x - x$

(c) The sum of the three expressions $5x + 2y + 3z$, $x - y - 2z$, and $2x - y + z$

Solution

(a) $5a + 6b + 2a - 3b \quad = \quad (5 + 2)a + (6 - 3)b$

ALGEBRA, FORMULAE, EQUATIONS AND GRAPHS   43

$$= 7a + 3b$$

(b) $\quad 4x + 3x - 2x - x \quad = (4 + 3 - 2 - 1)x$

$$= 4x$$

(c) $\quad (5x + 2y + 3z) + (x - y - 2z) + (2x - y + z)$

$$= (5 + 1 + 2)x + (2 - 1 - 1)y + (3 - 2 + 1)z$$
$$= 8x + 0y + 2z$$
$$= 8x + 2z$$

1.4 Evaluation of algebraic expressions

Numerical values of algebraic expressions can be calculated simply by substituting definite numbers for the letters.

For example suppose we have the expression $7a + 3b$ representing a problem that is common to several different businesses.

In Company 1 the value of a is 3 and the value of b is –1.

$$7a + 3b = (7 \times 3) + (3 \times -1)$$
$$= 21 - 3$$
$$= \underline{18}$$

In Company 2 the value of a is 5 and the value of b is 2.

$$7a + 3b = (7 \times 5) + (3 \times 2)$$
$$= 35 + 6$$
$$= \underline{41}$$

The letters a and b can also be called **'variables'**, because their values may vary in different situations, as in the example above.

1.5 Manipulation of algebraic expressions

> **KEY POINT**
>
> The rules for the manipulation of algebraic expressions are exactly the same as the rules for the manipulation of non-algebraic expressions that you learnt in Chapter 1.

The rules are **exactly the same** as those you learned in Chapter 1. Don't forget this, just because you have letters in some places instead of real numbers.

Brackets and algebra

(a) Items outside brackets multiply **everything** within:

$\quad a(x + y + z) \quad = \quad ax + ay + az$

$\quad 3(x + y + z) \quad = \quad 3x + 3y + 3z$

(b) Signs outside brackets multiply everything within:

$\quad -a(x + y + z) \quad = \quad -ax + -ay + -az$

$\quad -7(x + y - z) \quad = \quad -7x - 7y + 7z$

Activity 1

Expand the following expressions:

(a) $5(2x + 3y - 4z)$

(b) $-x(2 + 3x)$

(c) $-4(x - 2y + 3z)$

Feedback to this activity is at the end of the chapter.

Fractions and algebra

(a) Fractions may be added when reduced to a common denominator:

$$\frac{a}{x} + \frac{b}{y} = \frac{ay}{xy} + \frac{bx}{xy}$$

$$= \frac{ay + bx}{xy}$$

(b) When multiplying fractions, numerators and denominators are dealt with separately:

$$\frac{a}{x} \times \frac{b}{y} = \frac{ab}{xy}$$

(c) When dividing fractions, invert the divisor and multiply:

$$\frac{a}{x} \div \frac{b}{y} = \frac{a}{x} \times \frac{y}{b}$$

$$= \frac{ay}{xb}$$

2 Equations

2.1 Introduction

DEFINITION

An equation is a statement of the equality of two quantities.

An equation is a statement of the equality of two quantities.

In other words, it is a statement that something is the same as another thing! The simple formula A=L×B is an equation, where A, the area of a rectangle, can be found by multiplying the length (L) by the breadth (B). So, the value of A is the same as the value of L×B, and all we have to do to find our unknown quantity, A, is to measure L and B and then multiply their values.

This example also illustrates another aspect of equations: they generally describe a relationship between quantities. Here, it is the relationship between the area and the length and breadth of a rectangle. All these values can vary, but:

- area is the **dependent variable** as its value depends on the values of length and breadth.
- length and breadth are **independent variables**, as their values do not depend on any other variable.

Finding the unknown figure in equations, or solving equations, involves manipulation of the equations. These techniques are explored next.

2.2 Equations with one unknown

Where an equation contains only one unknown figure, say x, its solution may be found by simply manipulating the equation until x appears on the left-hand

(LH) side only, and then evaluating the right-hand (RH) side. The manipulation depends on the fact that an equation is like a pair of scales that are always in perfect balance. The **balance** will be maintained provided **both sides** are increased or decreased by the same amount. (It is a bit like double-entry bookkeeping: for every debit there must be a credit.)

Example 1

$$3x - 4 = 2 - 6x$$

Adding 6x to both sides gives:

$$3x - 4 + 6x = 2 - 6x + 6x \text{ (see note*)}$$
$$9x - 4 = 2$$

Adding 4 to both sides gives:

$$9x - 4 + 4 = 2 + 4 \text{ (see note*)}$$
$$9x = 6$$
$$x = \frac{6}{9} \quad \text{(dividing both sides by 9)}$$
$$= \frac{2}{3}$$

Note: by adding the same term to both sides, it looks as if that term has been taken over to the other side of the equation and given the opposite sign. This is what is done in practice, leading to the well-known rule 'change the side, change the sign'.

Example 2

$$7x + 2 = 10 - 5x$$

Take −5x over from RH side to LH side and change to +5x:

$$7x + 5x + 2 = 10$$

Take +2 over from LH side to RH side and change to −2:

$$7x + 5x = 10 - 2$$
$$12x = 8$$

Dividing both sides by 12 and cancelling:

$$\frac{12x}{12} = \frac{8}{12}$$
$$x = \frac{2}{3}$$

You can always check your result by substituting the value obtained into the **original** equation.

Thus if $x = \frac{2}{3}$,

$$7 \times \frac{2}{3} + 2 = 10 - 5 \times \frac{2}{3}$$

$$\frac{14}{3} + 2 = 10 - \frac{10}{3}$$

$$\frac{14+6}{3} = \frac{30-10}{3}$$

$$\frac{20}{3} = \frac{20}{3}$$

As this balances, the solution is correct.

3 Simultaneous equations

3.1 Introduction

KEY POINT

Simultaneous equations can be solved algebraically by eliminating one of the variables.

It's easy enough to solve an equation if there is only one unknown figure (x in the above examples) but in general we are required to find the value of **more than one unknown**. In order to be able to do this it is necessary that there are as many equations as there are unknowns.

The basic method is to eliminate one of the two unknowns between the equations. This is achieved by adding or subtracting the equations. This process is known as solving simultaneous equations.

3.2 Solving simultaneous equations with two unknowns

An example of simultaneous equations might be as follows.

You are told that both of the following relationships between two variables, x and y, are true.

$x + y = 10$ Equation (1)

and

$x - 4y = 0$ Equation (2)

Solution

Step 1

Firstly, by multiplying one or both of the equations, make the coefficients of either x or y equal.

The coefficients of x are already equal in this example, so there is no need to multiply either equation.

Step 2

Then, eliminate one of the unknowns by addition or subtraction.

By subtracting equation (2) from equation (1), x will be eliminated, leaving y.

(1): $x + y = 10$

(2): $\underline{x - 4y = 0}$ **subtract**

$5y = 10$

Note: that to subtract (–4y) change to (+4y) and add,

i.e. $y - (-4y) = y + 4y = 5y$.

Step 3

Obtain a value for y.

$5y = 10$

$\therefore \quad y = 2$

Step 4

This value of y is now substituted in equation (1) or (2) – whichever is the easier.

Substituting in (1): $x + 2 = 10$

$\therefore x = 10 - 2 = 8$

So the solution is x = 8, y = 2.

The result can be checked by substituting the values of x and y in the **other** equation. The original form of this equation should be used, as an error may have been made in re-arranging it.

Substituting x = 8, y = 2 in the equation $x - 4y = 0$:

$8 - 4 \times 2 = 0$

$8 - 8 = 0$

As this is a true statement, the answer is correct.

It is not always possible to eliminate one of the unknowns by simply adding or subtracting the equations. In such a case it will be necessary to multiply one or both of the equations to make the coefficients of x or y equal. One of the unknowns may then be eliminated by addition or subtraction of the amended equation(s).

Example

$2x + 3y = 42$ (1)

$5x - y = 20$ (2)

Solution

Step 1

By multiplying equation (2) by 3, the coefficients of y become equal.

(1): $2x + 3y = 42$

$3 \times (2)$: $15x - 3y = 60$ .... Equation (3)

Step 2

Equation (2) when multiplied is called equation (3). You can add equation (1) to equation (3) to eliminate y.

(1) $2x + 3y = 42$

(3) $\underline{15x - 3y} = \underline{60}$

$17x \qquad\qquad 102$

Step 3

Obtain a value for x by rearranging the equation:

$$17x = 102$$
$$x = \frac{102}{17}$$
$$x = 6$$

Step 4

Substitution into any of (1), (2) or (3) is possible but in this case (2) is most convenient giving:

$$(5 \times 6) - y = 20$$
$$30 - y = 20$$
$$30 - 20 = y$$
$$y = 30 - 20$$
$$= 10$$

So the solution is x = 6, y = 10

Check by substituting in (1)

$$2 \times 6 + 3 \times 10 = 42$$
$$12 + 30 = 42$$
$$42 = 42$$

As this is a true statement, the solution is correct.

3.3 Common errors

So long as you remember that you must **multiply both sides** of an individual **equation** by the same figure you can pick any number you like to multiply by: –5, 67, 0.324, 102.9, or whatever is appropriate.

However, you do **not** have to do the same thing to **both equations.** If you multiply both sides of equation (1) by 102.9, say, you need **not** also multiply equation (2) by 102.9. Equation (2) can stay as it is or be multiplied (on both sides!) by a completely different figure.

Try this out for yourself using real numbers instead of letters if you are unsure.

Activity 2

Solve the following:

$$\frac{x}{3} + \frac{y}{2} = \frac{2x}{3} - \frac{y}{6} = 7$$

Feedback to this activity is at the end of the chapter.

4 Linear equations and graphs

4.1 Graphing linear equations

DEFINITION

A linear equation (or 'equation of the first degree') is an equation containing no higher powers than the first of x and y, and is of the type y = a + bx where a and b are both constants.

A linear equation (or 'equation of the first degree') is an equation containing no higher powers than the first of x and y, and is of the type y = a + bx where a and b are both constants.

Consider the three equations:

(1) y = 2x (2) y = 4 + 2x (3) y = −2 + 2x

In order to draw graphs of these three equations it is necessary to decide on a range of values for x, say from −3 to +3, and then to calculate the corresponding values for y.

This is best displayed in the form of a table.

	x	−3	−2	−1	0	1	2	3
(1)	y = 2x	−6	−4	−2	0	2	4	6
(2)	y = 4 + 2x	−2	0	2	4	6	8	10
(3)	y = −2 + 2x	−8	−6	−4	−2	0	2	4

By convention, values of x are plotted on the horizontal axis and values of y on the vertical axis. A good way of remembering this is via the x in the word **relax**. The axis that is 'relaxing' (lying down, horizontally) is the x axis.

The three graphs will appear as follows:

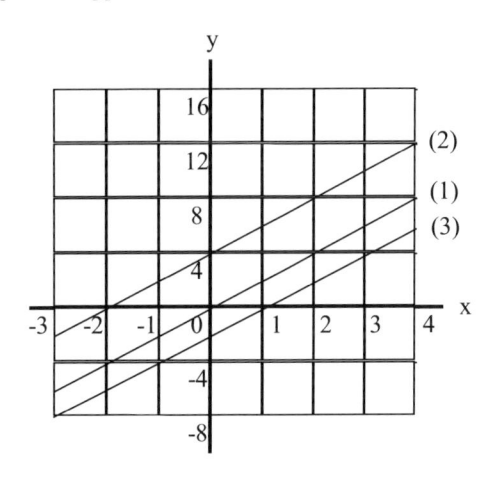

Several points are obvious from the graphs:

(a) The graphs are all straight lines.

(b) They are parallel to each other.

(c) Line (1) crosses the y axis at   x = 0, y = 0,   i.e. (0, 0), called 'the origin'

Line (2) crosses the y axis at   x = 0, y = 4,   i.e. (0, 4)

Line (3) crosses the y axis at   x = 0, y = −2, i.e. (0, −2)

The values of y are called the **intercepts on the y axis.**

(d) Line (1) crosses the x axis at   x = 0, y = 0,   i.e. (0, 0)

Line (2) crosses the x axis at $x = -2$, $y = 0$,   i.e. $(-2, 0)$
Line (3) crosses the x axis at $x = 1$, $y = 0$,   i.e. $(1, 0)$

These values of x are called the **intercepts on the x axis.**

4.2 The general equation of a straight line

KEY POINT

General equation of straight line is: y = a + bx where a is the intercept on the y-axis and b is the gradient.

Returning to the general form of the equation $y = a + bx$:

b   (the **coefficient** of x) is the **gradient** of the line, which is a measure of the 'steepness' of the line. This explains why the lines (1), (2) and (3) are parallel, since they all have a gradient of 2.

a   (the **constant**) is the **intercept** on the y axis, i.e. the value of y where the line cuts the y axis. For line (1) a = 0, line (2) a = 4, line (3) a = –2.

Equations of the first degree, i.e. of the form y = a + bx, always result in straight line graphs.

However, equations of the first degree will sometimes not be given in this straightforward form and will need to be rearranged prior to plotting the graph.

Example 1

To plot $2(x-1) = y + 1$, it is advisable to rearrange the expression so that y alone appears on the left hand side.

Solution

2x – 2 = y + 1	(multiplying out the bracket)
2x – 3 = y	(subtracting 1 from both sides)
y = 2x – 3	(transposing sides)

Hence it can be seen that the gradient is 2 and the intercept on the y axis is –3.

Example 2

Plot the graphs of the following equations and find the gradients and intercepts on the y axis.

(a) $4y = 6x - 5$ (x from 0 to +5)

(b) $\dfrac{x}{3} + \dfrac{y}{2} = 2$ (x from –2 to +3)

(c) $2(x - 3) = 4(y - 1)$ (x from –6 to +4 at even numbers only)

Solution

(a) $4y = 6x - 5$

$y = \dfrac{6x}{4} - \dfrac{5}{4}$ (Dividing through by 4)

$y = 1.5x - 1.25$

Comparing this with the general equation y = a + bx gives:

gradient = 1.5   (coefficient of x)

intercept = –1.25   (constant)

x	0	1	2	3	4	5
1.5x	0	1.5	3	4.5	6	7.5
y = 1.5x – 1.25	–1.25	0.25	1.75	3.25	4.75	6.25

ALGEBRA, FORMULAE, EQUATIONS AND GRAPHS 51

(b) $\dfrac{x}{3} + \dfrac{y}{2} = 2$

$\dfrac{y}{2} = 2 - \dfrac{x}{3}$

$\therefore y = 4 - \dfrac{2x}{3}$ (Multiplying through by 2)

Gradient $= -\dfrac{2}{3}$; intercept $= 4$

x	-2	-1	0	1	2	3
$\dfrac{-2x}{3}$	1.3	0.7	0	-0.7	-1.3	-2
$y = 4 - \dfrac{2x}{3}$	5.3	4.7	4	3.3	2.7	2

(c) $2(x - 3) = 4(y - 1)$

$2x - 6 = 4y - 4$

$\therefore 2x - 6 + 4 = 4y$

$2x - 2 = 4y$

$\dfrac{2x}{4} - \dfrac{2}{4} = y$ (Dividing through by 4)

$y = 0.5x - 0.5$

Gradient $= 0.5$, intercept $= -0.5$

x	-6	-4	-2	0	2	4
$0.5x$	-3	-2	-1	0	1	2
$y = 0.5x - 0.5$	-3.5	-2.5	-1.5	-0.5	0.5	1.5

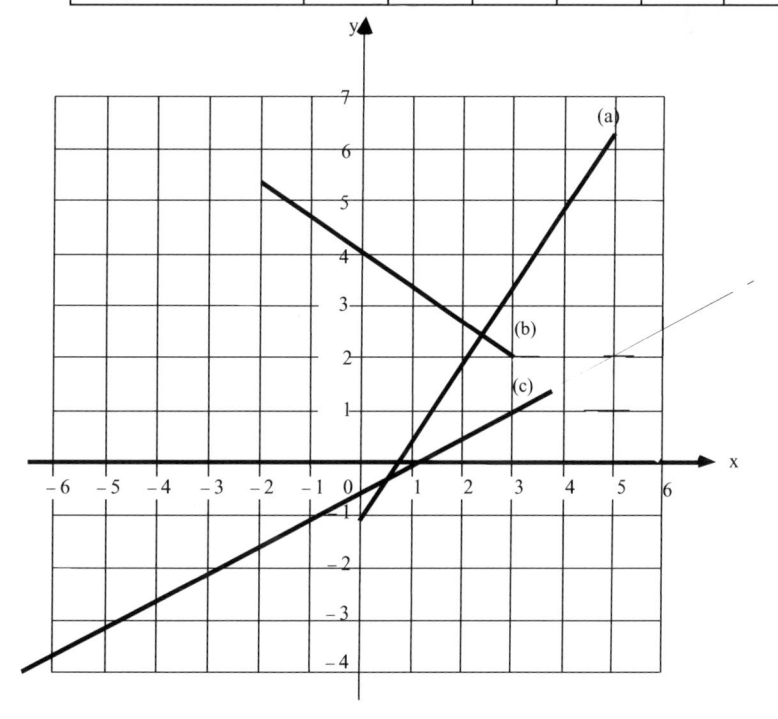

Note: in practice, once the equation is recognised as a straight line, it is only necessary to calculate and plot two points, as there is only one straight line that can pass through two given points. It is advisable, however, to plot three points as a check. If the three points do not lie on a straight line, a mistake has been made which must be located and corrected. It is never necessary to plot more than three points for a straight line graph. The points plotted must be well spaced out along the line. If the three points plotted are close together, the line cannot be drawn accurately.

5 Quadratic equations

5.1 Introduction

Whereas an expression of the first degree contains only terms in x, y and constants, a quadratic, or second order, expression may also contain terms in x^2 and/or y^2.

A quadratic equation is a quadratic expression which is set to be equal to zero. For example $x^2 + 3x = -2$ is not in this form, but if it is re-arranged:

$$x^2 + 3x + 2 = 0 \quad \text{is a quadratic equation}$$

In an equation like this there may be **two values of x** that satisfy the equation. These are called the **roots** of the equation.

> **DEFINITION**
>
> Whereas an expression of the first degree contains only terms in x, y and constants, a quadratic, or second order, expression may also contain terms in x^2 and/or y^2.

5.2 Factorisation

One method of solution of quadratic equations is by 'factorisation', but don't worry if you find this technique hard to follow. Not all quadratic equations factorise, and even if they do, factors will often be difficult to spot. It is more usual to use a formula to solve the equation. We'll cover that in a moment.

Factorisation is the reverse of multiplying out brackets. For example:

$$3x(x + 2) = 3x^2 + 6x$$

hence:

$3x^2 + 6x$ factorises to $3x(x + 2)$

Similarly,

$$(3x + 4)(2x - 5) = 3x(2x - 5) + 4(2x - 5)$$
$$= 6x^2 - 15x + 8x - 20$$
$$= 6x^2 - 7x - 20$$

Hence:

$6x^2 - 7x - 20$ factorises to $(3x + 4)(2x - 5)$

Three important factorisations that must be **memorised** are:

$$a^2 + 2ab + b^2 = (a + b)(a + b) = (a + b)^2$$
$$a^2 - 2ab + b^2 = (a - b)(a - b) = (a - b)^2$$
$$a^2 - b^2 = (a + b)(a - b)$$

(You can prove these to yourself by multiplying out the brackets.)

Example

The following expressions will be factorised:

(a) $12a^2m^3 - 15am^5$

(b) $am + bm + an + bn$

(c) $x^2 + 4x - 12$

(d) $10p^2 + 11pq - 6q^2$

Solutions

(a) $12a^2m^3 - 15am^5$

$3am^3$ is a common factor of both terms, hence:

$$12a^2m^3 - 15am^5 = 3am^3(4a - 5m^2)$$

(b) $am + bm + an + bn$

m is a factor of the first two terms, and n is a factor of the last two terms, hence:

$$am + bm + an + bn = m(a + b) + n(a + b)$$

$(a + b)$ is now seen to be a factor of both terms, hence:

$$m(a + b) + n(a + b) = (a + b)(m + n)$$

(c) $x^2 + 4x - 12$

In general, $(x + a)(x + b) = x^2 + (a + b)x + ab$

In this example, therefore, two numbers are required, whose product is -12 and whose sum is $+4$. By trial and error, these are found to be $+6$ and -2. Hence:

$$x^2 + 4x - 12 = (x + 6)(x - 2)$$

(d) $10p^2 + 11pq - 6q^2$

The factors will be of the form (ap + bq)(cp + dq). On multiplying out, the coefficient of p^2 will be ac which equals 10, the coefficient of q^2 will be bd, which equals –6. The coefficient of pq will be ad + bc which equals 11. Trial and error then shows that the required values are:

a = 5, b = –2, c = 2, d = 3

hence: $10p^2 + 11pq - 6q^2$ = (5p – 2q)(2p + 3q)

5.3 Using factorisation to solve quadratic equations

If a quadratic expression can be seen to factorise then this gives a quick and neat way of solving the equation. For example, in the case of the equation with which we began this section:

$x^2 + 3x + 2$ = 0

(x + 2)(x + 1) = 0

This helps to show why there may be two solutions to a quadratic equation: if the product of two factors is zero, then one or both factors must be zero.

∴ either   x + 2 = 0 or x + 1 = 0

∴   x = –2 or x = –1

5.4 Solution of quadratics by formula

Consider the general quadratic equation

$ax^2 + bx + c$ = 0

There is a formula for solving this which is usually given in exams, as follows.

$$x = \frac{-b \pm \sqrt{b^2 - 4ac}}{2a}$$

The most important part of this formula is $b^2 - 4ac$. There are three possibilities:

(a) If $b^2 - 4ac$ is zero there is only one solution to the quadratic equation. (Strictly speaking there are two solutions (roots), but they both have the same value and are said to be coincident.)

or

(b) If $b^2 - 4ac$ is positive there are two distinct solutions to the quadratic equations

or

(c) If $b^2 - 4ac$ is negative there are no real solutions to the quadratic equation since it is not possible to take the square root of a negative number (or not easily, as you can confirm on your calculator).

Example

The following equations will be solved using the formula:

(a) $9x^2 - 30x + 25$ = 0

(b) $(x + 3)^2$ = 25

Solution

Here is a reminder of the formula.

$$x = \frac{-b \pm \sqrt{b^2 - 4ac}}{2a}$$

(a) $9x^2 - 30x + 25 = 0$ so $a = 9, b = -30, c = 25$

$$\text{then } x = \frac{-(-30) \pm \sqrt{(-30)^2 - 4 \times 9 \times 25}}{2 \times 9}$$

$$= \frac{30 \pm \sqrt{0}}{18} \quad \text{(remember that } (-30)^2 = +900 \text{ as the product of two negative numbers is positive)}$$

$$= \frac{30}{18} = \frac{5}{3}$$

$b^2 - 4ac$ is zero and there is only one solution to the quadratic equation. Also, the quadratic will factorise:

$9x^2 - 30x + 25 = 0$

$(3x - 5)(3x - 5) = 0$

$(3x - 5)^2 = 0$

$\therefore 3x - 5 = 0$

$\therefore 3x = 5$ so $x = 5/3$ (Twice, each factor giving the same root.)

(b) $(x + 3)^2 = 25$ but $(x + 3)(x + 3) = x^2 + 6x + 9$

$\therefore x^2 + 6x + 9 = 25$

$x^2 + 6x + 9 - 25 = 0$

$x^2 + 6x - 16 = 0$ so $a = 1, b = 6, c = -16$

$$\text{then } x = \frac{-6 \pm \sqrt{6^2 - 4 \times 1 \times (-16)}}{2 \times 1}$$

$$= \frac{-6 \pm \sqrt{100}}{2}$$

$$= \frac{-6 \pm 10}{2}$$

$$= \frac{4}{2}, \text{ i.e. } 2 \text{ or } -\frac{16}{2}, \text{ i.e. } -8$$

5.5 Simultaneous equations – one linear, one quadratic

For example, $\quad x + y = 1 \quad (1)$

$\quad 3x^2 - xy + y^2 = 37 \quad (2)$

The general method of solving a problem like this is to find an expression for one of the variables from the linear equation (1) and replace this in the quadratic equation (2).

i.e. $\quad x + y = 1$

$\therefore y = 1 - x$

Substituting for y in (2):
$$3x^2 - x(1-x) + (1-x)^2 = 37$$
$$3x^2 - x + x^2 + (1 - 2x + x^2) = 37$$
$$5x^2 - 3x + 1 - 37 = 0$$
$$5x^2 - 3x - 36 = 0$$

It will now be necessary to solve this equation by factorisation or by using the formula.

By factorisation:

$$(5x + 12)(x - 3) = 0 \text{ (check by multiplying out the brackets)}$$

Either $5x + 12 = 0 \therefore x = \dfrac{-12}{5}$

or $x - 3 = 0 \therefore x = 3$

When $x = \dfrac{-12}{5}$ or -2.4, $y = 1 - (-2.4) = 3.4$

When $x = 3$, $y = 1 - 3 = -2$

So the solutions are:

$(x, y) = (-2.4, 3.4)$

or $(x, y) = (3, -2)$

6 Graphs of the quadratic function

Graphs will now be drawn of:

(a) $y = 2x^2$

(b) $y = 2x^2 + 3$

(c) $y = 2x^2 - 4$

For the values of x from -3 to $+3$

	x	-3	-2	-1	0	1	2	3
(a)	x^2	9	4	1	0	1	4	9
	$y = 2x^2$	18	8	2	0	2	8	18
(b)	$y = 2x^2 + 3$	21	11	5	3	5	11	21
(c)	$y = 2x^2 - 4$	14	4	-2	-4	-2	4	14

ALGEBRA, FORMULAE, EQUATIONS AND GRAPHS

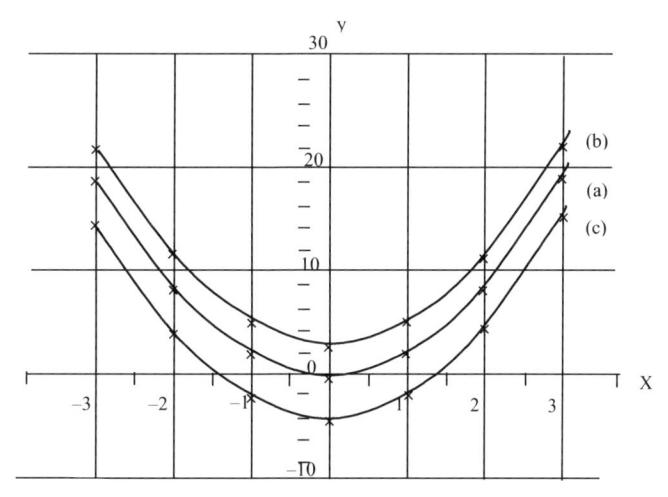

The graphs are symmetrical about the y axis, and they are clearly related to one another.

i.e. (b) $y = 2x^2 + 3$ is identical to (a), $y = 2x^2$ but it is raised three units higher.

i.e. (c) $y = 2x^2 - 4$ is identical to (a), $y = 2x^2$ but is it four units lower.

Therefore, the set of curves $y = 2x^2 \pm$ constant are identical except that they are higher or lower than the basic curve $y = 2x^2$ by the amount of the constant.

6.1 Example

The graph of $y = x^2 + 3x + 2$ will be drawn for values of x from −3 to +3.

x	−3	−2	−1	0	1	2	3
x^2	9	4	1	0	1	4	9
$3x$	−9	−6	−3	0	3	6	9
$y = x^2 + 3x + 2$	2	0	0	2	6	12	20

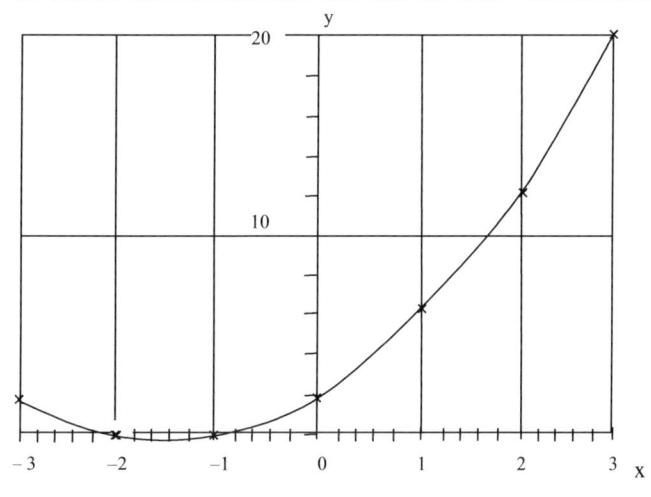

Although $y = 0$ at $x = -2$ and $x = -1$ the graph is a continuous curve between these points, it does not suddenly go flat.

Activity 3

The marketing department estimates that if the selling price of the new product A1 is set at £40 per unit then the sales will be 400 units per week, while if the selling price is set at £20 per unit, the sales will be 800 units per week. Assume that the graph of this function is linear.

The production department estimates that the variable costs will be £7.50 per unit and that the fixed costs will be £10,000 per week.

(a) Derive the cost, sales revenue, and profit equations.

(b) Graph the three equations derived in (a).

(c) From the graph, estimate the maximum profit that can be obtained, stating the number of sales units and the selling price necessary to achieve this profit.

Feedback to this activity is at the end of the chapter.

6.2 Graphical solution of simultaneous equations

> **KEY POINT**
>
> Simultaneous equations can be solved graphically by finding the point of intersection of the two lines.

The solution of simultaneous equations with two unknowns can be found at the point or points of intersection of the graphs of the equations. In practice, it is essential to use graph paper, otherwise accurate readings cannot be taken from the graph. (Solving the equations of the lines simultaneously will provide a more accurate and reliable result, which can be checked with the graph.)

Examples

Solve the following pairs of equations graphically.

(a) $4x - 5y = -5$
$5x + 4y = 20$ (drawing graphs in the range 0 to 5)

(b) $2x + 3 - x^2 = y$
$2x - 5y = -11$ (drawing graphs in the range -1 to 3)

Solutions

(a) From $4x - 5y = -5$ we get $y = \dfrac{4x+5}{5}$

x	0	2.5	5
$4x + 5$	5	15	25
$y = \dfrac{4x+5}{5}$	1	3	5

From $5x + 4y = 20$ we get $y = \dfrac{20-5x}{4}$

x	0	2	4
$20 - 5x$	20	10	0
$y = \dfrac{20+5x}{4}$	5	2.5	0

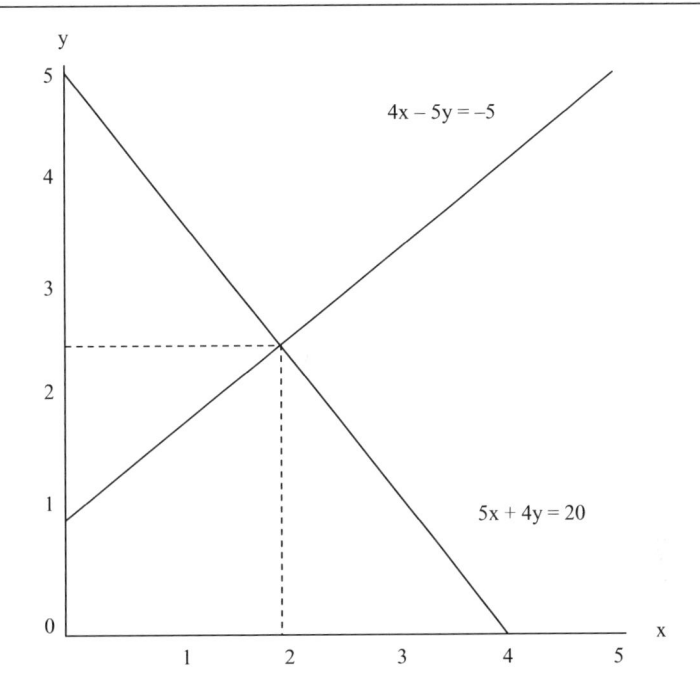

ALGEBRA, FORMULAE, EQUATIONS AND GRAPHS **59**

From the graph, the point of intersection of the lines is:

x ≈ 2

y ≈ 2½

Note: that if the two lines were parallel, they would not intersect and there would be no solution. (The true point of intersection, found by solving the equations simultaneously, is x = 1 $\frac{39}{41}$, y = 2 $\frac{23}{41}$.)

(b) $y = 2x + 3 - x^2$

x	−1	0	1	2	3
2x	−2	0	2	4	6
3	3	3	3	3	3
$-x^2$	−1	0	−1	−4	−9
$y = 2x + 3 - x^2$	0	3	4	3	0

From $2x - 5y = -11$ we get $y = \dfrac{2x + 11}{5}$

x	−1	0	1	2	3
2x + 11	9	11	13	15	17
$y = \dfrac{2x + 11}{5}$	1.8	2.2	2.6	3	3.4

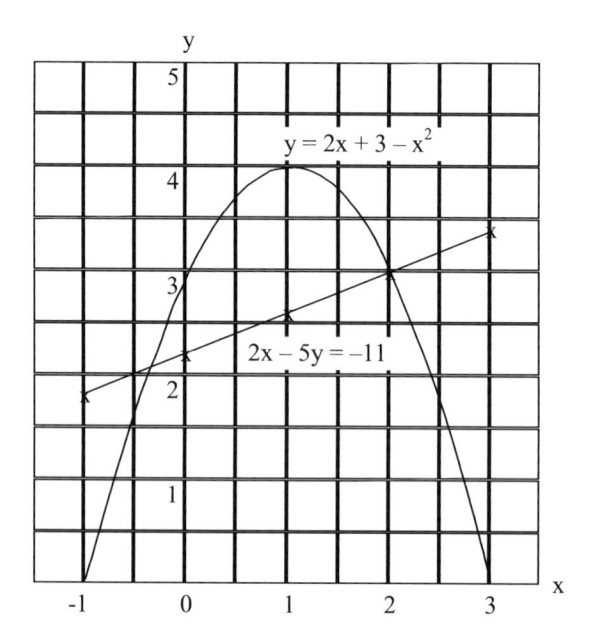

From the graph, the solutions are:

x ≈ −0.4, y ≈ 2.05 and

x ≈ 2.0, y ≈ 3.0

Note: that there may be two solutions, one solution or no solution, depending on whether the straight line cuts the curve, just touches it or misses it altogether. These correspond to the three possibilities listed earlier.

Activity 4

(a) Factorise:

    (i) $a^2 + 2a - 15$ (ii) $7b^2 + 10b + 3$

(b) Solve the simultaneous equations: $3p + 4q = 36$ $2p - 5q = 1$

(c) Solve the following by factorisation if possible, otherwise by using the formula:

    (i) $x^2 - 5x + 6 = 0$

    (ii) $x^2 + 6x + 7 = 0$

    (iii) $x^2 - 6x + 9 = 0$

    (iv) $2x^2 + 5x - 20 = 0$

Feedback to this activity is at the end of the chapter.

7 INEQUALITIES

7.1 Rules for manipulating inequalities

With algebraic expressions or equations where the left hand side *equals* the right hand side, the rule for manipulating and rearranging the expression is simple: 'as long as you do the *same* to both sides, then the equality will still hold'.

With inequalities, however, this is no longer true as some actions reverse the inequality.

Addition and subtraction

Addition and subtraction always preserve the original direction of the inequality.

$$\text{If } a>b, \text{ then } a+c > b+c$$

$$\text{If } a>b, \text{ then } a-c > b-c$$

For example:

(i) Adding 5 to each side of 3>2 gives 8>7

(ii) Subtracting 1 from each side of 3>2 gives 2>1

Multiplication and division

Multiplying or dividing by a positive number preserves the direction of an inequality but multiplying or dividing by a negative number reverses it.

$$\text{If } a>b, \text{ then } \quad a\times c > b\times c \text{ for positive } c$$

$$a \times c < b \times c \text{ for negative } c$$

$$a/c > b/c \text{ for positive } c$$

$$a/c < b/c \text{ for negative } c$$

For example:

(i) Multiplying both sides of 3>2 by 5 gives 15>10

(ii) Multiplying both sides of 3>2 by -5 gives -15<-10

(iii) Dividing both sides of 3>2 by 5 gives 0.6>0.4

(iv) Dividing both sides of 3>2 by -5 gives -0.6<-0.4

Reciprocals

Taking the reciprocal of an expression reverses the direction of the inequality.

$$\text{If } a>b, \text{ then } 1/a < 1/b$$

For example, 3>2 but 1/3<1/2.

Summary

Actions that leave the direction of the inequality unchanged	Actions that reverse the direction of the inequality
• Addition • Subtraction • Multiplication by a positive number • Division by a positive number	• Multiplication by a negative number • Division by a negative number • Taking a reciprocal

Activity 5

Rearrange the following expressions to make x the subject.

    (i)   3(5-2x)   ≤   4+2x

    (ii)   12/(4+x)   >   6

    (iii) 2 + 1/x   <   3

Feedback to this activity is at the end of the chapter.

7.2 Graphical interpretation of inequalities

When a line or curve is drawn on a graph it usually defines three areas – you can be on the line, above the line or below the line. Being on the line reflects equality in the original equation but to specify being above or below the lines requires inequalities.

For example, take the equation $y = 10 + 0.1x$.

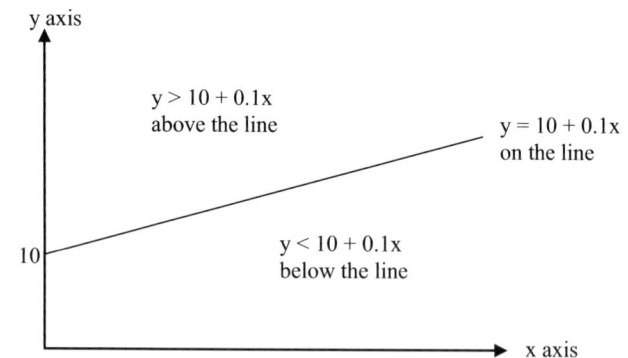

[Graph showing a line with y-intercept at 10, labelled regions: $y > 10 + 0.1x$ above the line; $y = 10 + 0.1x$ on the line; $y < 10 + 0.1x$ below the line]

Aspects of the graph can then be combined. For example the region $y \geq 10 + 0.1x$ would be shown as the following shaded area (note that the answer could be on or above the line):

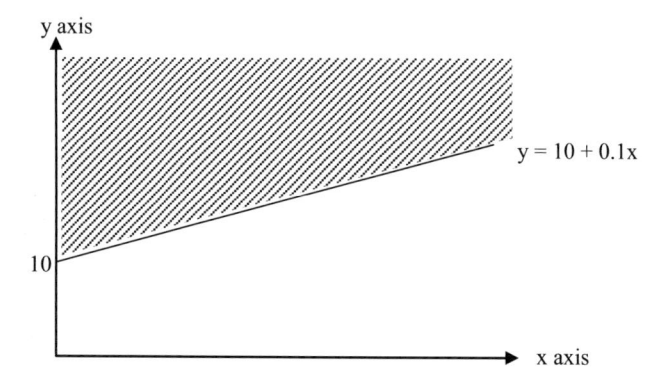

[Graph showing the line $y = 10 + 0.1x$ with the region above and on the line shaded]

Summary

- This chapter concentrated on equations: how they can be manipulated to find unknown quantities, and how they can be used to plot graphs. All the terminology and techniques learned in this chapter will be used in later chapters in practical situations.

Self-test questions

1. What is a coefficient? (1.2)

2. What are 'like terms'? (1.3)

3. What is a dependent variable? (2.1)

4. What shape do graphs of linear equations take? (4.1)

5. What is the general equation of a straight line? Explain the significance of the constants involved. (4.2)

6. What is the general form of a quadratic equation? (5.1)

7. What is the formula used to solve quadratic equations? (5.4)

8. With reference to the formula used to solve quadratic equations, how many solutions will there be if '$b^2 - 4ac$' is positive? (5.4)

9. Which actions on an algebraic expression reverse the direction of the inequality? (7.1)

Practice questions

Question 1

In the formula $Q = \sqrt{\dfrac{2DC}{PR}}$, if Q = 100, C = 10, P = 6 and R = 0.2, then D, to the nearest unit, is:

A   598

B   599

C   600

D   601

Question 2

The graph of Y = 2X is shown by which of the following lines?

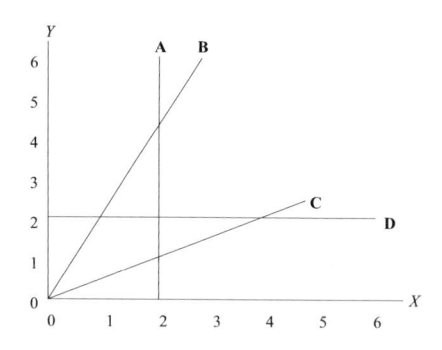

Question 3

A square-ended rectangular box has a volume of 1,458cm³. The length of the box is twice that of one side of the square end.

One side of the square end therefore measures

- **A** 6 cm
- **B** 9 cm
- **C** 18 cm
- **D** 24 cm

For the answers to these questions, see the 'Answers' section at the end of the book.

Practice questions

Question 1: Exercises in solving equations

Solve the following equations:

(a) $3x - 2 = 4x - 4$

(b) $4 - 5x = 14 + 12x$

(c) $\dfrac{12 - 3x}{4x + 5} = 4$

(d) $12x + 2y = 4$ and
$x - 2y = 9$

(e) $10x + 5y = 3 - 2x$ and
$4x + 10y = 8 - 3x$

(f) $(2x + 5)(x + 1) = 5$

(g) $6x^2 + 12x = 4(5x + 2)$

(h) $3x^2 - 2x + 7 = 0$

ALGEBRA, FORMULAE, EQUATIONS AND GRAPHS 65

(i) $2x^2 - 5x + 4xy = 60$

   $3x - y = 9$

For the answers to these questions, see the 'Answers' section at the end of the book.

Feedback to activities

Activity 1

(a)   Multiply everything within the bracket by 5.

   $10x + 15y - 20z$

(b)   Multiply everything within the bracket by $(-x)$.

   $-2x - 3x^2$

(c)   Multiply everything within the bracket by (-4).

   $-4x + 8y - 12z$

Activity 2

This means $\dfrac{x}{3} + \dfrac{y}{2} = 7$ (1)

and $\dfrac{2x}{3} - \dfrac{y}{6} = 7$ (2)

The first objective is to multiply through each equation by the lowest common denominator of that equation to remove the fractions, no attempt being made to eliminate x or y until the fractions are removed. Once this has been completed, and the equations are in the correct form, steps 1 to 4 can then be followed.

$(1) \times 6$: $6 \times \dfrac{x}{3} + 6 \times \dfrac{y}{2} = 6 \times 7 \quad \therefore 2x + 3y = 42$ (3)

$(2) \times 6$: $6 \times \dfrac{2x}{3} - 6 \times \dfrac{y}{6} = 6 \times 7 \quad \therefore 4x - y = 42$ (4)

Step 1

Multiply equation (4) by 3 to make the coefficients of y equal

   (3): $2x + 3y = 42$

$3 \times$ (4): $12x - 3y = 126$ (5)

Step 2

Add equation (3) to equation (5) to eliminate y.

   (3) $2x + 3y = 42$

   (5) $\underline{12x - 3y} = \underline{126}$

      $14x \qquad\quad\;\; 168$

66 BUSINESS MATHS

Step 3

Rearrange the equation to calculate a value for x.

$$14x = 168$$
$$x = \frac{168}{14}$$
$$\therefore x = 12$$

Step 4

Substitute the value for x into (4).

Substituting in (4): $4 \times 12 - y = 42$

$$48 - y = 42$$
$$-y = 42 - 48$$
$$-y = -6$$
$$\therefore y = 6$$

So the solution is x = 12, y = 6.

Check by substituting in (1) not (3):

$$\frac{12}{3} + \frac{6}{2} = 7$$
$$4 + 3 = 7$$
$$7 = 7$$

As this is true the solution is correct.

Activity 3

(a) **Cost equation**

Given: Selling price = £40/unit   Sales = 400 units/week
        Selling price = £20/unit   Sales = 800 units/week
        Variable costs = £7.50/unit
        Fixed costs = £10,000/week

Let output = x units/week

then Total cost: T = 10,000 + 7.5x

Sales revenue equation

Let price per unit = p (£/unit)

Then x = a + bp   since the graph of this function is linear.

Substituting each price and corresponding sales quantity into this equation,

when x = 400,   p = 40 $\therefore$ 400 = a + 40b   (1)

when x = 800,   p = 20 $\therefore$ 800 = a + 20b   (2)

(2) – (1):   400 = –20b

$\therefore$ $\frac{400}{-20}$ = b

                      –20 = b

Substituting in (1): $400 = a + 40 \times (-20)$

$400 = a - 800$

$400 + 800 = a$

$1{,}200 = a$

So $x = 1{,}200 - 20p$ (3)

Rearranging: $20p = 1{,}200 - x$

$\therefore \quad p = \dfrac{1{,}200 - x}{20} = 60 - \dfrac{x}{20}$

But sales revenue $R = x \times p$ (i.e. number of units sold × price per unit)

So sales revenue $R = x \times \left(60 - \dfrac{x}{20}\right)$

$\therefore \quad R = 60x - \dfrac{x^2}{20}$

Profit equation

Profit $P = R - T$

$= \left(60x - \dfrac{x^2}{20}\right) - (10{,}000 + 7.5x)$

$\therefore \quad P = -\dfrac{x^2}{20} + 52.5x - 10{,}000$

(b) In order to draw graphs of the above equations it is necessary to calculate a range of values for x and T, R and P. Taking x from 0 to 1,200 units:

x	0	200	400	600	800	1,000	1,200
7.5x	0	1,500	3,000	4,500	6,000	7,500	9,000
T = 10,000 + 7.5x	10,000	11,500	13,000	14,500	16,000	17,500	19,000
60x	0	12,000	24,000	36,000	48,000	60,000	72,000
$x^2/20$	0	2,000	8,000	18,000	32,000	50,000	72,000
R = 60x − x^2/20	0	10,000	16,000	18,000	16,000	10,000	0
P = R − T	−10,000	−1,5000	3,000	3,500	0	−7,500	−19,000

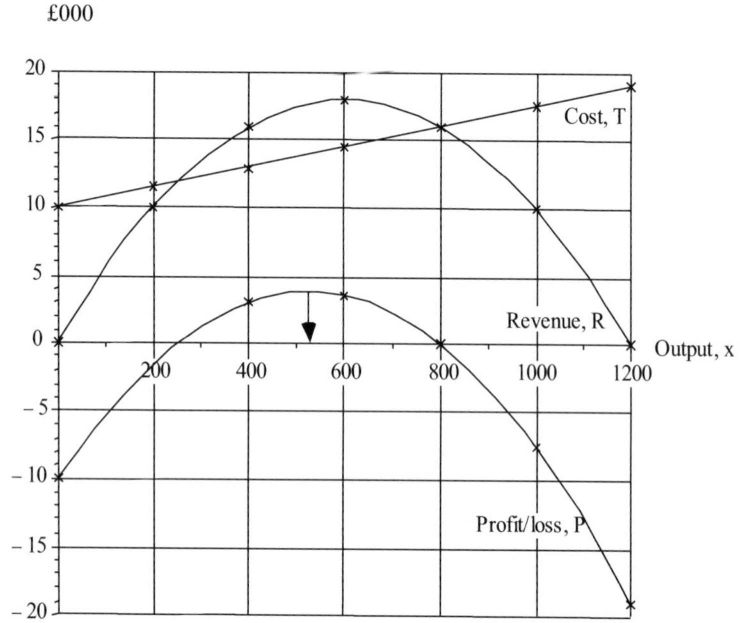

(c) From the graph it can be seen that a maximum profit of about £3,800 occurs at an output of 525 units/week.

$$\text{Selling price p} = \frac{1{,}200 - x}{20}$$

$$= \frac{1{,}200 - 525}{20}$$

$$= £33.75\text{/unit}$$

Activity 4

(a) (i) (a + 5)(a –3)

(ii) (7b + 3)(b + 1)

(b) p = 8, q = 3 (multiply the first equation by 2 and the second by 3 and subtract, eliminating p)

(c) (i) factorises x = 2 or 3

(ii) does not factorise x = –1.59 or –4.41(2dp)

(iii) factorises x = 3 twice

(iv) does not factorise x = 2.15 or –4.65 (2dp)

Activity 5

(i)
$3(5 - 2x) \le 4 + 2x$
$15 - 6x \le 4 + 2x$
$11 \le 8x$
$1.375 \le x$

(ii)
$12/(4 + x) > 6$
$1/(4 + x) > 6/12$ or 0.5
$4 + x < 1/0.5$ or 2
$x < -2$

(iii)
$2 + 1/x < 3$
$1/x < 1$
$x > 1$

5

INTRODUCTION TO FINANCIAL MATHEMATICS

Contents

1. Sequence and series
2. Arithmetical progressions
3. Geometrical progressions
4. Summary of formulae
5. Introduction to simple and compound interest
6. Present values and discounting
7. Further points on project appraisal

1 Sequence and series

> **DEFINITION**
>
> A **sequence** is a succession of numbers, of which each number is formed according to a definite law which is the same throughout the sequence. When each term in the sequence is summed the result is called a **series**.

A **sequence** is a succession of numbers, of which each number is formed according to a definite law which is the same throughout the sequence. When each term in the sequence is summed the result is called a **series**.

The series of most relevance are known as arithmetical and geometrical progressions.

2 Arithmetical progressions

> **DEFINITION**
>
> An **arithmetical progression** is one in which each term is formed from the preceding one by adding or subtracting a constant number, e.g.
>
> - 2, 3, 4, 5, ...
> - −7, 3, 13, 23, ...

An **arithmetical progression** is one in which each term is formed from the preceding one by adding or subtracting a constant number, e.g.

(a) 2, 3, 4, 5, ...

(b) −7, 3, 13, 23, ...

The constant number which is added or subtracted is known as the **common difference**.

In the examples above, for (a) the common difference is +1 and for (b) the common difference is +10. An arithmetical progression can be written in general terms as:

$$a, a + d, a + 2d, \ldots$$

where a is the first term and d is the common difference.

The nth term is:

$$a + (n - 1)d$$

The sum of the first n terms of an arithmetical progression (S_n) is given by the following formulae:

$$S_n = \frac{n}{2}[\text{First term} + \text{nth term}] = \frac{n}{2}[2a + (n - 1)d]$$

Example

(a) Find the tenth term and the sum of the first ten terms of the series 22, 20.5, 19 ...

(b) The first term of an arithmetic progression is 7 and the fourth term is 16. Find:

　(i)　The sum of the first four terms.

　(ii)　The sum of the first ten terms.

Solution

Use the formulae given above.

(a)　a = 22, d = −1.5

　　10th term　=　$a + 9d = 22 + (9 \times -1.5)$　=　8.5

　　S_{10}　=　$\frac{10}{2}[2 \times 22 + (9 \times -1.5)]$　=　152.5

(b) (i) $S_4 = \frac{4}{2}[\text{1st term} + \text{4th term}] = \frac{4}{2}[7 + 16] = 46$

(ii) 4th term $= a + 3d$ where $a = 7$

$\therefore 7 + 3d = 16$

$d = 3$

$S_{10} = \frac{10}{2}[2 \times 7 + 9 \times 3] = 205$

Activity 1

(a) Find the twenty-first term of the following series: 3, 5, 7, ...

(b) A new company makes 250 products in the first week. If the rate at which these are produced increases by 6 each week, find:

(i) How many will be produced in their 40th week of manufacture.

(ii) The expected total produced after 12 weeks.

Feedback to this activity is at the end of the chapter.

3 Geometrical progressions

3.1 Introduction

> **DEFINITION**
>
> A geometrical progression is a series in which each term is found by multiplying the previous term by a constant number. The constant is known as the **common ratio**, e.g.:
>
> - 1, 2, 4, 8, 16, ... common ratio = 2
> - $\frac{1}{3}, \frac{1}{9}, \frac{1}{27}, \frac{1}{81}, ...$ common ratio = $\frac{1}{3}$

A geometrical progression is a series in which each term is found by multiplying the previous term by a constant number. The constant is known as the **common ratio**, e.g.:

- 1, 2, 4, 8, 16, ... common ratio = 2

- $\frac{1}{3}, \frac{1}{9}, \frac{1}{27}, \frac{1}{81}, ...$ common ratio = $\frac{1}{3}$

A geometrical progression may be written in general terms as:

$A, AR, AR^2, AR^3, ...$

where A = the first term and R = common ratio.

The nth term is AR^{n-1}

R can be calculated by dividing the second term by the first.

The formula for calculating the sum of the first n terms of a geometrical progression is:

$S_n = \dfrac{A(1 - R^n)}{1 - R}$ for $R < 1$

$S_n = \dfrac{A(R^n - 1)}{R - 1}$ for $R > 1$

(The formulae are essentially the same, although they have been presented in ways that are convenient to use depending on the size of R.)

Example

Calculate the sixth term and sum of the first six terms of the series:

5, 2.5, 1.25 ...

Solution

Here A = 5

R = (2.5 ÷ 5) = 0.5

Hence 6th term = $AR^{n-1} = 5 \times 0.5^5$

= $5 \times 0.03125 = 0.15625$

$$S_6 = \frac{5 \times (1 - 0.5^6)}{(1 - 0.5)} = \frac{5 \times (1 - 0.015625)}{0.5}$$

= 9.84375

Activity 2

Calculate the 10th term and the sum of the first 10 numbers of the following series. 5, 7.5, 11.25, . . .

Feedback to this activity is at the end of the chapter.

3.2 Summing an infinite geometrical progression

Where the series is infinite it may still have a finite sum. This will only occur if R is between –1 and +1 (or –1 < R < +1, in shorthand). If this is the case then each term in the series is smaller than the last, although of itself this latter condition is not a sufficient condition to give a finite result.

Substituting back into the formula given above gives:

$$S_\infty = \frac{A(1 - R^\infty)}{(1 - R)} \quad \text{where } \infty \text{ means infinity.}$$

But if –1 < R < +1, as n gets larger R^n gets smaller, hence R^∞ becomes zero,

$$\therefore S_\infty = \frac{A}{1 - R}$$

As you will see later in this chapter, this formula for the sum of an infinite geometrical progression is important and should be learnt.

Example

Calculate the sum to infinity of the following series:

(a) $\frac{8}{3}, \frac{4}{9}, \frac{2}{27}, \ldots$

(b) $5, -1, \frac{1}{5}, \ldots$

Solution

(a) $A = \frac{8}{3}$, $R = \frac{4/9}{8/3} = \frac{4}{9} \times \frac{3}{8} = \frac{12}{72} = \frac{1}{6}$

$$S_\infty = \frac{8/3}{(1 - \frac{1}{6})}$$

$$= \frac{8/3}{5/6} = \frac{8}{3} \times \frac{6}{5} = \frac{48}{15}$$

$$= \frac{16}{5} = 3.2$$

(b) $A = 5, R = \dfrac{-1}{5}$

$S_\infty = \dfrac{5}{(1-(-\frac{1}{5}))}$

$= \dfrac{5}{(\frac{6}{5})} = \dfrac{5}{1} \times \dfrac{5}{6}$

$= \dfrac{25}{6} = 4.167$

Activity 3

Calculate the sum to infinity of the following series:

8, –1, 1/8, . . .

Feedback to this activity is at the end of the chapter.

4 Summary of formulae

4.1 Arithmetic progressions

The 'nth' term is $a + (n-1)d$

The sum of the first 'n' terms is $\dfrac{n}{2}[2a + (n-1)d]$

4.2 Geometric progressions

The 'nth' term is AR^{n-1}

The sum of the first 'n' terms is $\dfrac{A(1-R^n)}{1-R}$ for $R < 1$

or $\dfrac{A(R^n-1)}{R-1}$ for $R > 1$

The sum to infinity is $\dfrac{A}{1-R}$ for $-1 < R < 1$

5 Introduction to simple and compound interest

5.1 Simple interest

> **DEFINITION**
>
> When money is invested it earns interest; similarly when money is borrowed interest is payable. The sum of money invested or borrowed is known as the **principal**.

When money is invested it earns interest; similarly when money is borrowed interest is payable. The sum of money invested or borrowed is known as the **principal**.

With simple interest, the interest is payable or recoverable each year but it is not added to the principal. For example, the cumulative interest payable (or receivable) on £100 at 15% pa for 1, 2 and 3 years will be £15, £30 and £45.

The usual notation is:

$I = Xrt$

76 BUSINESS MATHS

where X = initial sum invested/borrowed (principal)
       r = interest rate % pa (expressed as a decimal; 15% = 0.15)
       t = time in years
       I = interest in £.

Example

A man invests £160 on 1 January each year. On 31 December simple interest is credited at 12% but this interest is put in a separate account and does not itself earn any interest. Find the total amount standing to his credit on 31 December following his fifth payment of £160.

Year (1 January)	Investment (£)	Interest (31 December)
1	160	$\frac{12}{100} \times 160 = £19.20$
2	160 + 160 = 320	$\frac{12}{100} \times 320 = £38.40$
3	160 + 320 = 480	$\frac{12}{100} \times 480 = £57.60$
4	160 + 480 = 640	$\frac{12}{100} \times 640 = £76.80$
5	160 + 640 = 800	$\frac{12}{100} \times 800 = £96.00$
Total		£288.00

Total amount at 31 December, Year 5 = £(800 + 288) (Principal and simple interest)

= £1,088

Activity 4

Calculate:

(a) the total amount of interest if a lump sum of £5,000 is invested for 5 years at 12% pa simple interest;

(b) the rate pa of simple interest if the amount of interest over 10 years on £800 is £400.

Feedback to this activity is at the end of the chapter.

5.2 Compound interest

With compound interest, the interest is added each year to the principal and for the following year the interest is calculated on their sum. For example, the compound interest on £1,000 at 10% pa for four years is calculated as follows:

Year	Principal (£)	Interest (£)	Total amount (£)
1	1,000	10/100 × 1,000 = 100	1,000 + 100 = 1,100
2	1,100	10/100 × 1,100 = 110	1,100 + 110 = 1,210
3	1,210	10/100 × 1,210 = 121	1,210 + 121 = 1,331
4	1,331	10/100 × 1,331 = 133.1	1,331 + 133.1 = 1,464.1

An alternative way of writing this is now shown:

Year	Principal (£)	Total amount (£)			
1	1,000	1,000(1 + 0.1)			= 1,100
2	1,000(1 + 0.1)	1,000(1 + 0.1)(1 + 0.1)	=	1,000(1 + 0.1)^2	= 1,210
3	1,000(1 + 0.1)^2	1,000(1 + 0.1)^2(1 + 0.1)	=	1,000(1 + 0.1)^3	= 1,331
4	1,000(1 + 0.1)^3	1,000(1 + 0.1)^3(1 + 0.1)	=	1,000(1 + 0.1)^4	= 1,464.1

So the value (V) at the end of the nth year is given by:

$V = X(1 + r)^n$

So the amounts at the end of successive years form a geometrical progression with common ratio (1 + r),

i.e. $(1 + r), (1 + r)^2, (1 + r)^3 \ldots$

Example 1

(a) Calculate the compound interest on £624 at 4% pa for 10 years.

(b) Find the sum of money which, if invested now at 5% pa compound interest, will be worth £10,000 in 10 years' time.

Solution 1

(a) Using V = $X(1 + r)^n$ with   X = £624
                                       r = 0.04
                                       n = 10

 then   V = £624 $(1 + 0.04)^{10}$
           = £624 $(1.04)^{10}$
           = £923.67

So the compound interest = £(923.67 – 624)
                          = £299.67

(b) Using V = $X(1 + r)^n$ with   V = £10,000
                                       r = 0.05
                                       n = 10

 then   £10,000 = $X(1 + 0.05)^{10}$

         X = $\dfrac{£10,000}{(1.05)^{10}}$

         X = £6,139.13

So £6,139.13 is the necessary sum of money.

Example 2

A country's population at the end of each year is greater by 2% than at the beginning of the year. Calculate the number of years required for the population to double.

Although this question is concerned with population rather than money it is still a **compounding** problem and the same basic formula can be adapted.

Using V = $X(1 + r)^n$ with   X = present population, p say
                                   V = double population, 2p
                                   r = 0.02

$$2p = p(1 + 0.02)^n$$
$$\therefore \quad 2p = p(1.02)^n$$
$$2 = (1.02)^n \quad \text{(Dividing both sides by p)}$$

As we saw in Chapter 1, we can solve this by using logarithms.

$$2 = 1.02^n$$
$$\log 2 = n(\log 1.02)$$

From log tables $\quad 0.3010 = n \times 0.0086$

$$\therefore \quad n = \frac{0.3010}{0.0086}$$
$$n = 35$$

Activity 5

In how many years will £1,000 amount to £3,207 at 6% pa compound interest?

Feedback to this activity is at the end of the chapter.

Activity 6

Find the interest rate percent pa at which £552 amounts to £896 in 11 years at compound interest.

Feedback to this activity is at the end of the chapter.

5.3 Annual percentage rate (APR)

For simplicity purposes previous compound interest examples have assumed that interest is calculated only once per year. However, this is not always the case; interest may be calculated on a monthly or even daily basis. The same formula can still be used, but there is a need to distinguish between the nominal and annual percentage rates.

There are usually two rates quoted by financial institutions, the first is the nominal rate, and the other, the rate actually earned, is known as the annual percentage rate (APR).

DEFINITION

Interest is not only calculated on an annual basis: it may be calculated daily, weekly, monthly, quarterly, half-yearly or at any other interval of time.
It is important that the rate of interest and the time are in compatible units.
For example, if the time is in months, then the rate of interest needs to be r% per month. If the time is in half-years, then the rate of interest must be r% per half-year.
As has already been shown, the general compounding formula can be applied to situations other than money problems.
For example, it can be applied to population statistics, index numbers or rates of increase and decrease generally.

Example

A credit card company charges 3.5% interest per month. Assume a customer has purchased £100 worth of goods on their card and does not pay anything against this sum for a full year. Calculate the amount they will owe after one year, and also the annual percentage rate (APR).

Solution

At the end of a 12 month period the amount which will be owed is:

$$V = X(1 + r)^n$$

where: X = original sum
  r = interest rate
  n = time period
  V = amount at end of period

So $V = 100 \times (1 + 0.035)^{12} = £151.11$

Note: in the formula r is always expressed as a decimal, hence 3.5% is expressed as 0.035.

The APR (which we shall call r_1 to avoid confusion with the r above) is therefore:

$$100 \times (1 + r_1) = 151.11$$

Hence:
$$100 \, r_1 = 51.11$$
$$r_1 = 0.5111 = 51.11\%.$$

The APR is 51.11%.

5.4 Compound depreciation

If a machine costs £1,000 and depreciates in value by 10% pa on written down value, its value in successive years is shown in the following table (all values in £).

Year	Amount of depreciation			Depreciated value		
0				1,000		
1	10% of 1,000	=	100	1,000 − 100	=	900
2	10% of 900	=	90	900 − 90	=	810
3	10% of 810	=	81	810 − 81	=	729
4	10% of 729	=	72.90	729 − 72.90	=	656.10

etc.

This is known as the **reducing balance** method of depreciation, as distinct from 'straight line' depreciation, which is depreciation by the same amount each year on cost (rather than on written down value.)

Compound depreciation is similar to compound interest except that instead of adding interest, we subtract depreciation. The law is therefore:

$$D = X(1-r)^n$$

where D = the depreciated value
X = the initial value
r = rate of depreciation
n = number of periods

Activity 7

A new machine costs £5,000 and is depreciated by 8% per annum. What is the book value of the new machine when it is five years old?

Feedback to this activity is at the end of the chapter.

Activity 8

A new machine costs £8,000 and has a useful life of ten years, after which it can be sold as scrap for £100. Calculate the annual rate of compound depreciation.

Feedback to this activity is at the end of the chapter.

5.5 Graphical representation

Consider £500 invested at 10% pa for 6 years at (a) simple interest and (b) compound interest.

(a) I = 0.1 × 500 = £50 pa.

So the total amount at the end of year 6 is:

Year	Principal and interest	Amount
1	500 + 50	£550
2	500 + 2 × 50	£600
3	500 + 3 × 50	£650
4	500 + 4 × 50	£700
5	500 + 5 × 50	£750
6	500 + 6 × 50	£800

(b) Using $V = X(1 + r)^n$ to calculate the amount at the end of the nth year where n = 1, 2, 3, 4, 5, 6.

Year	Principal and interest	Amount
1	$500(1 + 0.1)$	550
2	$500(1 + 0.1)^2$	605
3	$500(1 + 0.1)^3$	665.50
4	$500(1 + 0.1)^4$	732.05
5	$500(1 + 0.1)^5$	805.26
6	$500(1 + 0.1)^6$	885.78

Showing these graphically gives the following:

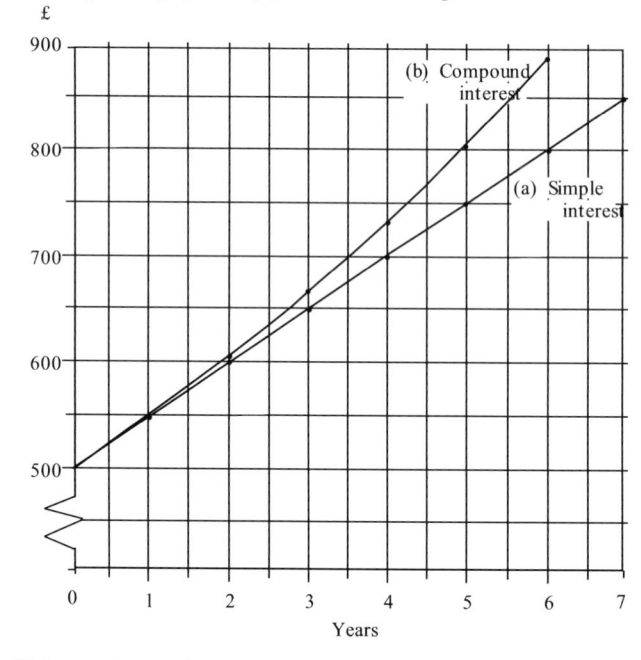

Notes on the graph

(a) The simple interest graph is a straight line.

(b) The compound interest graph is a curve.

(c) At any point in time, after the end of the first year, the amount at compound interest is greater than that at simple interest.

(d) The difference between these amounts becomes greater at later points in time.

5.6 Sinking fund

DEFINITION

A sinking fund is money put aside periodically to settle a liability or replace an asset. The money is invested to produce a required sum at an appropriate time. *(CIMA Official Terminology)*

A sinking fund is money put aside periodically to settle a liability or replace an asset. The money is invested to produce a required sum at an appropriate time. *(CIMA Official Terminology)*

Example

£2,000 is invested at the end of each year for five years at 8% compound interest. What is the accumulated amount at the end of five years?

The first contribution to the fund will earn interest for four years, the second contribution for three years and so on. Summarising in a table:

Instalment	Amount (£)	Duration (yrs)	Accumulated amount (£)
1	2,000	4	$2,000(1+0.08)^4$
2	2,000	3	$2,000(1+0.08)^3$
3	2,000	2	$2,000(1+0.08)^2$
4	2,000	1	$2,000(1+0.08)^1$
5	2,000	0	2,000

The total amount in the fund at the end of the period is the sum of the values in the final column. Thus, taking these from the bottom upwards:

Total = $2,000 + 2,000(1+0.08) + 2,000(1+0.08)^2 + 2,000(1+0.08)^3 + 2,000(1+0.08)^4$

This is a geometrical progression with A = 2,000, R = 1.08, n = 5.

Hence the total is $\dfrac{A(R^n - 1)}{R - 1}$ (R is the common ratio of the GP)

$= \dfrac{2,000 \times (1.08^5 - 1)}{1.08 - 1}$

$=$ £11,733

If the instalments are paid into the fund at the start of each year instead of the end, the first term will become $2,000(1.08)^5$ and the last, $2,000(1.08)$. Each term is therefore increased by a factor 1.08, so that the total would then be £11,733 × 1.08 = £12,672.

Activity 9

Sebastian wants to build up a fund to help pay for his unborn baby's school fees in just over five years' time. He intends to save £4,000 each year in a building society account which will earn interest at 9% (effective rate). He will save £4,000 immediately (today).

How much will he have by the time his child starts school at age five?

Feedback to this activity is at the end of the chapter.

Activity 10

Charlotte, an ambitious young student accountant, has put her name down on the waiting list for a Morgan Plus 8 sports car. The delivery time is seven years and she expects the price to be £35,000 at that time.

How much does she need to invest annually in a savings account earning 11% pa in order to be able to buy the car outright at that time?

Feedback to this activity is at the end of the chapter.

6 Present values and discounting

6.1 Discounting

Discounting is the reverse of compounding. It answers such questions as:

'I need £500 in two years' time. How much will I need to invest now at 10% compound to achieve this?',

and

'I have been offered an investment opportunity requiring an immediate single outlay of £850. It will generate cash inflows of £388 pa for the next three years. I will need to borrow the initial sum from the bank at 8%. Is it worthwhile?'.

The second of these will be considered later in this chapter.

Consider the first – we want to know the value of x where:

$x(1.1)(1.1) = 500$, or $x(1.1)^2 = 500$

(this just uses the compound interest formula where V = 500, r = 0.1 and n = 2)

i.e. $x = \dfrac{500}{(1.1)^2} = £413$ (to the nearest £)

Thus £413 will need to be invested for 2 years at 10% in order to yield £500.

£500 has been **discounted** to £413, which is known as its **present value**.

6.2 Present values

> **DEFINITION**
>
> The present value is the cash equivalent now of a sum receivable or payable at a future date. *(CIMA Official Terminology)*

The present value is the cash equivalent now of a sum receivable or payable at a future date. *(CIMA Official Terminology)*

The general formula for the present value (PV) of an amount A receivable/payable in n years' time at a discount rate of r% (as a decimal) is:

$$PV = \dfrac{A}{(1+r)^n}$$

The present value (PV) of an amount A receivable in n years' time is thus defined as that amount that must be invested now at r% pa to accumulate to A at the expiry of n years.

Example

Calculate the present value of £2,000 at 10% pa for 1 year, 2 years, or 3 years.

1 year: $PV = \dfrac{2{,}000}{(1+0.1)} = \dfrac{2{,}000}{1.1} = £1{,}818.18$

2 years: $PV = \dfrac{2{,}000}{(1+0.1)^2} = \dfrac{2{,}000}{1.1^2} = £1{,}652.89$

3 years: $PV = \dfrac{2{,}000}{(1+0.1)^3} = \dfrac{2{,}000}{1.1^3} = £1{,}502.63$

This means that £1,818.18 must be invested now to yield £2,000 in one year's time, £1,652.89 must be invested now to yield £2,000 in two years' time, etc.

6.3 The use of PV tables

Because discounting is so widely used in business problems, present value (PV) tables are available to shortcut the computations. A PV table is included at the beginning of this book.

This table provides a value (the 'discount factor') for a range of years and discount rates. Thus, the discount factor is the factor by which the future sum (A) is multiplied to get its present value:

$$\frac{1}{(1+r)^n}$$

where r is the discount rate
       n is the number of years.

In this table, the values are to three decimal places. This involves some rounding and loss of accuracy, but is adequate for most purposes.

You should note the timescale:

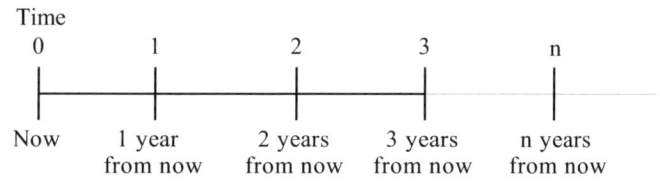

Time
0   1   2   3   n
|-----|---------|---------|---------|
Now   1 year   2 years   3 years   n years
      from now from now from now from now

(the discount factor for time 0 is always 1, so this is not included in the table).

Calculations involving discounting using PV tables are best laid out in tabular form.

Example

Calculate the present value of the given cash flows using a 15% discount rate.

Time	Cash flow	Discount factor	PV
	£		£
0	(60,000)	1.000	(60,000)
1	(10,000)	0.870	(8,700)
2	15,000	0.756	11,340
3	20,000	0.658	13,160
4	20,000	0.572	11,440
5	20,000	0.497	9,940
6	20,000	0.432	8,640

The above cash flows may represent the outflows and inflows of a particular investment project – this will be taken up later.

6.4 Annuities

DEFINITION

An annuity is a fixed periodic payment which continues either for a specified time, or until the occurrence of a specified event. (*CIMA Official Terminology*)

An annuity is a fixed periodic payment which continues either for a specified time, or until the occurrence of a specified event. *(CIMA Official Terminology)*

A ground rent is an example of an annuity, the holder of the freehold receiving an annual payment for the number of years specified in the lease.

Annuities and ground rent are constantly being bought and sold, and the method of present values can be used to calculate a fair price for the transaction.

Example

Find the present value of an annuity of £300 for 5 years, using compound interest at 4% pa, the first receipt being in one year's time.

This can be tackled using the simple discount factor identified in the previous section using the tabular approach; the factors can either be calculated directly or taken from the tables:

Time	Cash flow £	Discount factor	PV £
1	300	$\dfrac{1}{(1.04)^1} = 0.962$	289
2	300	$\dfrac{1}{(1.04)^2} = 0.925$	277
3	300	$\dfrac{1}{(1.04)^3} = 0.889$	267
4	300	$\dfrac{1}{(1.04)^4} = 0.855$	256
5	300	$\dfrac{1}{(1.04)^5} = 0.822$	247
	Total present value		1,336

This means that if £1,336 were invested now at a compound rate of 4%, the investor would be able to withdraw £300 a year for 5 years (at the end of which the investment would be down to nil). You can check this for yourself.

This type of calculation can get quite time-consuming, especially if the annuity continues for a lifetime! A quicker way is by the use of **annuity factors** or **cumulative discount factors,** which can again be obtained from a formula or from tables.

6.5 Annuity factor formula

The calculation in the table above could be written as:

$$\text{Total PV} = \frac{300}{1.04} + \frac{300}{(1.04)^2} + \frac{300}{(1.04)^3} + \frac{300}{(1.04)^4} + \frac{300}{(1.04)^5}$$

These terms form a geometrical progression with $A = \dfrac{300}{1.04}$, $R = \dfrac{1}{1.04}$ and $n = 5$

Using $S_n = \dfrac{A(1 - R^n)}{1 - R}$

$$= \frac{\frac{300}{1.04}\left(1 - \left(\frac{1}{1.04}\right)^5\right)}{\left(1 - \frac{1}{1.04}\right)}$$

This can be rearranged to:

$$300 \left[\frac{1}{0.04} - \frac{1}{0.04(1.04)^5} \right]$$

The expression in the square brackets represents the sum of the first five years' simple discount factors at 4%, with a value of 4.452.

Thus the Total PV may be calculated as:

300 × 4.452 = £1,336, as above.

The general formula for the annuity discount factor is as follows:

$$PV = \frac{1}{r}\left[1 - \frac{1}{[1+r]^n}\right]$$ or, in a single line, $1/r \times [1 - (1/(1+r)^n)]$

where r = discount rate (as a decimal)
       n = number of years for which the annuity continues

This can also be expressed as:

$$PV = \frac{1 - (1+r)^{-n}}{r}$$ or, in a single line, $[1 - (1+r)^{-n}]/r$

Use whichever you prefer. The second version is slightly quicker to tap into a calculator.

6.6 Cumulative present value tables

The annuity or cumulative discount factors for a range of values of r and t are given in the cumulative present value table, which can be found at the beginning of this book (t is denoted as n).

For n = 5, r = 4% the cumulative factor from the table = 4.452 as before.

Activity 11

(a) Calculate the amount to be invested now at 6% pa to provide an annuity of £5,000 pa for ten years commencing in five years' time.

(b) The cumulative present value tables only go up to 20%, only give you 20 years worth of factors and only deal with whole number percentages, not with percentages such as 6.25%. You will need to use your calculator's brackets functions as indicated in the 'single line' versions of the formulae given above.

If you have a calculator with a replay button this makes it much easier to calculate lots of discount factors, since you only need to alter the rate and the years once you have the operators and brackets in the right order.

Feedback to this activity is at the end of the chapter.

6.7 Loans, mortgages and amortisation

The term amortisation can be used to mean the repaying of a debt by regular instalments, as with a mortgage. Such repayments consist partly of interest and partly repayment of some of the loan. The amount of each instalment remains constant, but as the amount of the outstanding debt decreases, the proportion of the instalment which goes to paying the interest decreases, and the proportion which goes to paying off the outstanding debt increases.

From the point of view of the lender (mortgagee) this is equivalent to an annuity. The lender invests a lump sum in the borrower (mortgager) and receives a regular income in return.

DEFINITION

The term amortisation can be used to mean the repaying of a debt by regular instalments, as with a mortgage. Such repayments consist partly of interest and partly repayment of some of the loan. The amount of each instalment remains constant, but as the amount of the outstanding debt decreases, the proportion of the instalment which goes to paying the interest decreases, and the proportion which goes to paying off the outstanding debt increases.

Example

To find the annual repayment on a building society loan of £40,000 over five years at 12% pa.

This is equivalent to an annual income derived from an investment of £40,000.

Let the amount of each repayment = £A.

The first repayment is made at the end of the first year, the second at the end of the second year, and so on, so that:

$$£40,000 = \text{Present value of all repayments}$$

$$= A\left[\frac{1}{1.12^1} + \frac{1}{1.12^2} + \frac{1}{1.12^3} + \frac{1}{1.12^4} + \frac{1}{1.12^5}\right]$$

$$= A \times 3.605 \text{ (from cumulative PV table)}$$

$$\therefore A = \frac{40,000}{3.605}$$

$$= £11,096$$

The correctness of the result can be demonstrated by following through each transaction:

Year	Debt b/f	Interest	Debt & interest	Repaid	Debt c/f
	£	£	£	£	£
1	40,000	4,800	44,800	11,096	33,704
2	33,704	4,044	37,748	11,096	26,652
3	26,652	3,198	29,850	11,096	18,754
4	18,754	2,250	21,004	11,096	9,908
5	9,908	1,189	11,097	11,096	1

Thus the debt has been cleared by the end of the fifth year. The small residue of £1 is due to the use of tables which only run to 3 decimal places and rounding errors in the calculations. You could rework the calculations using the formula for the sum of a geometric progression to find the cumulative discount factor as 3.6048 to get more accuracy.

Activity 12

What is the annual repayment on a bank loan of £50,000 over eight years at 9% pa?

Feedback to this activity is at the end of the chapter.

6.8 Perpetuities

DEFINITION

A perpetuity is a periodic payment continuing for a limitless period. *(CIMA Official Terminology)*

A perpetuity is a periodic payment continuing for a limitless period. *(CIMA Official Terminology)*

Referring back to the formula for the annuity discount factor:

$$\frac{1}{r} - \frac{1}{r(1+r)^t}$$

if t gets very large (tends to infinity) the second term gets very small, and will be zero at t = infinity.

Thus the perpetuity discount factor is $\frac{1}{r}$.

Activity 13

How much needs to be invested now at 5% to yield an annual income of £4,000 in perpetuity?

Feedback to this activity is at the end of the chapter.

6.9 The relevance of discounting to business problems

One of the difficulties in many business problems is to evaluate, on a common scale, cash flows occurring at different points in time. Since businesses normally are either borrowing or lending money, interest is the cost/benefit to the business of cash at different points in time. Therefore, discounting provides a method of adjusting cash flows to a common base through the device of the notional interest charges.

For this reason discounting is widely used for financial evaluations, especially of new capital investment projects.

Example

Returning to the problem posed at the beginning of this section.

An investment opportunity is available which requires a single cash outlay of £850. Cash inflows of £388 will then arise at 12 month intervals for three years commencing in one year's time.

Bank overdraft finance is available at 8% pa.

You are required:

(a) to show the movement on the firm's bank account assuming that all cash flows associated with the project are paid into or out of the overdraft account;

(b) to compute the net terminal value of the project;

(c) to compute the net present value of the project;

(d) to comment upon your results and show the relationship between the numerical solutions derived in (a), (b) and (c).

Solution

(a)

Beginning of year	Opening balance £	Interest @ 8% £	Less repayments £	Closing balance £	End of year
1	(850)	(68)	388	(530)	1
2	(530)	(42)	388	(184)	2
3	(184)	(15)	388	189	3

Closing balance is £189 in hand.

(b) Net terminal value

The net terminal value of a project is equal to the net amount of all the cash flows associated with the project compounded forward to the end of the project's life.

Time	Cash flow	Compounding factor	Terminal value £
*0	(850)	$1.08^3 = 1.26$*	(1,071)
1	388	$1.08^2 = 1.17$	453
2	388	$1.08^1 = 1.08$	419
3	388	$1.08^0 = 1.00$	388
			189

* For convenience, in almost all investment appraisal methods, cash flows are assumed to arise at 12 monthly intervals, at the end of an integral number of years. By convention, 'now' is denoted as time 0 (the end of year 0, the beginning of year 1); 12 months' time is the end of year 1, the beginning of year 2 or, more particularly, time 1, and so on.

Although only 2 decimal places are shown it is worth using the figure that your calculator produces for 1.08^3 (1.259712) but then round the result for the terminal value (1,070.7552) to the nearest whole number.

(c) Net present value

The net present value of a project is the net amount of all cash flows associated with the project discounted back to the beginning of the project.

The neatest way to lay out the problem is to use the table seen below.

Time	Cash flow £	Discount factor	PV £
0	(850)	1.000	(850)
1	388	0.926	359
2	388	0.857	333
3	388	0.794	308
Net present value			£150

(d) As can be seen from (a) and (b), the net terminal value of the project is also equivalent to the net amount which would be in the bank if all cash flows associated with the project were paid into/out of a single bank account. Both of these are positive – i.e. there will be money left over after meeting all interest charges. Thus the project is worth considering.

The net present value (NPV) of £150 is related to the net terminal value (NTV) of £189 by:

$$£150 = \frac{£189}{(1.08)^3}$$

i.e. $$NPV = \frac{NTV}{(1+r)^3}$$

= the present value of the net terminal value.

It follows that if the NTV is positive, then the NPV will be also. Thus a positive NPV indicates a worthwhile investment.

6.10 Internal rate of return

DEFINITION

The internal rate of return is the annual percentage return achieved by a project, at which the sum of the discounted cash inflows over the life of the project is equal to the sum of the discounted cash outflows. *(CIMA Official Terminology)*

For so-called conventional projects, that is those where a single cash outflow is followed by subsequent cash inflows, it is often useful to compute the internal rate of return (IRR) of the project. This indicates the maximum discount rate at which the project is still worthwhile (positive NPV).

The internal rate of return is the annual percentage return achieved by a project, at which the sum of the discounted cash inflows over the life of the project is equal to the sum of the discounted cash outflows. *(CIMA Official Terminology)*

In general, it is necessary to compute the IRR by trial and error; that is to compute NPVs at various discount rates until the discount rate which gives an NPV of zero is found.

Example

Find the IRR of the project in the example above.

Solution

The NPV was computed at 8% and found to be £150. Our next estimate of the discount rate must be greater than 8% since the larger the discount rate, the lower the present value of future cash receipts.

Initially, try 15%; and since the 3 amounts of £388 represent an annuity, we can reduce the size of our calculation.

Year	Cash flow	Discount factor @ 15%	Present value
	£		£
0	(850)	1.000	(850)
1–3	388	2.283	886
Net present value			36

The NPV of £36 is lower than previously computed but still positive.

Therefore, increase the discount rate again a little more to say 20%:

Time	Cash flow	PV factor @ 20%	Present value
	£		£
0	(850)	1.000	(850)
1–3	388	2.106	817
Net present value			(33)

The IRR lies between 15% and 20%. A closer estimate can be found by linear interpolation.

If A is the lower discount rate (15%)
    B is the higher discount rate (20%)
    N_A is the NPV at rate A (£36)
    N_B is the NPV at rate B (– £33)

The IRR is given by:

$$\text{IRR} \approx A + (B - A) \times \left(\frac{N_A}{N_A - N_B} \right)$$

Note that this is only an approximate relationship (as indicated by the $\approx$ sign). Also note that N_B is negative, which means that care must be taken with the signs.

A useful mnemonic is that it spells out 'A BANANA – N.B.', but you still have to remember what the letters stand for and what to add, subtract, multiply and divide!

$$\text{IRR} \approx 15 + 5 \times \left(\frac{36}{36 - (-33)} \right)$$

$$\approx 17.6\%.$$

Since this is only an approximate relationship there is no point in quoting several decimal places. Even the first decimal place is suspect, 17½% might be more appropriate. The result could be found more accurately if two discount rates closer to 17½% were used.

6.11 Investment decisions

It is now possible to develop criteria for accepting or rejecting investment opportunities. Consider the situation where management can acquire funds at a known rate of interest and are considering whether to accept or reject an investment project. There are two possible approaches:

(a) **Internal rate of return approach** – is the IRR on the project greater than the borrowing rate? – if so, accept.

(b) **Net present value (NPV) approach** – at the borrowing rate, is present value of cash inflows, less initial cash outflows (i.e. the net present value) positive? – if so, accept.

DEFINITION

If the IRR on a project is greater than the borrowing rate, accept the project. If the NPV of a project at the borrowing rate is positive, accept the project.

Activity 14

An initial investment of £2,000 in a project yields cash inflows of £500, £500, £600, £600 and £440 at 12 monthly intervals. There is no scrap value. Funds are available to finance the project at 12%.

You are required to decide whether the project is worthwhile, using:

(a) Net present value approach.

(b) Internal rate of return approach.

Feedback to this activity is at the end of the chapter.

6.12 Relationship between IRR, NPV and discount rate

Example

Using the data in the previous activity, calculate additionally the NPV at 0%, 5% and 20%. Plot these, plus those already calculated, on a graph of net present value (y axis) against discount rate (x axis).

Solution

Year	Cash flow (= PV @ 0%)	Discount factor @ 5%	PV @ 5%	Discount factor @ 20%	PV @ 20%
	£		£		£
0	(2,000)	1.000	(2,000)	1.000	(2,000)
1	500	0.952	476	0.833	417
2	500	0.907	454	0.694	347
3	600	0.864	518	0.579	347
4	600	0.823	494	0.482	289
5	440	0.784	345	0.402	177
NPV	640		287		(423)

Graph of NPV against discount rate

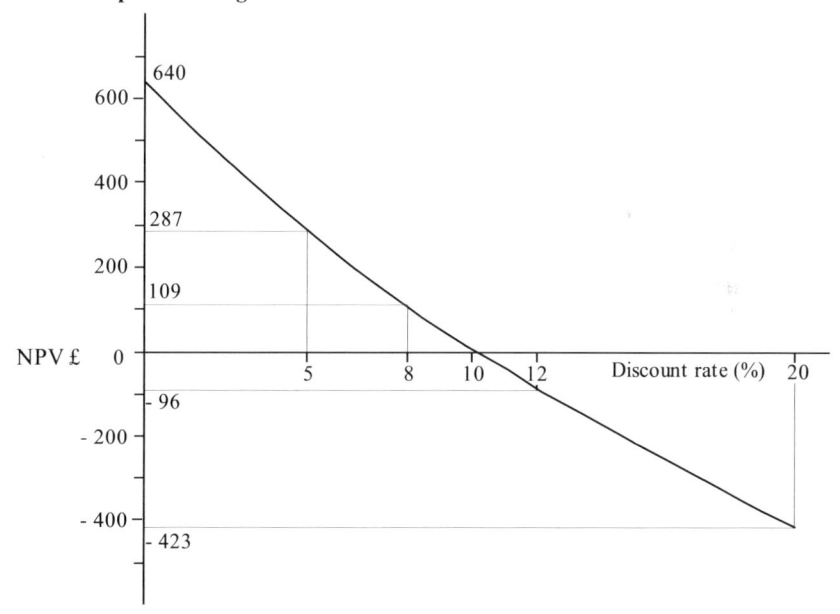

The graph shows that the higher the discount rate, the lower the NPV. Where the NPV is zero (i.e. cuts the x-axis), then we may read off the IRR.

Note: the 'curve' is nearly, but not quite, a straight line.

Thus, if a 'cut-off discount rate' is selected (e.g. the borrower's rate) of 12%, using the NPV criterion, we see that the NPV is negative; using the IRR criterion the x axis is cut at a lower discount rate than 12%. Either way the project is rejected.

7 Further points on project appraisal

7.1 Why cash flows rather than profits?

(a) **Cash is what ultimately counts** – profits are only a guide to cash availability, they cannot actually be spent.

(b) **Profit measurement is subjective** – which time period income or expenses are recorded in, and so on.

(c) **Cash is used to pay dividends** – the ultimate method of transferring wealth to equity investors.

You should note that in practice the cash flows of a project are likely to be similar to the project's effects on profits. Major differences will be:

- changes in working capital, and
- asset purchase and depreciation.

7.2 Problems in establishing which cash flows are relevant

(a) **Considering all alternatives** – any project becomes attractive if it is compared with a sufficiently bad alternative.

(b) **Opportunity costs** – if a project occupies premises which could otherwise be let at £1,000 pa, then that £1,000 pa could be regarded as a cash outflow (in fact it is a cash inflow forgone).

(c) **Interest payments** – since the analysis is based on discounting, it would be double counting to include the interest payments of the finance used to fund the project in the cash flows. Interest payments arise because money has a time value and it is precisely this time value which discounting/compounding is designed to account for. The only exception is when debt finance is raised specifically in connection with the acquisition of a particular asset.

(d) **Taxation payments** – are a cash outflow when they are paid; savings in tax payments through capital allowances or tax losses may be treated as cash receipts at the point in time when they reduce a tax payment.

(e) **Scrap or terminal proceeds** – where any equipment used in a project is scrapped, then the proceeds are a cash inflow.

7.3 Absolute and relative cash flows

When deciding between two projects (known as **mutually exclusive projects**) two approaches are possible.

(a) Discount the cash flows of each project separately and compare NPVs, or

(b) find the **differential** cash flow year by year, i.e. the **difference** between the cash flows of the two projects. Then discount those differential cash flows.

Either approach will give the same conclusion, although the second is only valid if you know that you **must** adopt one of the **two** projects.

Example

Two projects A and B are under consideration. Either A or B, but not both, may be accepted. The relevant discount rate is 10%. You are required to recommend A or B by:

(a) discounting each cash flow separately, and

(b) discounting relative (or differential) cash flows.

The cash flows are as follows:

Year	A £	B £
0	(1,500)	(2,500)
1	500	500
2	600	800
3	700	1,100
4	500	1,000
5	NIL	500

Solution

(a) **Discounting each cash flow separately**

Year	Discount factor at 10%	Project A Cash flow £	Project A PV of cash flow £	Project B Cash flow £	Project B PV of cash flow £
0	1.000	(1,500)	(1,500)	(2,500)	(2,500)
1	0.909	500	455	500	455
2	0.826	600	496	800	661
3	0.751	700	526	1,100	826
4	0.683	500	341	1,000	683
5	0.621	NIL	NIL	500	311
NPVs			£318		£436

Project B is preferred because its NPV exceeds that of A by £(436 − 318) = £118.

(b) **Discounting relative cash flows**

Year	Project A	Project B	Relative cash flow B − A	Discount factor at 10%	PV of relative cash flow
0	(1,500)	(2,500)	(1,000)	1.000	(1,000)
1	500	500	NIL	0.909	NIL
2	600	800	200	0.826	165
3	700	1,100	400	0.751	300
4	500	1,000	500	0.683	342
5	NIL	500	500	0.621	311

NPV of relative cash flow £118

In other words, the net present value of the cash flows of project B are £118 more than those of project A. B is preferred. *Note:* the result is exactly the same in (a) and (b). This gives a useful shortcut to computation when comparing two projects.

(However, method (b), whilst indicating that B is better than A, does not indicate that either are worthwhile. B may simply be less bad than A.)

Summary

This chapter has considered both arithmetic and geometric progressions and their relationships with simple and compound interest.

The principles of compound interest have then been used to discount future cash flows and thereby evaluate investment projects.

Self-test questions

1   What is the formula for the nth term of an arithmetic progression? (2)

2   What is meant by simple interest? (5.1)

3   What is compound interest? (5.2)

4   What is a sinking fund? (5.6)

5   Explain the meaning of 'present value'. (6.2)

6   What is an annuity? (6.4)

7   What is the meaning of 'net present value'? (6.9)

8   Explain the meaning of 'internal rate of return'. (6.10)

9   Explain the relationship between IRR, NPV and the discount rate. (6.12)

Practice questions

Question 1

An annual percentage interest rate (APR) of 30% is equivalent to a monthly compound interest rate closest to:

A   2.02%

B   2.21%

C   2.50%

D   2.66%.

Question 2

The present value of a stream of five annual revenues of £1,000, first one due now, is closest to (using tables and r = 8%):

A   £3,790

B   £3,990

C   £4,000

D   £4,310

Question 3

An annual rent of £1,000 is to be received for ten successive years. The first payment is due tomorrow.

Assuming the relevant interest rate to be 8%, the present value of this stream of cash flows is closest to:

A   £6,250

B   £6,710

C   £7,250

D   £7,710

Question 4

£2,500 was invested exactly three years ago, at a guaranteed rate of compound interest of 8% per annum. Its value now (to the nearest £) is:

A   £2,916

B   £3,100

C   £3,149

D   £3,401

Question 5

Which is worth most, at present values, assuming an annual rate of interest of 12%?

A   £1,200 in exactly one year from now

B   £1,400 in exactly two years from now

C   £1,600 in exactly three years from now

D   £1,800 in exactly four years from now

For the answers to these questions, see the 'Answers' section at the end of the book.

Practice questions

Question 1: Sum of a series

(a) Find the 20th term and the sum of 20 terms of the series

20, 17.5, 15 . . .

(b) Find the number of terms in an arithmetic progression whose first term is 2, common difference is 6 and sum is 420.

(c) Find the 10th term, sum of ten terms and the sum to infinity of the series

3, 1.2, 0.48 . . .

Question 2: Cash flows for projects A and B

The cash flows for two projects are expected to be as follows:

Project A		Project B	
Time	Cash flow £000	Time	Cash flow £000
0	−25	0	−25
1	10	1	0
2	10	2	5
3	10	3	10
4	10	4	30

(a) Use present value tables or first principles to compute the present values for each project at discount rates of 10%, 20%, 30% and 40%.

(b) Plot the two sets of points on a single sheet of graph paper, and join the two sets of points to produce two smooth curves.

(c) Use the graphs to read off the internal rate of return for the two projects.

For the answers to these questions, see the 'Answers' section at the end of the book.

Feedback to activities

Activity 1

(a)   a   =   3   The first term
      d   =   2   The common difference
      n   =   21   The number of terms

The nth term in the series will be $T_n = a + (n − 1)d$

So T_{21} =   3 + (21 − 1)2
              =   3 + 40
              =   43

(b) (i)   a   =   250
           d   =   6
           n   =   40
           T_{40} =   250 + (40 − 1)6
                    =   250 + 234
                    =   484

(ii) a = 250
d = 6
n = 12

The sum for the first n terms is

$$S_n = \frac{n}{2}(a + \text{nth term})$$

where the nth term is $(a + (n - 1)d)$

Step 1

Calculate the 12th term in the series:

$250 + (12 - 1)6 = 316$

Step 2

Calculate S_n

$$S_n = \frac{12}{2}(250 + 316)$$

$= 3{,}396 \text{ units}$

Activity 2

A = 5

R = $7.5 \div 5 = 1.5$

The 10th term = AR^{10-1}

= 5×1.5^9

= 192.22

The sum of the first 10 terms = $\frac{A(R^{10} - 1)}{R - 1}$

$= \frac{5 \times (1.5^{10} - 1)}{1.5 - 1}$

$= \frac{5 \times (56.665)}{0.5}$

= 566.65

Activity 3

A = 8

R = $\frac{-1}{8}$

$$S_\infty = \frac{A}{1-R} = \frac{8}{1-(\frac{-1}{8})} = \frac{8}{9/8} = \frac{64}{9} = 7\frac{1}{9} \text{ or } 7.11$$

98 BUSINESS MATHS

Activity 4

(a) $X = £5{,}000$, $r = 0.12$, $t = 5$

$I = Xrt = 5{,}000 \times 0.12 \times 5 = £3{,}000$

(b) $X = £800$, $t = 10$, $I = £400$

$r = \dfrac{I}{XT} = \dfrac{400}{800 \times 10} = 0.05$ or 5% pa

Activity 5

Using $V = X(1 + r)^n$ with $V = £3{,}207$
$X = £1{,}000$
$r = 0.06$

$3{,}207 = 1{,}000 \times (1 + 0.06)^n$

$\dfrac{3{,}207}{1{,}000} = (1.06)^n$

$3.207 = 1.06^n$

Taking logs of both sides gives: $\log 3.207 = \log(1.06^n)$
$= n \log 1.06$

From tables $0.5060 = n \times 0.0253$

$n = \dfrac{0.5060}{0.0253}$

$n = 20$

Activity 6

Using $V = X(1 + r)^n$ with $V = £896$
$X = £552$
$n = 11$

∴ $896 = 552 \times (1 + r)^{11}$

∴ $\dfrac{896}{552} = (1 + r)^{11}$

$1.623 = (1 + r)^{11}$

∴ $\sqrt[11]{1.623} = 1 + r$

$1.045 = 1 + r$

so $r = 1.045 - 1 = 0.045$

$r = 4.5\%$

INTRODUCTION TO FINANCIAL MATHEMATICS

Activity 7

$X = £5,000$

$r = 8\% = \frac{8}{100} = 0.08$ $n = 5$

$$\begin{align}
D &= X(1-r)^n \\
&= £5,000 \times (1-0.08)^5 \\
&= £5,000 \times 0.6591 \\
&= £3,295
\end{align}$$

Activity 8

$D = £100$
$X = £8,000$
$n = 10$

So $100 = 8,000(1-r)^{10}$

$(1-r)^{10} = \frac{100}{8,000} = 0.0125$

$(1-r) = \sqrt[10]{0.0125}$
$ = 0.6452$

$\begin{align}
r &= 1 - 0.6452 \\
&= 0.3548 \text{ or } 35.48\%
\end{align}$

Activity 9

In total there will be six instalments and the amount saved will be:

$S_n = \frac{A(R^n - 1)}{R - 1}$ where $A = £4,000$, $R = 1.09$, $n = 6$

$ = \frac{£4,000 \times (1.09^6 - 1)}{1.09 - 1}$

$ = £30,093$

Activity 10

Rearranging the formula in Activity 9 we have:

$A = \frac{S_n(R-1)}{(R^n - 1)}$ Where $S_n = £35,000$
$\phantom{A = \frac{S_n(R-1)}{(R^n - 1)}}$ $n = 8$
$\phantom{A = \frac{S_n(R-1)}{(R^n - 1)}}$ $R = 1.11$

$A = \frac{£35,000 \times 0.11}{(1.11^8 - 1)}$

$ = £2,951$

Activity 11

(a) The first income payment will be received at the end of five years from now and has a present value of $\dfrac{£5,000}{(1.06)^5}$.

The second payment has a present value of $\dfrac{£5,000}{(1.06)^6}$, etc.

The total PV of the ten payments will therefore be:

$$PV = 5,000\left[\dfrac{1}{(1.06)^5} + \dfrac{1}{(1.06)^6} + \dfrac{1}{(1.06)^7} + \ldots + \dfrac{1}{(1.06)^{14}}\right]$$

The terms inside the square brackets can be regarded as the cumulative PV of £1 for the first 14 years minus the cumulative PV of £1 for the **first four** years. (It is worthwhile checking that years 5 to 14 inclusive correspond to years 1 to 14 less years 1 to 4.) Thus:

$$PV = £5,000 \times [9.295 - 3.465] \text{ (from the tables)} = £29,150$$

(b) This is an activity for you to practise on your own until you know the formulae off by heart. All the answers for whole number interest rates up to 20% and periods of up to 20 years can be checked via the present value tables at the beginning of this book, so there are no excuses for not practising ... and trust us – you'll be very glad you did in your later studies!

Activity 12

Let annual repayment be A.

Present value of 8 repayments of A at 9% = £50,000.

A × 5.535 = £50,000

∴ A = £9,033

Note: as the calculations in the book show, there is no point in stating results to the nearest penny since the tables do not allow for that accuracy.

Activity 13

The PV of the perpetuity is $£4,000 \times \dfrac{1}{0.05} = £80,000$

If £80,000 is invested now at 5%, £4,000 could be withdrawn each year indefinitely (this represents the withdrawal of the annual interest, i.e. 5% of £80,000 = £4,000).

Activity 14

(a) **Net present value approach**

Year	Cash flow (£)	Discount factor @ 12%	Present value (£)
0	(2,000)	1.00	(2,000)
1	500	0.893	447
2	500	0.797	399
3	600	0.712	427
4	600	0.636	382
5	440	0.567	249
Net present value			(96)

Since the present value is negative, the project should be rejected.

(b) **Internal rate of return approach**

Calculating IRR requires a trial and error approach. Since it has already been calculated in (a) that NPV at 12% is negative, it is necessary to decrease the discount rate to bring the NPV towards zero – try 8%.

Year	Cash flow (£)	Discount factor @ 8%	Present value(£)
0	(2,000)	1.000	(2,000)
1	500	0.926	463
2	500	0.857	429
3	600	0.794	476
4	600	0.735	441
5	440	0.681	300
Net present value			109

Thus, the IRR lies between 8% and 12%. We may estimate it by interpolation (or 'using the "banana" formula', if that helps you to remember what to do!).

$$\text{IRR} \approx A + (B - A) \times \frac{N_A}{N_A - N_B}$$

$$\approx 8\% + (12\% - 8\%) \times \left(\frac{109}{109 - (-96)}\right)$$

$$\approx 8\% + 4\% \times \left(\frac{109}{109 + 96}\right)$$

$$\approx 10.13\%$$

The formula produces an IRR of 10%.

Note: however, that a linear relationship is assumed between discount rates and NPV. This is not accurate and, in fact, the actual rate of return is somewhat lower at almost exactly 10%. We can conclude that the project should be rejected, i.e. the same conclusion as in (a) above, because the IRR (10.13%) is less than the cost of capital to finance the project (12%).

6

DATA COLLECTION

Contents

1. Data and information
2. Tabulation of data
3. Frequency distributions

1 Data and information

1.1 The difference between data and information

Information is different from **data**. Although the two terms are often used interchangeably in everyday language, it is important to make a clear distinction between them, as follows.

The word '**data**' means facts. Data consists of numbers, letters, symbols, raw facts, events and transactions which have been recorded but not yet processed into a form which is suitable for making decisions.

Information is data which has been processed in such a way that it has a meaning to the person who receives it, who may then use it to improve the quality of decision making.

> Data + meaning = information

For example, in management accounting the accounting system records a large number of facts (data) about materials, times, expenses and other transactions. These facts are then classified and summarised to produce accounts, which are organised into reports which are designed to help management to plan and control the firm's activities.

Note that as data is converted into information, some of the detail is eliminated and replaced by summaries which are easier to interpret. The preparation of accounts is concerned with the optimum way of exchanging detail for easy understanding. The debate about the form and content of published accounts revolves around the extent to which some methods of summary might show the financial results in a light which is more 'true and fair' than other methods.

DEFINITION

Information is data which has been processed in such a way that it has a meaning to the person who receives it, who may then use it to improve the quality of decision making.

1.2 The management of information requirements

Just as raw materials can be turned into a good product or a sub-standard one, so raw data can be processed into good or bad information. Good information is information which has **value** to the user. It is **useful** to the recipient, can be relied upon and helps in the decision-making process.

The basic qualities of good information are that it should be:

- complete
- relevant
- timely
- as accurate as is required
- understandable
- significant
- communicated to the right person
- communicated via an appropriate channel.

Three further properties may be added:

- good information commands the confidence of the user
- information is only useful so long as its value is higher than the cost of generating it
- if information is inaccurate, the probability and level of inaccuracy are known.

This last point has an effect on all others. For example, information should be as complete or as accurate as possible without incurring costs which are higher than its value. The trade-off between cost and value of information is examined in a later section. This section continues by looking at the required qualities of good information in more detail.

1.3 Communication via an appropriate channel

Information must be communicated using an appropriate channel. There are many channels available, including:

- conversations
- telephone calls
- computer screens
- written reports
- postal communications
- fax
- email
- computer networks.

The appropriate channel depends on many factors including:

- the nature of the information
- how quickly the user requires it
- what format the user requires
- what channel is most likely to motivate the user
- geography (i.e. how far the information has to travel)
- cost of communication.

The following examples illustrate some of the relevant factors.

(a) **A fire breaks out in the stores**

Clearly the information must be transmitted immediately, using a fire alarm, internal and external telephone.

(b) **A cutting machine becomes badly adjusted and starts to produce components which are too short**

The machine operators must communicate verbally with their superior immediately. It is pointless waiting for the routine daily or weekly inspection.

(c) **An accounts clerk is processing petty cash vouchers which have not been authorised by appropriate officials**

The most efficient method of communicating information to several people internally, as is required in this case, is by memorandum. However, before sending out a memo, the effect on people's behaviour must be estimated. It would usually be appropriate to see people individually first in order to explain company policy.

(d) **Summary results of a subsidiary company in India need to be sent to the head office in the UK for consolidation**

Fax could be used but this makes it difficult to process the data further by computer. An email attachment or a network link would be preferable.

(e) **A telephone order clerk needs to check the availability of a stock item before accepting a customer order**

The most efficient method is to give the clerk a PC connected to the main computer network and able to access the inventory system: this allows for direct interrogation of stock levels.

Activity 1

We have looked at the information but must remember that information is data that has been processed in such a way as to be meaningful to the person who received it. Identify the processing operations carried out in your department at work.

Feedback to this activity is at the end of the chapter.

1.4 The value of information

The value of information results from actions by decision makers who use the information to improve profitability. Examples include:

(a) **Reducing unnecessary costs** – An investigation into the causes of adverse cost variances may uncover inefficiencies and wastage which can be eliminated in future.

(b) **Adopting better marketing strategies** – Analysis of sales by product line from point-of-sale terminals may direct management's attention to those products and locations which show the highest profit potential. Market research studies enable managers to make decisions on the qualities of products which consumers value the most.

(c) **Better analysis of 'cost drivers'** – Detailed information about the causes of costs and the factors which 'drive costs' (activity based costing) enables more realistic budgets to be set which in turn should result in scarce resources being applied in the most profitable manner.

(d) **Optimising techniques** – Information from operational research techniques such as linear programming (to determine optimal product mixes) or critical path analysis (to identify the quickest way to carry out a major project) is worthwhile if it enables resources to be applied more profitably.

Information has no value if it is not used. Neither has it any value if it is known already (no 'surprise value'). In order to assess the value of information, the following questions can be asked:

- Who uses the information?
- What is it used for?
- How often is it used?
- How often is it provided but not used?
- What is achieved by its use?
- Are there alternatives to this source of information?

It is increasingly recognised that information has a value as a strategic resource.

1.5 The cost of information

The cost of information can be classified under three general headings:

(a) The **cost of designing and setting up the system** which produces the information: this includes:

    (i) systems design

    (ii) testing

    (iii) capital costs of equipment

    (iv) installation

    (v) training.

(b) The **day-to-day running costs** of the system providing the information, including:

    (i) staff salaries

    (ii) supplies (paper, disks, etc)

    (iii) telephone charges.

(c) **Storage costs** including:

    (i) hardware costs

    (ii) space costs

    (iii) retrieval costs.

1.6 Conclusion

> **KEY POINT**
>
> The mnemonic RC Cactus helps to remember what makes management information useful.

The mnemonic RC Cactus helps to remember what makes management information useful:

R elevant
C omplete
C ommunicated to the right person
A s accurate as is required
C ommunicated via an appropriate channel
T imely
U nderstandable
S ignificant

Also:

- commanding confidence
- value higher than cost of generation
- level of accuracy known.

2 Tabulation of data

2.1 Principles of data construction

When tabulating data to make it easier to comprehend, the following principles need to be borne in mind.

(a) **Simplicity**: the material must be classified and detail kept to a minimum.

(b) **Title:** the table must have a comprehensive and self explanatory title.

(c) **Source:** the source of the material used in drawing up the table should always be stated (usually by way of a footnote).

(d) **Units:** the units of measurement that have been used must be stated, e.g. *000s* means that the units are in thousands. This can be done in the title, to keep the number of figures to a minimum.

(e) **Headings:** all column and row headings should be concise and unambiguous.

(f) **Totals:** these should be shown where appropriate, and also any subtotals that may be applicable to the calculations.

(g) **Percentages and ratios:** these are sometimes called **derived statistics** and should be shown if meaningful, with an indication of how they were calculated.

Example

Alpha Products plc has two departments, A and B. The total wage bill in 20X7 was £513,000, of which £218,000 was for department A and the rest for department B. The corresponding figures for 20X8 were £537,000 and £224,000. The number employed in department A was 30 in 20X7 and decreased by 5 for the next year. The number employed in department B was 42 in 20X7 and increased by 1 for the year 20X8.

Tabulate this data to bring out the changes over the two year period for each department and the company as a whole.

Solution

Alpha Products plc
Changes in Labour Force 20X7 to 20X8

	Dept A 20X7	Dept A 20X8	Change %	Dept B 20X7	Dept B 20X8	Change %	Total 20X7	Total 20X8	Change %
Wage Bill (£000)	218	224	+2.8	295	313	+6.1	513	537	+4.7
Number employed	30	25	−16.7	42	43	+2.4	72	68	−5.6

Source *Company records*

2.2 Further principles

The object of a table is to enable the reader to see quickly and easily patterns and relationships between the data. To achieve this most effectively certain rules should generally be observed, unless otherwise instructed.

(a) Round numbers to 2 significant figures.

(b) Reorder the numbers – sort the data so as to highlight significant relationships. This is of course easy if you are using a spreadsheet to produce the table.

(c) Interchange rows and columns – significant relationships should be shown down columns, not across rows.

(d) Use summary measures, e.g. averages.

(e) Minimise use of spaces and lines – gridlines, e.g. from a spreadsheet, interfere with visualising patterns. Some lines may be needed to make sure that the eye does not slip.

(f) Labelling should be clear but not obtrusive – abbreviated labels may lead to lack of understanding.

(g) Use a verbal summary – a brief summary of the main points emerging is often useful.

3 Frequency distributions

3.1 Classification of data

Before data can be tabulated and interpreted it must be **classified**, since, in its raw form, data is impossible to handle quickly and easily. Classification is the **bringing together of items with a common characteristic**.

Example

Fifty university students were selected at random and their heights were measured in inches. The following values were found and recorded:

67	71	61	70	66
68	72	71	76	72
77	71	66	70	72
71	64	70	72	66
70	67	71	66	69
73	74	68	70	73
67	69	69	70	71
69	74	68	72	70
70	65	69	75	67
72	70	68	73	67

By careful inspection of the above **raw** or **ungrouped data** it is possible to ascertain the height of the tallest student (77") and that of the shortest student (61"), but very little else. It is necessary, therefore, to arrange the data in a tabular form. This may involve a loss of detail, but will result in a gain in comprehensibility.

3.2 Grouped frequency distribution

In statistics, the term **total frequency** means the number of items being considered. A class frequency is the number of items in the class.

A grouped frequency distribution is constructed as follows:

Step 1

Pick out the highest and lowest figures from raw data.

Step 2

Determine the range of values, i.e. the difference between the highest and lowest values.

Step 3

Decide upon the class intervals. There should normally be between 5 and 15 classes and, wherever possible, 'the intervals' should be equal and of a 'convenient' width.

Step 4

Take each figure in the raw data and insert a tally (or check) mark against the appropriate class, e.g.

2 is represented by ||

5 is represented by ⊬⊦⊦|

11 is represented by ⊬⊦⊦| ⊬⊦⊦| |

Step 5

By totalling the tally marks find the class frequencies. The totalling is made easier by grouping the tally marks in five's as shown above. This may seem unnecessary for fifty items, but would become more important in practice if tens of thousands of items had to be classified (although in that case it is more likely that data would be collected and analysed by computer, e.g. with a spreadsheet).

Example

Using the data given in the last example, a grouped distribution is constructed of the university student's heights.

Highest value is 77", lowest value is 61"; therefore, range of values = 16".

Taking 3" class intervals of 60" and less than 63", 63" and less than 66", etc. the distribution becomes:

Class interval	Tally	Frequency
Height (inches)		Number of students
60" and less than 63"		1
63" and less than 66"		2
66" and less than 69"		13
69" and less than 72"		20
72" and less than 75"		11
75" and less than 78"		3
Total		50

If you compare this table with the one on the previous page you will see that it gives a much clearer picture of what the data means. This style of analysis also has considerable implications for many of the statistical methods that we will be studying in the chapters that follow.

3.3 Class intervals and class limits

The following points should be **carefully** noted as regards the construction of such a frequency distribution:

(a) **Number of classes**

The number of classes should be **relatively few** so that the information given is easily grasped and retained, but not so few that the inevitable loss of detail from grouping becomes too pronounced. Often it will be found that 6 or 7 classes are appropriate.

(b) **Class intervals (or width)**

> **KEY POINT**
>
> Class intervals should all be equal if possible.

These should all be **equal if possible**. The exception is generally for opening and closing classes where there may be one or two extreme values. Thus, in the above example, if there was a student of height 81" the final class would probably be 78" and above in order to include them and yet not have one class interval with zero frequency in between 78" and 80". It may also be more informative to divide one of the large central classes into smaller intervals in order to retain some detail of the original data.

(c) **Open ended class intervals**

Classes such as '78 and over' or 'less than 60', which have only one boundary specified, are said to be open ended. For the purpose of statistical calculations, each such class is assumed to have the same interval as the class next to it. In this example, 'less than 60' would be taken as '57 and less than 60' to make it have the same interval as '60 and less than 63', and '78 and over' would be taken as '78 and less than 81' to have the same interval as '75 and less than 78'. Since open ended classes are only used when the number of items in the class is small, any error resulting from this assumption will usually be negligible.

(d) **Class limits (their mathematical meaning)**

The limits of a class indicate what values from the original data will be included in each class, and therefore it is important to clarify the various ways in which class limits can be stated.

The most commonly used method of defining classes is shown in the following example (the actual numbers used are an example only, and in practice would depend on the total range of values):

0	and less than	10	
10	and less than	20	
20	and less than	30	etc.

This may also be shown as

≥ 0 but < 10

≥ 10 but < 20

≥ 20 but < 30

The upper class boundary is thus inferred from the lower boundary of the next class.

The above method is unambiguous; a value of exactly 10 (say) would be put in the second class. For discrete whole number data, 'less than 10' would mean 'up to and including 9' so that in this case, the classes could be:

0	–	9
10	–	19
20	–	29 etc.

This must not be used for continuous data, as there would be nowhere to put values between 9 and 10, 19 and 20, etc.

The following is sometimes used, but should be avoided.

0	to	10
10	to	20
20	to	30 etc.

In this case, we cannot logically decide in which group a value of exactly 10 (say) should be put.

It is important not to round the data before classifying it. In the above example, if the data had been rounded before classifying, any value between 9.5 and 10 would have been rounded to 10 and then classified in the group 10 and less than 20 instead of the correct group of 0 and less than 10.

If the data has been rounded before classifying, it would be more correct to define the group intervals as 0 to 9.5, 9.5 to 19.5, 19.5 to 29.5, etc. Such boundaries are awkward and mean that the first group has a different class interval (9.5 units) to subsequent groups (10 units), which will present problems later on.

Summary

- The distinction between data and information, and the qualities of information that make it useful to managers, was examined. The chapter went on to describe how data is acquired and processed into a more useful form. The next chapter will develop the idea of presentation of data.

Self-test questions

1. How might management information be communicated? (1.3)

2. What might represent the 'value' of information? (1.4)

3. What constitutes the 'cost' of the information? (1.5)

4. What is a class limit? (3.3)

Practice question

Data and information

(a) Define and distinguish between 'data' and 'information'.

(b) What do you consider to be the qualities that should be possessed by good information?

For the answer to this question, see the 'Answers' section at the end of the book.

Feedback to activity

Activity 1

The processing operations could include:

- classifying
- sorting
- calculating
- summarising
- interpreting
- updating
- destroying.

7

PRESENTATION OF DATA

Contents

1 Diagrammatic representation of data
2 Graphical representation of data
3 Histograms and ogives
4 Data in business reports

1 Diagrammatic representation of data

1.1 Introduction

There are several advantages of presenting a mass of data in tabular form. The figures can easily be located, comparisons between classes can be made at a glance, patterns of figures are highlighted and tables are easily understood by non-statisticians.

However, charts, diagrams and graphs are more popular ways of displaying data simply. Such visual representation of facts plays an important part in everyday life since diagrams can be seen daily in newspapers, advertisements and on television. These can be misleading and give entirely the wrong impression. It is, therefore, important to adhere to the same basic principles as were listed under table construction.

1.2 Construction of graphs and diagrams

Principles to be followed are:

- All diagrams (and graphs) must have a title.
- The source of data must be stated.
- The units of measurement that have been used must be given.
- The scale must be stated.
- The axes must be clearly labelled.
- Neatness is essential.

1.3 Advantages of diagrams and graphs

If these principles are followed then a diagram will have several advantages over a table:

- It is easier to understand than a mass of figures in a table.
- Relationships between figures are shown more clearly.
- A quick, lasting and accurate impression is given of the significant and pertinent facts.

1.4 Types of diagram

There are various methods of representing data diagrammatically. The first set of methods to be considered are:

- pictograms
- bar charts – simple, component and multiple
- pie charts.

Each of these is considered in turn with examples to illustrate the method of construction.

1.5 Pictograms

These are, as the name implies, pictures (or symbols) which can readily be associated with the data under consideration. One picture or symbol is used to represent a unit of the variable.

Example

The following pictogram represent the car sales for British Mayland for the three consecutive years 20X1 to 20X3:

Car sales British Mayland, 20X1 to 20X3

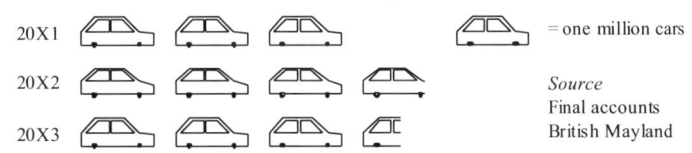

20X1 🚗 🚗 🚗   🚗 = one million cars

20X2 🚗 🚗 🚗 🚗   *Source*
                          Final accounts
20X3 🚗 🚗 🚗 🚗   British Mayland

A higher value should be shown by a greater number of pictorial units (as in this example) not by increasing the size of the pictorial units, as this can be deceptive. For instance, if both the width and the height of a picture double, its area increases by a factor of 4.

1.6 Bar charts

When information is of a quantitative form, it is often represented by a bar chart. Bars of equal width, either vertical or horizontal, are constructed with their lengths proportional to the value of the variable.

1.7 Simple bar chart

Example

The following bar chart represents the production of wheat in the UK for the years 20X1 to 20X3:

Wheat production UK, 20X1 to 20X3

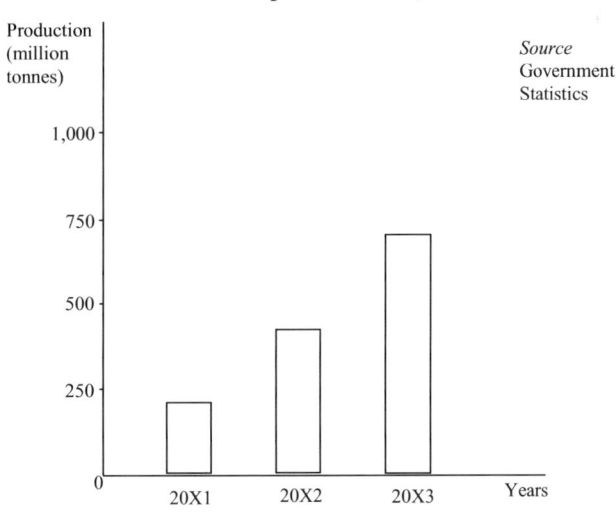

Source
Government Statistics

Note: it is bad practice to use a base line, horizontal axis, other than zero. If in the above chart the base line had started at (for example) 150 with the object of saving space, the relative heights of the bars would be visually incorrect and the chart misleading.

1.8 Component bar chart

A component bar chart is drawn when each total figure is built up from several component parts.

Example

The following bar chart represents the grain production (rye, barley and wheat) in the UK for the years 20X4 to 20X6:

Grain production UK, 20X4 to 20X6

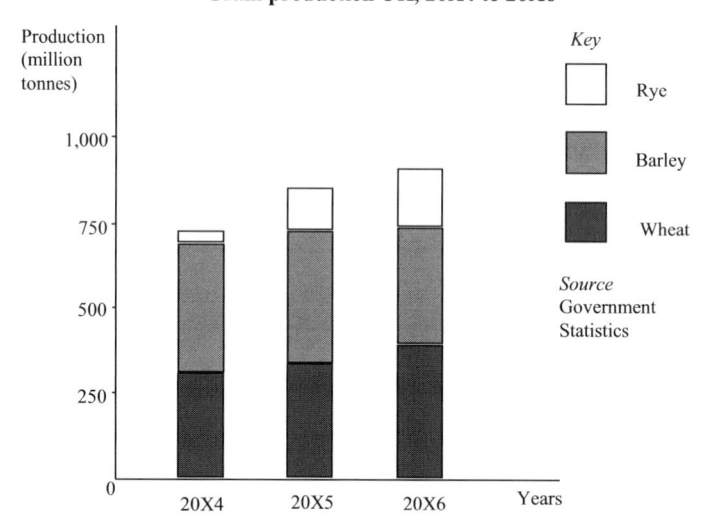

Key
- Rye
- Barley
- Wheat

Source Government Statistics

Notes:

(a) The rectangle for barley must start at the top of the rectangle for wheat, and rye start at the top of barley, so that the total height represents the total production of all three cereals. A common mistake is to commence all rectangles from the same base line so that they overlap instead of appearing one above the other. (This would then form another type of bar chart shown later.)

(b) The components of a bar, when taken together, should form a logical whole; in this case, total grain production each year. This would not be the case if the data were plotted the other way round using each bar to represent a different type of grain instead of different years.

1.9 Percentage component bar chart

This is a component bar chart in which the component values are expressed and drawn as percentages of the bar total. Each bar will have the same total height, representing 100%. They can be misleading: an actual increase can appear as a decrease and vice-versa in relative terms.

1.10 Multiple bar chart

This is drawn where two or more related items are to be compared. The bars are placed next to each other and each represents a different item.

Example

The following bar chart represents the sales of root vegetables (turnips, carrots and parsnips) in Noddy Land for the years 20X4 to 20X6:

Root vegetables Noddy Land, 20X4 to 20X6

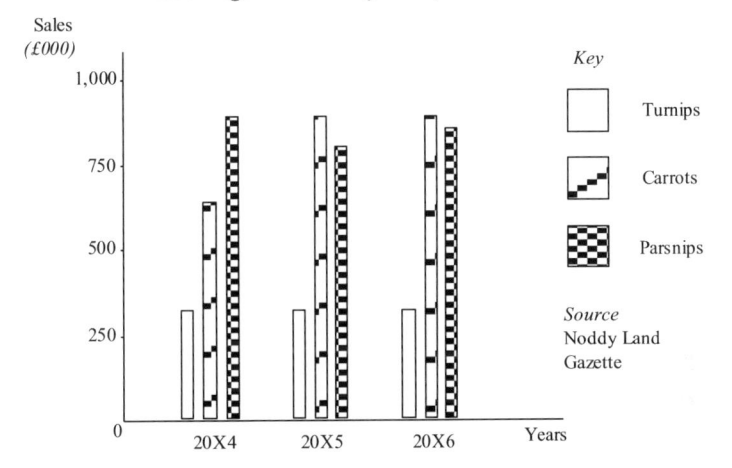

Key
- Turnips
- Carrots
- Parsnips

Source
Noddy Land Gazette

1.11 Pie charts

These are usually drawn when the proportion of each class to the whole is important, rather than the absolute value of each class. A circle is drawn, and divided into sectors such that the area of each sector is proportionate to the size of the figure represented. They are analogous to the component bar chart.

1.12 Comparison with component bar charts

Advantage: with bar charts, all components have the same base line, making comparison within and across years easier.

Disadvantage: they do not show the total for each year. This is achieved in pie charts by ensuring that the area of each circle is proportional to this total.

Example

The following pie chart represents the proportion of each type of grain produced in Disney Land in the year 20X5:

Grain production Disneyland, 20X5

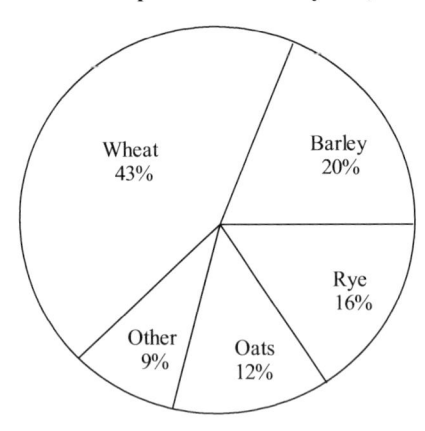

Source
Disney Land
Ministry of
Home Affairs

(Pie chart: Wheat 43%, Barley 20%, Rye 16%, Oats 12%, Other 9%)

Construction of pie chart

The angles are calculated as proportional parts of 360°. For example, in the above chart, given the percentages:

Grain	*%*	*Angle of sector (degrees)*		
Wheat	43	$360 \times \dfrac{43}{100}$	=	155
Barley	20	$360 \times \dfrac{20}{100}$	=	72
Rye	16	$360 \times \dfrac{16}{100}$	=	58
Oats	12	$360 \times \dfrac{12}{100}$	=	43
Other	9	$360 \times \dfrac{9}{100}$	=	32
	100			360

If two or more years are to be compared, a separate pie chart would be needed for each year. The area of each circle should be proportional to the total, which means that the radius must be proportional to the square root of the total. Thus if the total grain production for 20X5 was 5 million tonnes and for 20X6 was 6 million tonnes, the radii should be in the ratio $\sqrt{5}:\sqrt{6}$ or $1:\sqrt{6/5}$ which equals 1:1.095. If the circle for 20X5 was constructed with a radius of 3cm, the circle for 20X6 should have a radius of 3.3cm.

1.13 Diagrams and charts compared

Pictograms may be time-consuming to draw and lack accuracy. They are attractive to the eye but should really only be used to convey simple information.

Bar charts are the easiest type of diagram to understand and to draw. They are accurate, and actual values can be read off the vertical scale.

Pie charts are more difficult to draw than bar charts. They are less accurate, and actual values cannot usually be read off the chart. It is also very difficult to compare pie charts, especially if different sized circles have been drawn.

1.14 Diagrams and spreadsheet packages

Most spreadsheet packages have a facility to generate charts and diagrams directly from data in a spreadsheet.

The following example is a bar chart from closing cash balances produced using Microsoft Excel.

Closing Cash Balances during 20X1

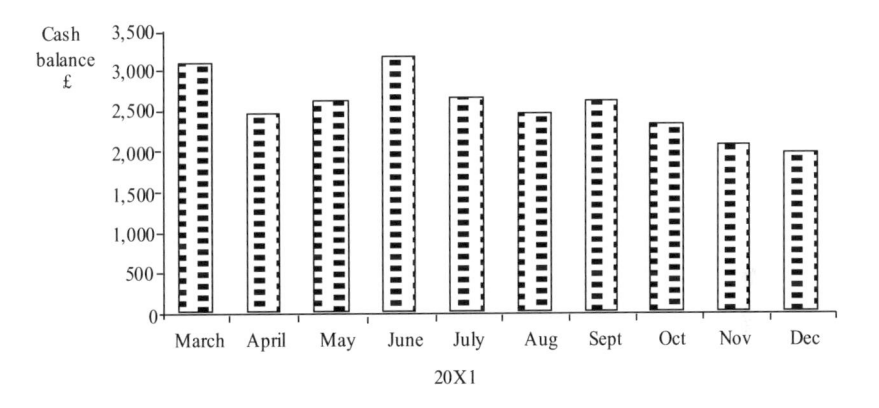

The next example, using the same spreadsheet, is a pie chart of area sales.

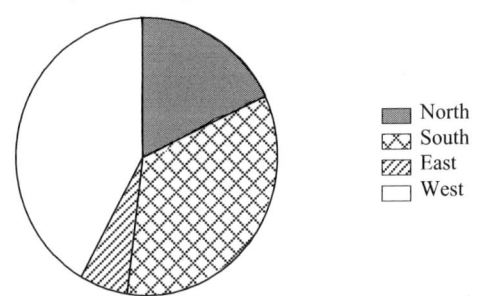

The main problem, given the wide availability of these packages, is to discourage users from filling reports with too many diagrams.

2 Graphical representation of data

The graphical representation of data may take the following forms:

- histograms and ogives
- frequency polygons
- frequency curves.

3 Histograms and ogives

3.1 Introduction

DEFINITION

A **histogram** is a special form of column or bar chart that is used to represent data given in the form of a grouped frequency distribution. The important difference is that the area of each rectangle rather than the height represents the frequency of a particular class interval.

A **histogram** is a special form of column or bar chart that is used to represent data given in the form of a grouped frequency distribution. The important difference is that the **area** of each rectangle rather than the height represents the frequency of a particular class interval.

There are various types of histogram described below.

3.2 Equal class intervals

KEY POINT

If the class intervals are all equal then the heights of the rectangles in the histogram are proportional to the frequencies.

If all the class intervals are of the same size (as in the example below) then the rectangles have the same length of base (or width) and the heights will be proportional to the frequencies (just as in a bar chart).

Example

Class interval	Range of class	Frequency (f)
Age (years)		Number of people
11 and less than 16	5	9
16 and less than 21	5	17
21 and less than 26	5	22
26 and less than 31	5	18
31 and less than 36	5	10

The standard width of a class interval is five years.

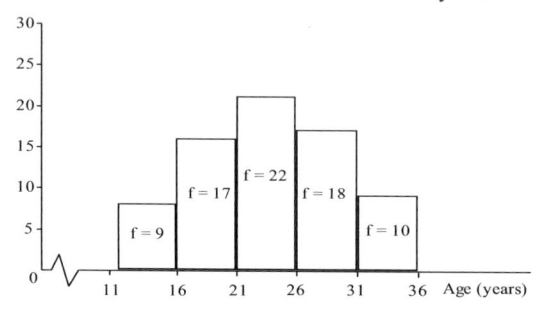

Part of the horizontal axis has been omitted for clarity. The omission is shown by a jagged line.

Note: the vertical lines are always drawn at the mathematical class limits, so there are no gaps as in a bar chart. If class intervals are equal, as here, there is no need to put the frequency in each bar (except for additional accuracy reading the diagram). It is a useful technique if class intervals are unequal.

3.3 Unequal class intervals

If the distribution has unequal class intervals, as in the example below where the third and fourth class intervals have twice the range of the others, it is necessary to adjust the heights of the bars to compensate for the fact that the rectangles do not have all the same length of base. Only by doing this will the area of the rectangle represent the frequency.

Example

The following data refers to the weights (in kg) of 42 crates of frozen fish landed at Grimsby:

Class intervals	Range of class	Frequency(f)	Height of bar (h)
Weights (kgs)		Number of crates	
10 and less than 15	5	2	2
15 and less than 20	5	5	5
20 and less than 30	10	12	12/2 = 6
30 and less than 40	10	16	16/2 = 8
40 and less than 45	5	7	7

The standard width of a class interval is 5kg. Therefore, since the third and fourth intervals are twice as wide, it is necessary to halve the frequencies of these two classes to find the actual heights of the rectangles.

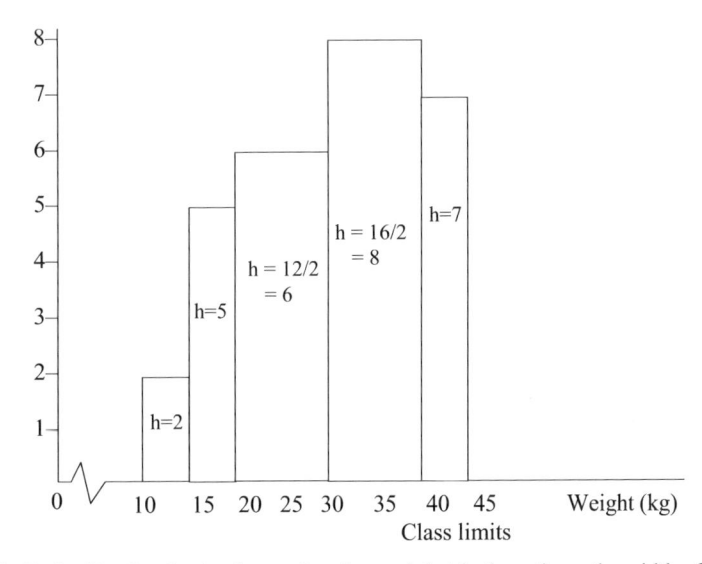

Similarly, if a distribution has a class interval that is three times the width of the standard class interval, the frequency of that class must be divided by three to find the height of the rectangle.

In the above example it was the central classes which were wider than standard. Usually it will be the tail-end classes which are wider, in order to avoid classes with no members if possible.

Interpretation must always be in terms of the standard width of class interval. For example, the height of the third rectangle is 6 units. This does not mean that there are 6 items in the class 20 to 30 kg, but that there is an average of 6 in **each** of the classes 20 to 25 kg and 25 to 30 kg. The vertical axis no longer represents frequency, but 'frequency density'.

Activity 1

A frequency distribution of a sample of incomes is as follows:

£	Frequency
40 and less than 80	7
80 and less than 100	16
100 and less than 120	28
120 and less than 130	21
130 and less than 140	8
	80

In the histogram of this data, the rectangle for the £80 – £100 class has a height of 8cm.

What should be the height of the rectangles for the following classes:

(a) £100 to £120?
(b) £130 to £140?

Feedback to this activity is at the end of the chapter.

3.4 Frequency polygons

DEFINITION

If the mid-points of the tops of the rectangles in the histogram are joined by straight lines, the figure is known as a frequency polygon.

If the mid-points of the tops of the rectangles in the histogram are joined by straight lines, the figure is known as a **frequency polygon**.

The lines at each end of the diagram must be taken to the base line at the centres of the adjoining corresponding class intervals. This is because these two class intervals have, in effect, a zero frequency since they contain no items.

Example

A frequency polygon is constructed using the data from the earlier equal class interval example.

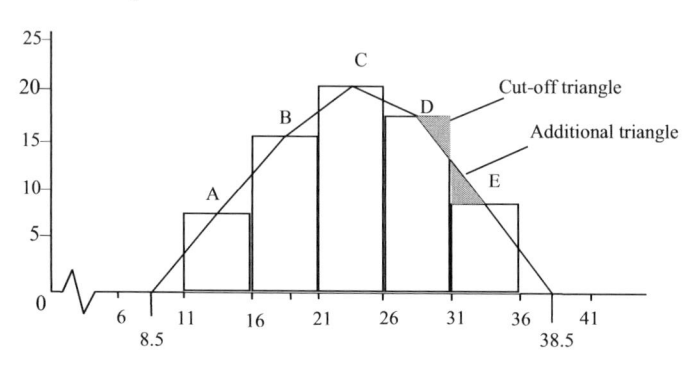

3.5 Area of a frequency polygon

Compared to the histogram, some areas are cut off when the polygon is drawn and some extra areas are enclosed. The area of the frequency polygon is equal to the area of the histogram because the areas of the cut-off triangle and of the additional triangle (shaded areas) are equal at each stage.

KEY POINT

A frequency polygon tends to a frequency curve as more data is collected to allow more class intervals to be shown of progressively smaller widths.

3.6 Frequency curves

If a smooth, freehand curve is drawn rather than joining up the mid-points with straight lines, this is known as a frequency curve and it is especially useful if two or more frequency distributions are to be compared and contrasted.

The area of a frequency curve should be the same as that of the original histogram.

DEFINITION

Ogive – a graph which displays cumulative frequencies.

3.7 Cumulative frequency curves or ogives

If the cumulative frequencies are plotted against the **upper class limits** the resulting graph is called an **ogive**, or a 'cumulative frequency curve'.

Example

The following is the frequency distribution of the weights (to the nearest gram) of 100 articles. They have been grouped into intervals of 10 grams.

Class interval	Frequency	Cumulative frequency
Weight (grams)	Number of articles	
100 and less than 110	1	1
110 and less than 120	2	1 + 2 = 3
120 and less than 130	5	3 + 5 = 8
130 and less than 140	11	8 + 11 = 19
140 and less than 150	21	19 + 21 = 40
150 and less than 160	20	40 + 20 = 60
160 and less than 170	17	60 + 17 = 77
170 and less than 180	11	77 + 11 = 88
180 and less than 190	6	88 + 6 = 94
190 and less than 200	6	94 + 6 = 100

The cumulative frequencies are plotted against the upper class limits because:

$$1 \text{ article weighs less than } 110g$$

$1 + 2$ = 3 articles weigh less than 120g

$1 + 2 + 5$ = 8 articles weigh less than 130g

$1 + 2 + 5 + 11$ = 19 articles weigh less than 140g, etc.

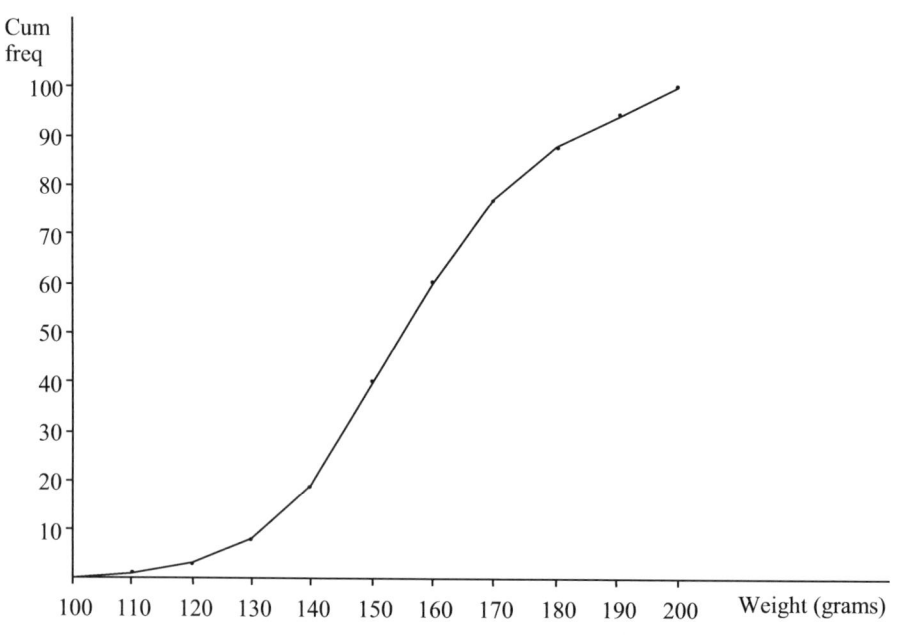

[Cumulative frequency ogive graph: Cum freq (0–100) vs Weight in grams (100–200)]

Note: that the cumulative frequency is always plotted at the upper mathematical class limit. It is only at this stage that the cumulative class frequency has been attained.

The above curve is called a 'less than' ogive because it shows the number of items less than a given value of the variable. Alternatively, the frequencies can be cumulated from the bottom upward and plotted against the **lower** class boundaries, i.e.

	6	items weigh 190 grams or more
6 + 6 = 12		items weigh 180 grams or more
12 + 11 = 23		items weigh 170 grams or more, etc.

The curve obtained by plotting these values is called a 'more than' ogive.

Plot the complete graph for yourself and compare it with the 'less than' curve.

Notes: A cumulative frequency curve has the points joined with one smooth continuous curve. A cumulative frequency polygon has the points joined by a series of straight lines.

Sometimes it is necessary to compare the ogives of two different distributions, but, unless the total frequencies of the two distributions are the same, the above method does not yield much useful information. For comparison purposes, it is better to plot cumulative percentage graphs, i.e. the cumulative frequencies are expressed as percentages of the total frequencies.

Ogives can be used to estimate the value of any item in the distribution (say, the twentieth item) by identifying the item on the vertical axis and reading off the value on the horizontal axis. The main use, however, will be met in the next chapter when medians and quartiles are being calculated. These are defined and explained elsewhere.

A common mistake is to use the class mid-points for the graph. This is always wrong for an ogive. For a 'less than' ogive the upper class boundaries, and for a 'more than' ogive the lower class boundaries, must be used.

KEY POINT

A common mistake is to use the class mid-points for the graph. This is always wrong for an ogive. For a 'less than' ogive the upper class boundaries, and for a 'more than' ogive the lower class boundaries, must be used.

4 Data in business reports

4.1 Introduction

Information is only effective when it is communicated well, so here are some suggestions for improving presentation.

4.2 Using graphs and diagrams

In general, people find information in graphs and diagrams much easier to quickly grasp and interpret. However, such diagrams have their limitations, especially when handling more complex data or being used to further analyse the data.

In summary:

Advantages of graphs/diagrams

- good at attracting attention and adding variety to reports.

Limitations of graphs/diagrams

- can be confusing if used for too complex data
- not suitable for reference purposes.

4.3 Data analysis

Accountants are expected to analyse data, to 'read figures'. This requires a systematic approach to handling any tabulated data. The following provides a general step by step approach to the problem.

Step 1

Reduce the data

Generally, tables contain too many numbers, usually because they are available and the producer is unclear what is important. Therefore, the data should be reduced to that which is essentially required for the analysis.

Step 2

Re-present the data

The seven rules for re-presenting data in tables were set out in the previous chapter, but here is a quick reminder:

(a) round numbers to 2 significant figures
(b) order rows and columns
(c) interchange rows and columns if appropriate
(d) use summary measures
(e) minimise spaces and grid lines
(f) ensure labelling is clear
(g) provide verbal summary.

Step 3

Build a 'model'

This means looking for relationships, e.g. sales grew at 5% pa; production per employee in factories A and B both grew at 2% pa, but that in B remained 20%

higher than that in A. Alternatively, the model may be a mathematical one e.g. sales, y, are related to time, t, by:

$$y = 1,459 + 0.023t$$

A good model summarises a great deal of data. It can be used to identify exceptions. With caution, it can form the basis of a predictive model for saying what will happen in future.

Step 4

Exceptions

Having established a pattern, it becomes meaningful to look for exceptions. In management these can be most important.

When an exception is found, note that the first stage is to look for an error in recording data as the cause. If this is eliminated, management faces three choices in relation to an exception: correct it, leave it alone, or conduct a management investigation.

Step 5

Comparisons

The opportunity should always be sought to compare data. There is nearly always some possible source of comparison, e.g. other companies, other countries, or simply the same company for earlier periods. If the results coincide, this further validates the model. If they differ, then the reasons may be investigated – is the model wrong, or are there some different factors? If the latter, are there some lessons that can be learnt?

Summary

This chapter has considered the compilation of statistics from data and the various forms that the presentation of such data may take. Finally the use of such presentation techniques was considered in connection with the preparation of business reports.

Self-test questions

1. What is a pictogram? (1.5)
2. How does a simple bar chart differ from a component bar chart? (1.7 & 1.8)
3. What is a pie chart? (1.11)
4. What is a histogram? (3)
5. What is a frequency polygon? (3.4)
6. What is an ogive? (3.7)

Practice questions

Question 1

In a histogram in which one class interval is one and a half times as wide as the remaining classes, the height to be plotted in relation to the frequency for that class is:

A × 0.67
B × 0.75
C × 1.00
D × 1.50

Question 2

In a pie-diagram representing a total of £550,000 operating costs, the segment for wages is represented by 89 degrees.

The amount of wages is approximately:

A £6,180
B £135,972
C £137,556
D £489,500

Question 3

A pie-chart shows total sales of £350,000 and a second pie-chart shows total sales of £700,000. If drawn correctly to scale, the ratio of the radius of the second pie-chart to the first pie-chart, to two decimal places, should be:

A 1.41 times
B 2 times
C 2.82 times
D 3.14 times

Question 4

An ogive is:

A another name for a histogram
B a chart showing any linear relationship
C a chart showing a non-linear relationship
D a graph of a cumulative frequency distribution

For the answers to these questions, see the 'Answers' section at the end of the book.

Additional questions

Question 1: Pie charts and bar charts

The following data has been extracted from the annual report of a manufacturing company:

Annual Sales (£m)

	20X8	20X7
United Kingdom	35.0	31.5
EC (other than UK)	47.4	33.2
North America	78.9	40.3
Australia	18.2	26.1

Represent this data by:

(a) pie charts

(b) component bar charts.

State the advantages and disadvantages of the two types of chart for representing this data.

Question 2: Students' statistics

From the following data prepare:

(a) a histogram

(b) a frequency polygon, and

(c) an ogive.

Height of students (ins)	Number of students
$\geq 60 < 63$	5
$\geq 63 < 66$	18
$\geq 66 < 69$	42
$\geq 69 < 72$	27
$\geq 72 < 75$	8
	100

For the answers to these questions, see the 'Answers' section at the end of the book.

Feedback to activity

Activity 1

(a) 14cm

(b) 8cm

8

AVERAGES

Contents

1 Averages
2 Arithmetic mean
3 Median
4 Mode

1 Averages

1.1 Choice of average

> **DEFINITION**
>
> An average is a measure of location sometimes called a measure of central tendency.

An average is a measure of location sometimes called a measure of central tendency.

In the sections that follow the three measures stated in the introduction are examined in detail, and the calculations for both grouped and ungrouped data are explained. Bear in mind the following points:

(a) The choice of average depends on the purpose for which the average is required.

(b) All are correct measures; they are simply different ways of summarising the same data.

(c) Measures for grouped data are always estimates, because of the loss of information when the raw data is grouped into classes.

2 Arithmetic mean

> **DEFINITION**
>
> The arithmetic mean is the best known type of average. It is defined as **the total value of the items divided by the total number of items**.

The arithmetic mean is the best known type of average. It is defined as **the total value of the items divided by the total number of items**.

2.1 Calculation for ungrouped data

Ungrouped data is data that has not been summarised (grouped) in the form of a frequency distribution.

Assuming a set of data consists of n items, $x_1, x_2, ..., x_n$, then the arithmetic mean (denoted by $\bar{x}$, pronounced 'x bar') is given by the formula:

$$\bar{x} = \frac{x_1 + x_2 + x_3 + ... + x_n}{n}$$

i.e. $\bar{x} = \dfrac{\sum x}{n}$

where $\sum x$ (sigma x) denotes the **sum of** the individual values of x.

Example

The arithmetic mean of 3, 6, 10, 14, 17, 19 and 22 is calculated as follows:

$$\bar{x} = \frac{\sum x}{n}$$

where $x_1 = 3, x_2 = 6, ...$ etc, and $n = 7$

$$\bar{x} = \frac{3+6+10+14+17+19+22}{7}$$

$$= \frac{91}{7}$$

$$\bar{x} = 13$$

2.2 Estimation of mean for grouped data

KEY POINT

For grouped data it is assumed that in each class all items are spread evenly about the mid-value. Hence,

mean = $\dfrac{\Sigma fx}{\Sigma f}$ where x is the mid-value.

For **grouped data** (data in a frequency distribution) it is necessary to decide on one value that best represents each class interval. The mid-value of each class is conventionally taken, i.e. it is assumed that the items in each class are spread evenly about the mid-value.

The formula is:

$$\bar{x} = \dfrac{f_1 x_1 + f_2 x_2 + \ldots + f_n x_n}{f_1 + f_2 + \ldots + f_n}$$

i.e. $\bar{x} = \dfrac{\Sigma fx}{\Sigma f}$

where $x_1, x_2, \ldots, x_n$ denote the mid-values of the class intervals and $f_1, f_2, \ldots, f_n$ denote the corresponding frequencies and Σf is the total frequency.

This is an example of a **weighted average**; the x-values are weighted with the class frequencies. The general formula for a weighted average is:

$$\bar{x} = \dfrac{\Sigma wx}{\Sigma w}$$

where $w_1, w_2, w_3 \ldots$ are the weights of $x_1, x_2, x_3 \ldots$ respectively.

Example

The following table shows the frequency distribution of 100 articles. The arithmetic mean is calculated as shown beneath the table.

Class interval Weight (grams)	Mid-value x	Frequency f	fx
100 and less than 110	105	1	105
110 and less than 120	115	2	230
120 and less than 130	125	5	625
130 and less than 140	135	11	1,485
140 and less than 150	145	21	3,045
150 and less than 160	155	20	3,100
160 and less than 170	165	17	2,805
170 and less than 180	175	11	1,925
180 and less than 190	185	6	1,110
190 and less than 200	195	6	1,170
Totals		$\Sigma f = 100$	$\Sigma fx = 15,600$

$$\bar{x} = \dfrac{\Sigma fx}{\Sigma f} = \dfrac{15,600}{100} = 156 \text{ grams}$$

Notes:

(a) Because 'less than 110' means 'up to 109.999...' the difference between the upper limit and 110 is infinitesimal. The error is infinitesimal in taking the class interval as 10 and the interval mid-point as 105. Similarly for the other classes.

(b) If the data was discrete whole numbers, '100 and less than 110' would have meant '100 to 109'. In this case, the mid-value would have been:

$$\dfrac{100 + 109}{2} = 104.5$$

Similarly for the other classes. Take care in identifying the mid-points and note this difference between discrete and continuous variables.

(c) Open ended classes are closed by assuming that they have the same class interval as the adjacent closed classes.

2.3 Advantages and disadvantages of the mean

Advantages	Disadvantages
• It is easy to understand and calculate. • All the data in the distribution is used, and so it can be determined with arithmetical precision, and is representative of the whole set of data. • It can be calculated when nothing more than the total value or quantity of items and the number of items are known. • It can be used in more advanced mathematical statistics.	• It may give undue weight to or be influenced by extreme items, i.e. high or low values. For example, the mean life of a sample of 100 electric light bulbs might be 2,000 hours, but it would only require one additional 'dud' bulb with a life of zero to reduce the mean to 1980 hours, a drop of 20 hours. • The value of the average may not correspond to any item in the distribution. For example, the average number of children per family is approximately 1.8, but there is no family with that number of children.

Activity 1

The following table shows the heights of a sample of 100 cabinets. Calculate the arithmetic mean.

Class interval Height (cm)	Frequency f
$\geq 150 < 160$	1
$\geq 160 < 170$	9
$\geq 170 < 180$	12
$\geq 180 < 190$	16
$\geq 190 < 200$	26
$\geq 200 < 210$	19
$\geq 210 < 220$	8
$\geq 220 < 230$	6
$\geq 230 < 240$	2
$\geq 240 < 250$	1
	$\Sigma f = 100$

Feedback to this activity is at the end of the chapter.

2.4 When not to use the arithmetic mean

The arithmetic mean is the most generally used measure of central tendency. There are however situations where it is not appropriate. Three examples are as follows:

(a) Distortion of the mean by extreme values, e.g. a company where 10 employees earn £6,000 pa, and the managing director earns £40,000 pa.

(b) The arithmetic mean is not always the correct average to use for rates of change, and care has to be taken when finding averages of percentages (or averages of averages). For example, if one group of workers has a wage increase of 10% and another group 20%, the average increase is not 15% unless both groups are the same size.

(c) If the data is split into 'clusters' the arithmetic mean is not suitable, e.g. the number of people seeing a given number of episodes of a TV series tends to cluster at the very low and very high ends.

2.5 Arithmetic mean of combined data

If one group of 10 people has a mean height of 175cm, and another group of 15 people has a mean height of 172cm, the mean of the whole group is found as:

$$\text{Mean} = \frac{\text{Sum of heights of all people in combined groups}}{\text{Total number of people in combined groups}}$$

The sum of the heights of the 10 in the first group is 175×10 = 1,750cm

The sum of the heights of the 15 in the second group is 172×15 = 2,580cm

The sum of all 25 heights is therefore $1,750 + 2,580$ = 4,330cm

The mean height is therefore $\frac{4,330}{25}$ = 173.2cm

This should be recognised as another example of a weighted average. The average for the whole group is the weighted average of the individual groups, using the number of people in the group as the weight.

3 Median

DEFINITION

The median is the value of the middle item in a distribution once all the items have been arranged in order of magnitude.

3.1 Calculation for ungrouped data

Once the items have been arranged in order, starting with either the largest or smallest, then:

- if the number of items is odd, the median is simply the value of the middle item.
- however, if the number of items is even, the median is the arithmetic mean of the two middle items.

Example 1

The median of 3, 6, 10, 14, 17, 19 and 22 is 14 since this is the value of the middle item.

Therefore, median = 14

Example 2

The median of 3, 6, 10, 14, 17, 19, 22 and 25 is found by taking the arithmetic mean of 14 and 17.

Therefore, median = $\frac{14+17}{2}$

= 15.5

If there are n items in the distribution:

the median is the value of the $\frac{n+1}{2}$ th item.

3.2 Estimation of median for grouped data

When data has been categorised into classes, each containing a range of values, then:

the median is the value of the $\frac{n}{2}$ th item.

KEY POINT

The median can be estimated from a cumulative frequency curve by going to the mid-point on the frequency range (on the y-axis) and then reading the corresponding value on the x-axis.

n is taken rather than n + 1 because, for grouped data, n is always large, otherwise the data would not have been grouped, and when n is large, the difference between n and n + 1 is negligible.

The median can be estimated from a cumulative frequency graph (ogive) as follows.

The value of the middle item is read off the horizontal axis as M:

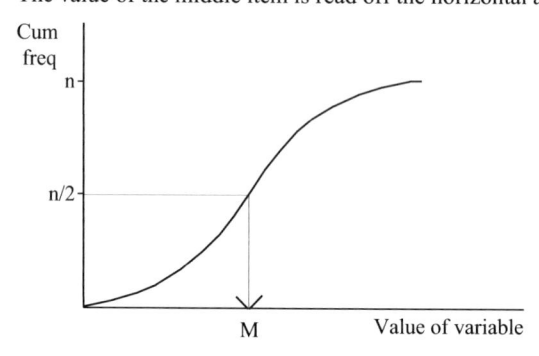

where n is the total frequency (Σf) and M is the median value.

Clearly, for reasonable estimates of the median to be made it is necessary to draw an accurate graph.

Example

Using the same data as earlier, the median is estimated as follows:

Weight (grams)	Frequency	Cumulative frequency
100 and less than 110	1	1
110 and less than 120	2	3
120 and less than 130	5	8
130 and less than 140	11	19
140 and less than 150	21	40
150 and less than 160	20	60
160 and less than 170	17	77
170 and less than 180	11	88
180 and less than 190	6	94
190 and less than 200	6	100

The cumulative frequency curve is shown below.

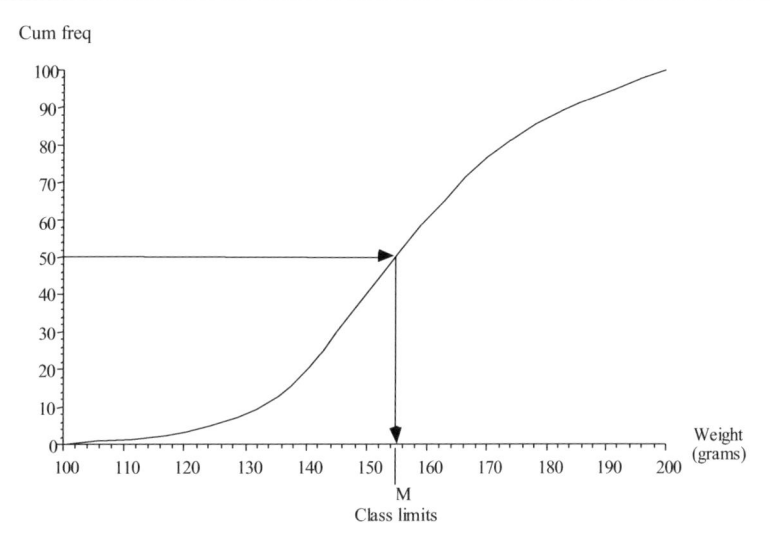

The median (M) is approximately 155 grams.

For accurate readings to be taken from the graph, it is essential that graph paper is used.

3.3 Advantages and disadvantages of the median

Advantages	Disadvantages
• It is simple to understand.	• If there are only a few items, it may not be truly representative.
• It is not affected by extreme values of the variable. In example 1, changing the last item from 22 to, say, 50 would have no effect on the median.	• It is unsuitable for use in mathematical statistics.
	• Data has to be arranged in order of size which is a tedious operation.
• It can be obtained even when the values of the extreme items are not known. It is unaffected by unequal class intervals or open-ended classes.	
• It can be the value of an actual item in the distribution.	

4 Mode

> **DEFINITION**
>
> The mode is the value that occurs most frequently amongst all the items in the distribution. When dealing with data grouped into class intervals, it is usual to refer to the modal class.
>
> *Note:* it is possible to have two (or more) modal values or modal classes.

The mode is the value that occurs most frequently amongst all the items in the distribution. When dealing with data grouped into class intervals, it is usual to refer to the modal class.

4.1 Calculation for ungrouped data

The mode can usually be determined by observation and no real calculation as such is necessary, although it is much easier if the data has been presented as a frequency distribution.

However, it is possible for a distribution to have more than one mode or, indeed, no mode at all.

Example 1

11 boys were asked what size shoes they were wearing. The following distribution resulted:

5, 7½, 6, 6, 7, 5½, 6, 5, 6, 5, 5.

5½, 7 and 7½ occur once.

5 occurs four times and 6 occurs four times.

The modal values are therefore 5 and 6.

Example 2

An interviewer called at ten houses and enquired as to how many children there were in each family. The following data resulted:

0, 4, 1, 2, 2, 0, 1, 2, 3, 2.

3 and 4 occur once.

0 and 1 occur twice.

2 occurs four times.

The modal value is therefore 2.

The mode is the value with the highest frequency.

4.2 Estimation of mode for grouped data

In a grouped frequency distribution, the modal class is the class with the largest frequency. This can easily be found by observation. The value of the mode within the modal class can then be estimated from a histogram.

Having located the modal class it is necessary to draw in the dotted lines shown in the following diagram:

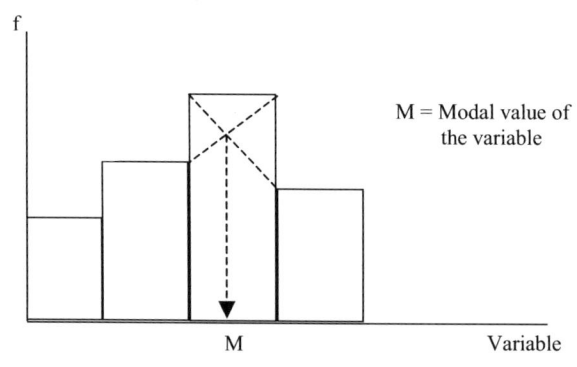

M = Modal value of the variable

Students should appreciate that it is normally continuous variables which are summarised using class intervals. For continuous variables, no two items can ever be said to have exactly the same value and therefore when dealing with continuous variables the mode should be used with extreme caution, and preferably only discussed in terms of the modal class.

Example

Using the same data as earlier the mode is estimated from a histogram. The mode (M) is 149 grams (approximately).

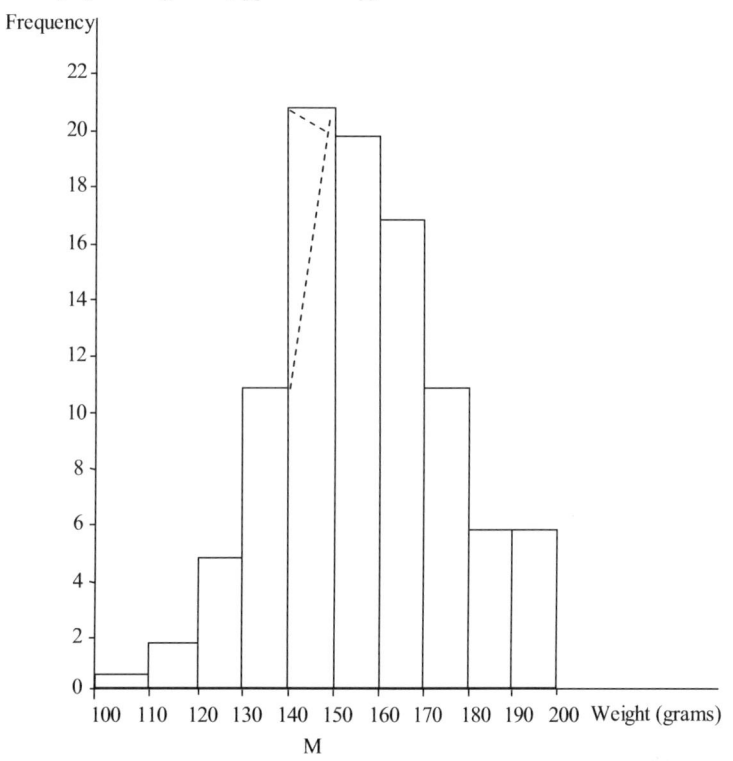

In order to estimate the mode graphically it is only really necessary to draw the modal class and the two adjoining classes. However, it is usual to be asked to draw the complete histogram. For an accurate reading, graph paper must be used, and the width of the rectangles be made as large as possible. It is worth noting before performing any calculation that the mode lies in the interval 140 grams to 150 grams, but is clearly much closer to 150 grams.

4.3 Advantages and disadvantages of the mode

The mode has many uses in both business and government.

For example, when planning a new housing estate, the architect needs to know the modal size of family in order to be able to design suitable houses.

Advantages	Disadvantages
• It is easy to understand.	• There may be no modal value or more than one may exist.
• It is not affected by extreme values.	
• It can be calculated even if not all the values in the distribution are known.	• Data has to be arranged to ascertain which value occurs most frequently and this can be tedious.
• It can be the value of an actual item in the distribution.	• It is not suitable for mathematical statistics.

Summary

The average is a useful measure which conveys information about the central value of a set of data.

There are three measures commonly used: arithmetic mean, median and mode. Their calculation depends upon whether the data is grouped or ungrouped.

Self-test questions

1. What is the formula for calculating the arithmetic mean of ungrouped data? (2.1)

2. What is the meaning of the symbol Σ? (2.1)

3. What do x and f denote when finding the mean of grouped data? (2.2)

4. Give two circumstances when use of the arithmetic mean is not appropriate. (2.4)

5. What is the definition of the median? (3)

6. The median can be estimated by use of a cumulative frequency graph or ogive. Explain how this is achieved. (3.2)

7. Give one disadvantage of using the median. (3.3)

8. Explain how the mode can be determined from a histogram. (4.2)

Practice questions

Question 1

The average (mean) cost of producing 10 units of X is £1, of producing 20 units of Y is £2 and of producing 30 units of Z is £3. The average (mean) unit cost of producing all items is closest to:

A   £2.00

B   £2.33

C   £2.50

D   £2.67

Question 2

A trader spends £900 on each of four different items costing £10, £12, £18 and £20 per unit.

The mean price paid per unit is closest to:

A £13.00

B £14.00

C £15.00

D £16.00

Question 3

The arithmetic mean of the following ten invoice values is £20:

£X £15 £22 £14 £21 £15 £20 £18 £27 £X

Therefore £X equals:

A £19

B £20

C £24

D £48

Question 4

A factory employs staff in four departments for which the average (mean) wage per employee per week is as follows:

Department	W	X	Y	Z
Mean wage	£50	£100	£70	£80
Number of employees	20	5	10	5

The average (mean) wage per employee per week in this factory is:

A £50

B £65

C £70

D £75

Question 5

The median of the scores 34, 23, 78, 12, 56, 43, 28, 9, 24 and 87 is

A 31.0

B 39.4

C 48.0

D 49.5

For the answers to these questions, see the 'Answers' section at the end of the book.

Additional questions

Question 1: Automatic filling machines

A sample of 12 packets taken from an automatic filling machine had the following weights in kilograms:

504, 506, 501, 505, 507, 506, 504, 508, 503, 505, 502, 504

Find:

(a) (i) the median weight

(ii) the modal weight

(iii) the arithmetic mean weight

(b) The effect on the median, mode and arithmetic mean if one extra value of 495 were included.

Question 2: Frequency distributions II

The production of each manufacturing department of your company is monitored weekly to establish productivity bonuses paid to members of that department.

250 items have to be produced each week before a bonus will be paid. The production of one department over a forty week period is shown below:

382	367	364	365	371	370	372	364	355	347
354	359	359	360	357	362	364	365	371	365
361	380	382	394	396	398	402	406	437	456
469	466	459	454	460	457	452	451	445	446

You are required:

(a) to form a frequency distribution of five groups for the number of items produced per week.

(b) to construct the ogive or cumulative frequency diagram for the frequency distribution established in (a).

(c) to establish the value of the median from the ogive.

(d) to contrast the use of the median and the mean as measures of location.

For the answer to these questions, see the 'Answers' section at the end of the book.

Feedback to activity

Activity 1

Step 1

Find the mid-point of each class interval, x, and produce a table showing x, f and fx.

Step 2

Multiply x by f and calculate Σfx.

Mid-value x	Frequency f	fx
155	1	155
165	9	1,485
175	12	2,100
185	16	2,960
195	26	5,070
205	19	3,895
215	8	1,720
225	6	1,350
235	2	470
245	1	245
Totals	$\Sigma f = 100$	$\Sigma fx = 19,450$

Step 3

Calculate the arithmetic mean.

$$\text{The arithmetic mean} = \frac{\Sigma fx}{\Sigma f} = \frac{19,450}{100} = 194.5 \text{cms}$$

Notice that, if the original data had units, the mean should have units. It might be worth practising calculating means on your scientific calculator.

9

VARIATION

Contents

1. Measuring dispersion
2. Range
3. Standard deviation
4. Symmetry and skewness
5. The Pareto distribution and the '80:20' rule

1 Measuring dispersion

1.1 Types of measure of dispersion

There are three commonly used measures that can be calculated for a set of data. They are:

(a) the range
(b) the semi-interquartile range } used for presenting data to non-statisticians
(c) the standard deviation

Each is a different method of choosing a single number to measure the spread of the items.

2 Range

2.1 Calculation

> **DEFINITION**
>
> Range is by far the simplest measure of dispersion, being the difference between the extreme values of the distribution.

The range is by far the simplest measure of dispersion, being the difference between the extreme values of the distribution.

Range = Highest value − lowest value

Example

The range of values 3, 5, 8, 11 and 13 is simply 10, since the highest and lowest values are 13 and 3 respectively, and 13 − 3 = 10.

2.2 Advantages and disadvantages of the range

Since this measure yields no information about the dispersion of items lying in the interval between the highest and lowest values, it is of very little practical use except in elementary quality control, where a measure is required that can be calculated very quickly.

Advantages	*Disadvantages*
• It is very simple and quick to calculate. • It is very simple to understand. • It is used as a measure of dispersion in quality control work, where rapid results are essential.	• It can be very misleading if the data contains one extremely high or low value. • Only two values are used from the distribution, it is not therefore representative of the whole data. • It cannot be used precisely in mathematical statistics.

Activity 1

Calculate the range of the following data:

9, 6, 8, 2, 4, 7, 3.

Feedback to this activity is at the end of the chapter.

3 Standard deviation

3.1 Calculation for ungrouped data

> **DEFINITION**
>
> Standard deviation is the most valuable and widely used measure of dispersion. However, it is also the most complex to calculate and the most difficult to understand. The standard deviation is a measure of the amount by which the values in a set of numbers differ from the arithmetic mean. It is defined as the **square root of the mean square deviations of the values from the mean**. The defining formula is therefore:
>
> Standard deviation
>
> $$= \sqrt{\frac{\Sigma(x - \bar{x})^2}{n}}$$
>
> where n is the number of x values. The standard deviation is usually denoted by σ (the Greek lower case sigma) or by the abbreviation SD.

> **KEY POINT**
>
> Easier computational formula for standard deviation is:
>
> $$\sigma = \sqrt{\frac{\Sigma x^2}{n} - \left(\frac{\Sigma x}{n}\right)^2}$$

Standard deviation is the most valuable and widely used measure of dispersion. However, it is also the most complex to calculate and the most difficult to understand.

The standard deviation is a measure of the amount by which the values in a set of numbers differ from the arithmetic mean.

It is defined as the **square root of the mean square deviations of the values from the mean**. The defining formula is therefore:

$$\text{Standard deviation} = \sqrt{\frac{\Sigma(x - \bar{x})^2}{n}}$$

where n is the number of x values. The standard deviation is denoted by σ (the Greek lower case sigma) or by the abbreviation SD.

While the formula above defines the standard deviation, it is rarely used for calculations, as there is an alternative formula which is algebraically equivalent, but is easier and quicker for computation. This formula is:

$$\sigma = \sqrt{\frac{\Sigma x^2}{n} - \left(\frac{\Sigma x}{n}\right)^2}$$

Example

Calculate the standard deviation of 3, 5, 8, 11, 13.

Solution

Statistical calculations of this nature are always best set out in columns thus:

x	x^2
3	9
5	25
8	64
11	121
13	169
$\Sigma x = 40$	$\Sigma x^2 = 388$

$$\begin{aligned}
\text{Hence } \sigma &= \sqrt{\frac{388}{5} - \left(\frac{40}{5}\right)^2} \\
&= \sqrt{77.6 - 64} \\
&= \sqrt{13.6} \\
&= 3.69 \text{ to 2dp}
\end{aligned}$$

Example using the formula

Just to prove to you that the other formula gives the same result but takes more effort, here is the same five-number problem again, solved the long way round.

$\bar{x}$ is $\Sigma x/n = 40/5 = 8$

x	$\bar{x}$	$(x - \bar{x})$	$(x - \bar{x})^2$
3	8	-5	25
5	8	-3	9
8	8	0	0
11	8	3	9
13	8	5	25
40			Σ 68

$$\sqrt{\frac{\Sigma(x-\bar{x})^2}{n}} = \sqrt{\frac{68}{5}} = \sqrt{13.6} = 3.69$$

Activity 2

Use the formula to calculate the standard deviation for the data 3, 4, 6, 8, 9, and show all your workings.

Feedback to this activity is at the end of the chapter.

Activity 3

It is well worth finding out how the standard deviation function on your scientific calculator works. As with other calculator functions we recommend you get a calculator with a 'replay' facility (see Chapter 1).

Here are some more sets of numbers to practise on. Use your scientific calculator's standard deviation function to calculate the standard deviation and write down the answer to two decimal places in the end column.

(a)	29	26	42	57	2			
(b)	73	58	91	82	16			
(c)	45	76	44	84	54			
(d)	26	36	22	76	40	78	39	87
(e)	714	494	637	815	666	427	784	
(f)	119	311	258	619	702			
(g)	13	2	59	37	70			
(h)	72	39	87	64	23			
(i)	26	40	52	76	64			
(j)	354	133	43	187	97			

Feedback to this activity is at the end of the chapter.

3.2 Calculation for a frequency distribution

The defining formula now becomes:

$$\sigma = \sqrt{\frac{\Sigma fx^2}{\Sigma f} - \left(\frac{\Sigma fx}{\Sigma f}\right)^2} \text{ or } \sqrt{\frac{\Sigma fx^2}{\Sigma f} - \bar{x}^2}$$

Example

Using the data of the earlier example (shown below):

Weight (stones)	Mid-value x	frequency f	fx	fx²
8–9	8.5	4	34	289.0
9–10	9.5	10	95	902.5
10–11	10.5	14	147	1,543.5
11–12	11.5	22	253	2,909.5
12–13	12.5	16	200	2,500.0
13–14	13.5	12	162	2,187.0
14–15	14.5	2	29	420.5
Totals		80	920	10,752.0

Note: that algebraically, $fx^2 = fx \times x$, therefore:

Column 5 = column 4 × column 2

(It is worth working across this table in rows to reduce the amount of button-clicking needed on the calculator.)

Substituting in the computational formula:

$$\sigma = \sqrt{\frac{10{,}752}{80} - \left(\frac{920}{80}\right)^2}$$

$$= \sqrt{134.4 - (11.5)^2}$$

$$= \sqrt{2.15}$$

$$= 1.47 \text{ stones.}$$

Note: only one additional column (fx^2) is required to the calculation of the arithmetic mean. In practice, both parameters are usually calculated at the same time from the same table.

3.3 Advantages and disadvantages of the standard deviation

Advantages	Disadvantages
• It is the most commonly used measure of dispersion in statistical work. • The value of every item of data is used. • It is the only measure that can be used in mathematical statistics.	• The calculation is complex. • It is difficult for the layman to understand. • It can give more than a proportional weight to extreme values because of squaring the deviations.

3.4 Variance

DEFINITION

The variance is the square of the standard deviation.
∴ Variance = $\frac{\Sigma(x-\bar{x})^2}{n}$ for ungrouped data.

Variance = $\frac{\Sigma fx^2}{\Sigma f} - \bar{x}^2$ for a frequency distribution.

The variance is simply the square of the standard deviation.

$$\text{Variance} = \frac{\Sigma(x-\bar{x})^2}{n} \text{ for ungrouped data.}$$

$$\text{Variance} = \frac{\Sigma fx^2}{\Sigma f} - \bar{x}^2 \text{ for a frequency distribution.}$$

The variance is of importance when **combining** frequency distributions.

Certain problems involve more than one distribution. As long as the distributions are independent, the following relationships can be used.

The mean of a sum = the sum of the means.

The variance of a sum = the sum of the variances.

An example will make this a bit clearer.

Example

Bloggs Ltd, an engineering firm, produces an item which, in the course of assembly, has to pass through three workshops – A, B and C. A record of the times taken in each workshop was kept and the following summary shows the mean and standard deviations of these times (all in hours).

	Mean	Standard deviation
Workshop A	3.48	0.25
Workshop B	4.56	0.30
Workshop C	1.91	0.20

Assuming that these times are independent, the mean and the standard deviation of the time taken to completely assemble the item is:

Mean (A + B + C) = 3.48 + 4.56 + 1.91

= 9.95 hours

Variance (workshop A) = $(0.25)^2$ = 0.0625

Variance (workshop B) = $(0.30)^2$ = 0.0900

Variance (workshop C) = $(0.20)^2$ = 0.0400

∴ Variance (A + B + C) = 0.0625 + 0.0900 + 0.0400

= 0.1925

Standard deviation (A + B + C) = $\sqrt{0.1925}$ = 0.44 hours

The important thing to note is that while you can add together the separate means to get the mean for the combined distributions you cannot add together the standard deviations.

Similarly if the problem involves a **difference** rather than a **sum** then:

The mean of a difference = the **difference** of the means

The variance of a difference = the **sum** of the variances

3.5 Coefficient of variation

DEFINITION

Coefficient of variation is a measure expressing the standard deviation as a percentage of the mean. It is a way of comparing variability between data sets.

When comparing the dispersion in two or more sets of data, the **mean** of each set of data must be taken into account. For example, a variation of 2 units in a set of data with a mean of 5 is of much greater significance than a variation of 2 units in a set of data with a mean of 50. To compare the amount of variation, or dispersion, between sets of data, the coefficient of variation is often used, which expresses the standard deviation as a percentage of the mean.

$$\text{Coefficient of variation} = \frac{\text{Standard deviation} \times 100}{\text{Arithmetic mean}}$$

Example

Two machines are used for filling bags of fertiliser. One machine is set to deliver a nominal weight of 1 kilo, and the other machine, 7 kilos. Tests on the actual amounts delivered gave the following results:

Machine	Mean weight (kilo)	Standard deviation (kilo)
1	1.05	0.062
2	7.13	0.384

Which machine varies most in weight delivered?

Solution

In absolute terms the answer is clearly machine 2, but:

Machine 1: Coefficient of variation $= \dfrac{0.062 \times 100}{1.05} = 5.9\%$

Machine 2: Coefficient of variation $= \dfrac{0.384 \times 100}{7.13} = 5.4\%$

Therefore machine 1 has a slightly greater variation in weight of output than machine 2, relatively speaking.

Activity 4

Given the following data concerning A and B, which has the higher coefficient of variation?

	Mean	Standard deviation
A	5.46	1.29
B	16.38	4.21

Feedback to this activity is at the end of the chapter.

3.6 Conclusion

KEY POINT

When stating the mean of a population, you should also state the corresponding standard deviation.

Of all the measures of dispersion that have been calculated, the standard deviation is by far the most important, its main uses and applications being in the field of more advanced statistics.

In general, the mean and standard deviation are calculated for a distribution. This is the most common 'pairing' of average and dispersion.

4 Symmetry and skewness

4.1 Introduction

If a frequency curve is drawn for a distribution, then the position of the peak of the curve is very important. If the peak is in the centre of the distribution, then it is said to be **symmetrical**.

If the peak of the curve lies to one side of the centre, the distribution is said to be **skewed**.

The further the peak lies from the centre, the greater is the degree of skewness of the distribution.

> **DEFINITION**
>
> Skewness – the tendency in a distribution to deviate from symmetry. Can be positive or negative.

4.2 Types of distribution

Normal distribution

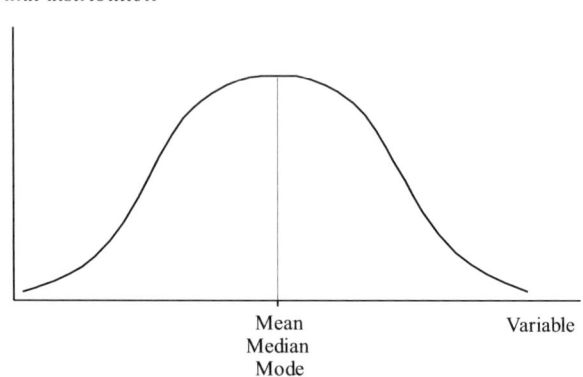

```
f
```
Mean
Median
Mode

Variable

The peak of the frequency curve is at the centre of the distribution, the curve on either side of this being the same shape, i.e. the curve is symmetrical about the dotted line.

The mean, median and mode all coincide at this point.

A positively skewed distribution

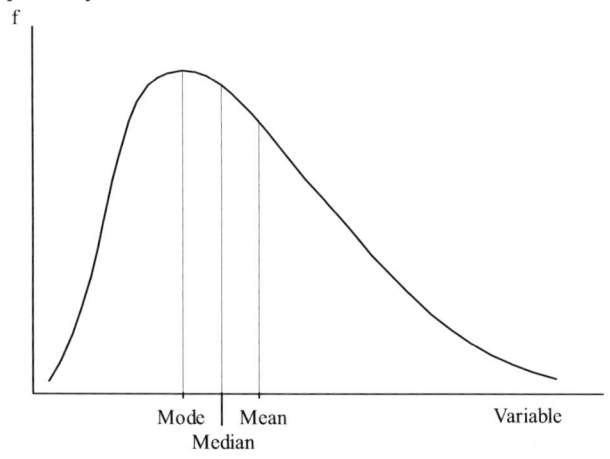

```
f
```
Mode   Mean
   Median

Variable

This occurs when the majority of the frequencies are located at the lower values of the variable. The peak of the curve therefore lies to the left of the centre of the distribution.

An example could be the distribution of salaries within a company.

A negatively skewed distribution

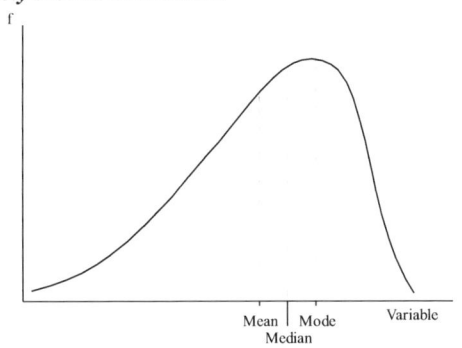

This is the exact opposite of a positively skewed distribution; it occurs when the majority of the frequencies are located at the higher values of the variable. The peak of the frequency curve will be to the right of the centre of the distribution.

An example would be age at death.

These diagrams are not drawn to scale. In actual fact, the mean, median and mode would be much closer to each other than as shown, and the median will be nearer to the mean than to the mode.

4.3 Relationship between skewness and averages

(a) In a **symmetrical distribution**, the mean, median and mode all have the same value, and are located at the same point on the frequency curve.

(b) In a **skewed distribution**, the mean will be drawn away from the mode, which is always found at the peak of the curve. The median lies between the mean and the mode. (Remember the order mean, median, mode – alphabetical order.)

5 The Pareto distribution and the '80:20' rule

5.1 Background

The Pareto distribution was named after Vilfredo Pareto who, in the late 18th century, studied the distribution of wealth in Europe and found that 80% of the wealth was held by 20% of the population – an example of a very skewed distribution.

The 80:20 aspect of this has been encapsulated into the '80:20' rule which has many variations, including

- 80% of a company's business comes from 20% of its customers
- 80% of process defects arise from 20% of the process issues.
- 20% of your sales force produces 80% of your company revenues
- 80% of delays in schedule arise from 20% of the possible causes of the delays.
- 20% of the people cause 80% of the problems
- managers spend only 20% of their time to complete 80% of their work

5.2 Pareto charts

Pareto charts can be used to highlight key areas for management.

For example, suppose a distribution/warehousing department was investigating the causes of time delays and identified five main causes with the following total delays caused:

Cause	Effect = time wasted
• Goods not in stock	• 100 hours
• Goods sent to the wrong address.	• 50 hours
• Wrong items sent	• 700 hours
• Faulty goods	• 70 hours
• Goods damaged in transit	• 80 hours

These could be shown in the following Pareto chart:

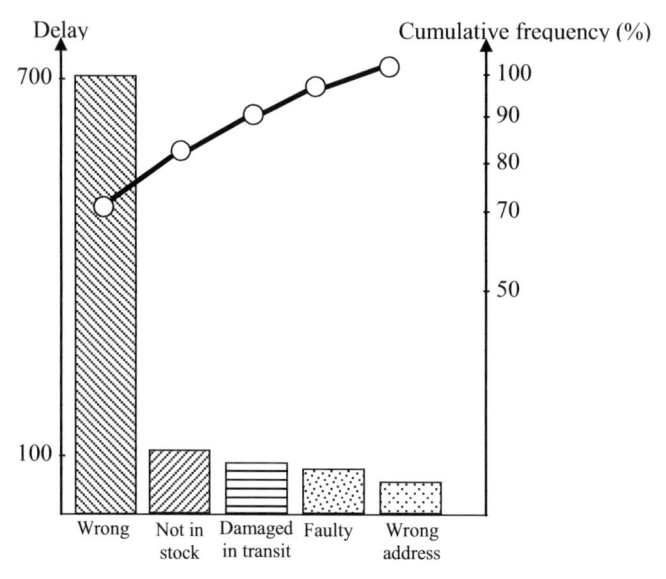

The cumulate frequency shows that 80% of delays are due to just two causes. Focussing on these first will ensure maximum management efficiency.

Summary

This chapter has considered the different measures of dispersion which may be used to analyse data, and has shown how each of them are calculated.

Self-test questions

1. What are the advantages of the 'range' as a measure of dispersion? (2.2)

4. What is the standard deviation? (3.1)

5. What is the variance? (3.4)

6. What is the coefficient of variation? (3.5)

7. If a frequency distribution is said to be positively skewed, which value would be greater, the mode or the mean? (4.2)

8. Describe what is meant by the '80:20' rule. (5.1)

Practice questions

Question 1

Quality control of four independent production processes reveals the length of certain parts (in mm) to be as follows:

Process	Mean	Standard deviation
W	100	10
X	40	5
Y	80	8
Z	150	12

The process(es) with the largest relative variation, as measured by the coefficient of variation, is/are:

A   X only

B   Z only

C   X and Y

D   W and Y

Question 2

Several groups of invoices are being analysed. For each group the coefficient of variation has been calculated.

The coefficient of variation measures:

A   the range of values of the invoices

B   the correlation between the invoice values

C   the relative dispersion of the invoice values

D   the variation between the sample mean and the true mean

Question 3

The interval between the upper quartile and the lower quartile is known as the:

A   mean

B   inter-quartile range

C   standard deviation

D   mode

For the answers to these questions, see the 'Answers' section at the end of the book.

Additional practice questions

Question 1: Dispersion of sales values

The following sales values were recorded per month over a period of 12 months in £000:

$$225, 227, 222, 227, 224, 225, 223, 220, 219, 221, 225, 228.$$

For this data calculate the standard deviation.

Question 2: Manco plc

The price of the ordinary 25p shares of Manco plc quoted on the Stock Exchange at the close of business on successive Fridays is tabulated below:

126	120	122	105	129	119	131	138
125	127	113	112	130	122	134	136
128	126	117	114	120	123	127	140
124	127	114	111	116	131	128	137
127	122	106	121	116	135	142	130

Required:

(a) Group the above data into eight classes.

(b) By constructing the ogive calculate the median value

(c) Calculate the mean and standard deviation of your frequency distribution.

(d) Compare and contrast the values that you have obtained for the median and mean.

For the answer to these questions, see the 'Answers' section at the end of the book.

Feedback to activities

Activity 1

9 − 2 = 7

Activity 2

$\Sigma x = 3 + 4 + 6 + 8 + 9 = 30$, $\Sigma x^2 = 9 + 16 + 36 + 64 + 81 = 206$,

$$\sigma = \sqrt{\frac{206}{5} - \left(\frac{30}{5}\right)^2}$$

$$= 2.28$$

Activity 3

These are the answers you should have got. If you want even more practice just generate a short column of random numbers using Excel and use the STDEVP function to find out what answer you should get when you use your calculator.

(a) 18.26

(b) 26.36

(c) 16.41

(d) 23.99
(e) 132.96
(f) 221.90
(g) 25.96
(h) 23.04
(i) 17.55
(j) 106.50

Activity 4

A   Coefficient of variation $= \dfrac{1.29 \times 100}{5.46} =$ 23.63%

B   Coefficient of variation $= \dfrac{4.21 \times 100}{16.38} =$ 25.70%

B has the higher coefficient of variation.

10

INDEX NUMBERS

Contents

1. Index numbers
2. Simple indices
3. Weighted indices
4. Chain base index numbers
5. Index numbers and inflation

160 BUSINESS MATHS

1 Index numbers

1.1 Why use index numbers?

An index number is a single value that measures change in a series. They are useful in a variety of accounting contexts.

DEFINITION

An index number is a single value that measures change in a series.

- Inflation has been a familiar feature of life for a number of years albeit currently running at a relatively low level. It explains the ever-increasing prices paid over time for the same commodity. The cause of and the cure for inflation have been much argued over by economists. Most accountants would acknowledge that the accounts of businesses are distorted when no allowance is made for the effects of inflation. The use of index numbers is often required for the preparation of inflation-adjusted accounts.

- Over time, most products are improved, and a direct price comparison ignores that improvement. For example, while the hi-fi system at the end of the 1980s included a compact disc player and cassette recorder, the 1960 model would have included little more than a gramophone and a wireless. The same problem exists with most products. There are no simple answers to these problems, but what they do mean is that index numbers, if carefully constructed, provide valuable information. They certainly do not, however, provide any absolute measure of price changes even in relation to a limited group of commodities.

1.2 Types of index number

The following types of index number will be considered:

- Simple indices.
- Weighted indices.
- Chain base indices.

2 Simple indices

2.1 Percentage relatives

Percentage relatives are based on a single item. There are two types:

DEFINITION

Price relative – a number expressing a current year money value of a series as a percentage of a base year money value of the same series.

- Price relatives – a number expressing a current year money value of a series as a percentage of a base year money value of the same series.

- Quantity relatives – the same, except not expressed in money.

The **base year** is the year with which all changes in the series are compared, in other words the reference point of the series.

DEFINITION

Base year is the year with which all changes in the series are compared. The reference point of the series.

The formulae for calculating these index numbers are:

Simple price or price relative index $\qquad = \qquad \dfrac{P_1}{P_0} \times 100$

Simple quantity or quantity relative index $\qquad = \qquad \dfrac{Q_1}{Q_0} \times 100$

KEY POINT

Price relative = $\frac{P_1}{P_0} \times 100$

Where P^0 is the price at time 0
       P^1 is the price at time 1
       Q^0 is the quantity at time 0
       Q^1 is the quantity at time 1

Note: the concept of time 0, time 1 and so on is simply a scale counting from any given point in time. Thus, for example, if the scale started on 1 January 20X0 it would be as follows:

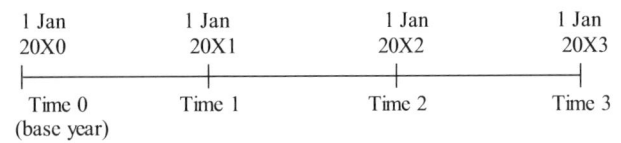

1 Jan 20X0	1 Jan 20X1	1 Jan 20X2	1 Jan 20X3
Time 0 (base year)	Time 1	Time 2	Time 3

The starting point is chosen to be most convenient for the problem under consideration.

Example 1

If a commodity costs £2.60 in 20X4 and £3.68 in 20X5, calculate the simple price index for 20X5, using 20X4 as base year (i.e. time 0).

Solution 1

$$\text{Simple price index} = \frac{P_1}{P_0} \times 100$$

$$= \frac{3.68}{2.60} \times 100$$

$$= 141.5$$

This means that the price has increased by 41.5% of its base year value, i.e. its 20X4 value.

Example 2

6,500 items were sold in 20X8 compared with 6,000 in 20X7. Calculate the simple quantity index for 20X8 using 20X7 as base year.

Solution 2

$$\text{Simple quantity index} = \frac{Q_1}{Q_0} \times 100$$

$$= \frac{6,500}{6,000} \times 100$$

$$= 108.3$$

This means that the quantity sold has increased by 8.3% of its 20X7 figure.

Activity 1

A product which cost £12.50 in 20X0, cost £13.65 in 20X1. Calculate the simple price index for 20X1 based on 20X0.

Feedback to this activity is at the end of the chapter.

162 BUSINESS MATHS

KEY POINT

By using appropriate weights, price relatives can be combined to give a multi-item price index.

2.2 Multi-item indices

Usually, an index number is required to show the variation in a number of items at once rather than just one as in the examples above. By using appropriate weights, price relatives can be combined to give a multi-item price index. The Retail Price Index (RPI) is such an index and consists of a list of items as diverse as the price of bread, the cost of watch repairs, car repairs and cinema tickets.

3 Weighted indices

3.1 Weighted average of price relatives

As the name suggests, a weighted average of price relatives compares the price of each item in one year with the price of each item in the base year, expressing each as a percentage relative, and then finds the weighted average. It is calculated as follows:

$$\frac{\sum W \frac{P_1}{P_0} \times 100}{\sum W}$$

where W = weight, P_1 = prices at time 1, P_0 = prices at time 0

KEY POINT

Weighted average price relative =
$$\frac{\sum W \times P_1/P_0 \times 100}{\sum W}$$

Example

From the following information, construct an index of the weighted average of price relatives, with 20X5 as the base year. Don't worry about how the weights were chosen – we'll look at that in a moment.

	Price (pence)		
Item	20X5	20X6	Weights
A	10	20	100
B	25	26	182
C	35	33	132
D	12	13	13
			427

Solution

P_0	P_1	Price relative $\frac{P_1}{P_0} \times 100$	Weights W	Weights × price relative $W \times (\frac{P_1}{P_0} \times 100)$
10	20	200.0	100	20,000.0
25	26	104.0	182	18,928.0
35	33	94.3	132	12,447.6
12	13	108.3	13	1,407.9
		Σ	427	52,783.5

Index of the weighted average of price relatives

$$= \frac{\sum W \frac{P_1}{P_0} \times 100}{\sum W} = \frac{52,783.5}{427} = 123.6$$

3.2 Selecting weights

The weights applied to price relatives should, in general, reflect the **amount spent** or total value of each item purchased, rather than simply the quantities purchased (however standardised). The reason is that this eliminates the effect of a relatively low-priced item having a very high price relative from only a small price rise.

Example

The price of peas and bread, and the amount consumed in both years is as follows:

Item	20X5 price	20X6 price	Units consumed (both years)
Peas	2p	3p	2
Bread	15p	16p	5

You are required:

(a) to construct a price-relative index using:
  (i) quantity weights
  (ii) value weights

(b) to explain why the value weighted price relative is the more useful.

Solution

(a)

$$\frac{\sum W \frac{P_1}{P_0} \times 100}{\sum W}$$

Let the quantity weights be W_A and the value weights be W_B. We need to find figures for $\sum W_A$ and $\sum W_B$.

Item	P_0 20X5	P_1 20X6	Q (same pattern for both years)	W_A Quantity weight (= Q)	W_B Value weight (= $P_0 \times Q$)
	Pence	Pence			
Peas	2	3	2	2	$2 \times 2 = 4$
Bread	15	16	5	5	$15 \times 5 = 75$
				$\Sigma\ 7$	79

Now we can calculate figures for the top half of the formula.

Item	Price relative	Quantity weight × price relative	Value weight × price relative
	$\frac{P_1}{P_0} \times 100$	$W_A \times \frac{P_1}{P_0} \times 100$	$W_B \times \frac{P_1}{P_0} \times 100$
Peas	150.0	300.0	600.0
Bread	106.7	533.5	8,002.5
		$\Sigma\ 833.5$	8,602.5

(i) Therefore, using quantity weights only, the index is:

$$\frac{\sum W_A \frac{P_1}{P_0} \times 100}{\sum W_A} = \frac{833.5}{7} = 119.1$$

This would imply an average increase in prices of 19.1%.

(ii) Using value weights, the index is:

$$\frac{\Sigma W_B \frac{P_1}{P_0} \times 100}{\Sigma W_B} = \frac{8{,}602.5}{79} = 108.9$$

This implies an average increase of 8.9%.

(b) The fact that the **value** weighted average of price relatives is the more realistic can be shown by considering total expenditure.

Item	Expenditure 20X5	Expenditure 20X6	% increase
Peas	2 × 2 = 4p	3 × 2 = 6p	50.00%
Bread	15 × 5 = 75p	16 × 5 = 80p	6.70%
Total Budget	79p	86p	8.86%

Thus, an equal **money** price rise of 1p for two items will cause a higher percentage price rise for the lower priced item (peas), but this is compensated for when the weights used are the value or expenditure on each item, since this reduces the importance of the lower priced item.

Algebraically, as $W = Q \times P_0$ then the weighted average of price relatives, which is:

$$\frac{\Sigma W \frac{P_1}{P_0} \times 100}{\Sigma W}, \text{ becomes } \frac{\Sigma QP_0 \times \frac{P_1}{P_0}}{\Sigma QP_0} \times 100 = \frac{\Sigma QP_1}{\Sigma QP_0} \times 100$$

Activity 2

A production process uses 10 sacks of product A and 30 of product B per year. The costs are as follows:

Item	20X1	20X2
Product A	£6.50	£6.90
Product B	£2.20	£2.50

Construct a price relative index using:

(a) quantity weights
(b) value weights.

Feedback to this activity is at the end of the chapter.

4 Chain base index numbers

DEFINITION

A chain base index number expresses each year's value as a percentage of the value for the previous year.

If a series of index numbers are required for different years, such that the rate of change of the variable from one year to the next can be studied, the chain base method is used.

A chain base index number expresses each year's value as a percentage of the value for the previous year.

This simply means that each index number is calculated using the previous year as base. If the rate of change is **increasing** then the index numbers will be rising; if it is **constant**, the numbers will remain the same and if it is **decreasing** the numbers will be falling.

4.1 Example

A shopkeeper received the following amounts from the sale of radios:

20X1 £1,000
20X2 £1,100
20X3 £1,210
20X4 £1,331
20X5 £1,464

Is it correct to say that the annual rate of increase in revenue from sales of radios is getting larger?

KEY POINT

Chain base index = $\dfrac{\text{This year's value}}{\text{Last year's value}} \times 100$

Year	Sales	Chain base index
20X1	£1,000	
20X2	£1,100	$\dfrac{1,100}{1,000} \times 100 = 110$
20X3	£1,210	$\dfrac{1,210}{1,100} \times 100 = 110$
20X4	£1,331	$\dfrac{1,331}{1,210} \times 100 = 110$
20X5	£1,464	$\dfrac{1,464}{1,331} \times 100 = 110$

Although the sales revenue from radios has increased each year, the chain base index numbers have remained static at 110. Therefore, the annual rate of increase of sales revenue from radios is remaining constant rather than increasing.

The chain base is also a suitable index to calculate if the weights ascribed to the various items in the index are changing rapidly. Over a period of years, this index would have modified itself to take account of these changes whereas in a fixed-base method after a number of years the whole index would have to be revised to allow for the changed weighting.

4.2 Conclusion

It is normal to periodically revise the commodities and weights used as a basis for index calculation. In order to maintain comparability, the new index is **linked** to the old series so as to establish one single index series with periodic revision of the weights.

In using any index, consideration should be given to the basis of revision, and whether the current weights are appropriate. Thus, for example, the Cost of Living Index (now the Retail Price Index) was not revised from 1914 to 1947. Towards the end of the period, the index was, arguably, meaningless, and indeed this was used deliberately by the government in the Second World War which, by controlling the price of a few commodities in the index, was able to hold down the rate of increase of the index and claim a much lower rate of inflation than was actually taking place.

The weights used in the Retail Price Index are now revised annually. However, other indices, both in the UK and overseas, may not be subject to regular revision.

5 Index numbers and inflation

5.1 Measuring UK inflation

DEFINITION

The RPI and CPI measure the percentage changes month by month in the average level of prices of goods and services purchased by most households in the UK.

The Retail Prices Index (RPI) was the UK's main indicator of inflation before 2003. Since then, the Government has focussed policy on the Consumer Prices Index (CPI), although RPI figures are still widely quoted and used.

Like the RPI, the CPI measures the average change from month to month in the prices of consumer goods and services. However it differs in the particular households it represents, the range of goods and services included, and the way the index is constructed.

The most useful way to think about both the CPI and RPI indices is to imagine a 'shopping basket' containing those goods and services on which people typically spend their money. As the prices of the various items in the basket change over time, so does the total cost of the basket. Movements in the CPI and RPI indices represent the changing cost of this representative shopping basket.

In principle, the cost of the basket should be calculated with reference to all consumer goods and services purchased by households, and the prices measured in every shop or outlet that supplies them. In practice, both the CPI and RPI are calculated by collecting a sample of prices for a selection of representative goods and services in a range of UK retail locations. Currently, around 120,000 separate price quotations are used very month in compiling the indices, covering some 650 representative consumer goods and services for which prices are collected in around 150 areas throughout the UK.

Within each year, the RPI and CPI are calculated as fixed quantity price indices – only the prices of goods affect the index from month to month.

However, the contents of the baskets of goods and services and their associated weights are updated annually. This is important in helping to avoid potential biases in consumer price indices that might otherwise develop over time, for example, due to the development of entirely new goods and services, or the tendency for consumers to substitute purchases away from those particular goods and services for which prices have risen relatively rapidly. For example, frozen chicken nuggets were included in the basket for the first time in 2005.

One major source of information comes from the diaries filled in by people taking part in the Office of National Statistics (ONS) *"Expenditure and Food Survey"*, a continuous survey of over 6000 households each year.

5.2 Rebasing an index

From time to time it may be desirable to **rebase** an index to a more recent year. For example if an index was started in 1967 (at 100) it may now have reached, say, 520, but this will not mean very much to most people, because they won't have any clear memory of what life was like in 1967, and conditions were completely different.

An index number for any year can be rebased using the following formula.

$$\frac{\text{Old value for year in question}}{\text{Old value in new base year}} \times \text{New base index (usually 100)}$$

Example

The following table shows the index of prices (2000 = 100) for a certain commodity over the period 2000–2005.

2000	2001	2002	2003	2004	2005
100	105	115	127	140	152

It has been decided to rebase the index so that 2003 = 100. Construct the new index, rounding to whole numbers.

Solution

$$\frac{\text{Old value for year in question}}{\text{Old value in new base year (here 127)}} \times \text{New base index (here 100)}$$

For example for the year 2001 the new figure is $105/127 \times 100 = 83$ (rounded).

2000	2001	2002	2003	2004	2005
79	83	91	100	110	120

Note that the new base index does not have to be 100: it could be 1, in which case the index would be in decimals, or it could be, say 32, if those happened to be your instructions. A base index of 100 is the most usual.

5.3 Deflating a monetary series

Deflating a monetary series shows the 'real term' effect of price changes.

$$\text{Deflated value} = \frac{\text{Actual value}}{\text{Index value (e.g. RPI)}} \times 100$$

Example

The following example illustrates the method, using the Retail Prices Index as the measure of inflation to deflate a set of sales values.

Year	Actual sales (£000)	RPI	Deflated sales (£000)
1	275	100	$\frac{275}{100} \times 100 = 275$
2	305	112	$\frac{305}{112} \times 100 = 272$
3	336	122	$\frac{336}{122} \times 100 = 275$
4	344	127	$\frac{344}{127} \times 100 = 271$
5	363	133	$\frac{363}{133} \times 100 = 273$

It will be seen that although actual sales have increased in value by a fairly large amount, in real terms there has been a slight decrease.

Summary

Indexing is a technique for comparing changes over a period of time, by expressing current quantities as a percentage of a base year.

We have discussed and calculated a variety of indices, the most well known of indices is the Retail Price Index (RPI), where the index is calculated as a weighted average of price relatives.

Self-test questions

1   What is a price relative? (2.1)

2   When is 'time 0'? (2.1)

3   What is the formula for a weighted average of price relatives? (3.1)

4   Why is a value weighted price relative more useful than a quantity weighted price relative? (3.2)

5   How is a chain base index calculated? (4.1)

6   What is the Retail Price Index (RPI)? (5.1)

7   How can you deflate a monetary series? (5.3)

Practice questions

Question 1

An index-linked pension of £10,000 a year became payable on 1 January 1992. Details of the Index of Retail Prices are shown below:

Index of Retail Prices each January (January 1987 = 100)

1987	1991	1992	1993	1994
100	130.2	135.6	137.9	142.0

(Source: Monthly Digest of Statistics, February 1994)

The annual pension payable from 1 January 1994 is closest to:

A   £10,297

B   £10,472

C   £13,560

D   £14,200

Question 2

The price index for a commodity in the current year is 135 (base year = 100). The current price for the commodity is £55.35 per kg.

What was the price per kg in the base year?

A   £35

B   £41

C   £74.72

D   £100

Question 3

In 1994, a price index based on 1980 = 100 stood at 126. In that year it was re-based at 1994 = 100. By 1996, the new index stood at 109. For a continuous estimate of price changes since 1980, the new index may be expressed, to two decimal places, in terms of the old as

A   85.51

B   137.34

C   135.00

D   135.68

For the answers to these questions, see the 'Answers' section at the end of the book.

Additional question

Salaries of systems analysts

You have been requested by a client to research into the area of salaries paid to their systems analysis team, to prepare a report in order that a pay review may be carried out.

The following table shows the salaries, together with an officially published wages and salary index, for the years 20X0 to 20X8.

Year	Average salary £	Published index
20X0	9,500	89.2
20X1	10,850	94.6
20X2	13,140	97.8
20X3	14,300	101.9
20X4	14,930	106.9
20X5	15,580	115.2
20X6	16,200	126.1
20X7	16,800	133.5
20X8	17,500	138.5

Required:

(a)   What is the purpose of an index number?

(b)   Tabulate the percentage increases on a year earlier for the average salary and the published index.

(c)   Revalue the average salary each year to its equivalent 20X8 value using the published index.

(d) Using the results of (b) and (c) above, comment on the average salary of the systems analysts of your client.

For the answer to this question, see the 'Answers' section at the end of the book.

Feedback to activities

Activity 1

Simple price index $= \dfrac{P_1}{P_0} \times 100$ where P_1 is the price in 20X1 and P_0 is the price in 20X0

$= \dfrac{13.65}{12.50} \times 100$

$= 1.092 \times 100$

$= 109.20$

This means that the price has increased by 9.2% on its base year price of £12.50.

Activity 2

Start by preparing a table of all the information required to answer the question, i.e.

Item	P_0 20X1	P_1 20X2	Q	Quantity weight only $W_A (= Q)$	Value weight $W_B (= P_0 \times Q)$
Product A	6.5	6.9	10	10	65
Product B	2.2	2.5	30	30	66
Σ				40	131

Item	$\dfrac{P_1}{P_0} \times 100$	$W_A \dfrac{P_1}{P_0} \times 100$	$W_B \dfrac{P_1}{P_0} \times 100$
Product A	106.2	1,062	6,903.0
Product B	113.6	3,408	7,497.6
Σ		4,470	14,400.6

(a) To calculate the index using quantity weights, we need to insert the data into the formula

$$\dfrac{\Sigma W_A \times \dfrac{P_1}{P_0} \times 100}{\Sigma W_A} = \dfrac{4{,}470}{40} = 111.75$$

(b) To calculate the index using value weights, we need to insert the data into the formula.

$$\dfrac{\Sigma W_B \times \dfrac{P_1}{P_0} \times 100}{\Sigma W_B} = \dfrac{14{,}400.6}{131} = 109.93$$

11

PROBABILITY: BASIC RULES

Contents

1. Probability
2. Laws of probability
3. Conditional probability

1 Probability

1.1 Measurement of probability

KEY POINT

Probability is measured on a scale from 0 to 1, where 0 represents impossibility and 1 represents certainty.

Probability is measured on a scale from 0 to 1, where 0 represents impossibility and 1 represents certainty.

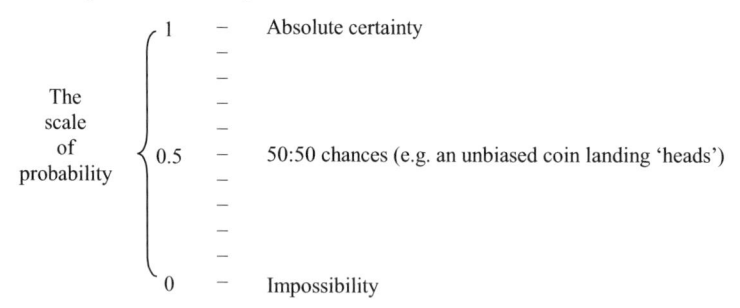

The scale of probability:
- 1 — Absolute certainty
- 0.5 — 50:50 chances (e.g. an unbiased coin landing 'heads')
- 0 — Impossibility

Example 1

When an unbiased dice is thrown, each of the numbers 1 to 6 has an equal chance of falling uppermost. What is the probability that the outcome of a single throw is:

(a) the number 4

(b) an even number

(c) a number less than 3

(d) a number greater than 6, and

(e) a number less than 7?

Solution 1

When an unbiased dice is thrown, there are six equally likely outcomes: 1, 2, 3, 4, 5, 6.

For each answer, (a) to (e) above, the number of 'favourable' outcomes must be determined, and this is expressed as a proportion of the total number of possible outcomes.

The probability of event 'A' occurring is represented by the symbol P(A).

(a) P(number 4):

P(4) = 1/6, because one of the six possible outcomes is the number 4.

(b) P(even) = 3/6 (or 1/2), because three of the six possible outcomes are even numbers: 2, 4 and 6.

(c) P(a number less than 3):

P(<3) = 2/6 (or 1/3), because two of the six outcomes are less than 3, i.e. 1 and 2.

(d) P(a number greater than 6):

P(>6) = 0/6 (or 0), because none of the six outcomes is greater than 6. This is an impossible situation.

(e) P(a number less than 7):

P(<7) = 6/6 (or 1), because all six outcomes are less than 7. It is therefore certain that the result will be a number less than 7.

Example 2

An ordinary pack of playing cards consists of 52 cards. If the pack is well shuffled and one card selected at random, the following probabilities can be calculated.

(a) the card is the ace of clubs

(b) the card is a king

(c) the card is a heart, and

(d) the card is red.

Solution 2

When a card is selected at random, there are 52 equally likely outcomes.

(a) P(ace of clubs) = 1/52 because there is only one ace of clubs in the pack.

(b) P(king) = 4/52 (or (1/13) because there are four kings in a pack.

(c) P(heart) = 13/52 (or 1/4) because there are 13 hearts in a pack.

(d) P(red) = 26/52 (or 1/2) because there are 26 red cards out of the total of 52.

1.2 A priori, empirical and subjective probability

The discussion of the scale of probability suggests that the concept of probability is always the same. This is not so; probabilities can be arrived at by different methods, and have quite different significance for their users. The simplest way of explaining this is in terms of the way in which probability estimates are obtained. These may be summarised as follows:

(a) **A priori probability**

The probability of an event is calculated by a process of logical reasoning. In the scale of probability above, it was stated that there was a 0.5 probability of an unbiased coin landing 'heads'. This was deduced without any reference to any experiment, but is confirmed from previous personal experience of the way coins behave. This is a form of objective probability, but based on logic: 'A priori' means 'from what was before'.

(b) **Empirical probability**

Where a particular situation can be repeated a large number of times, an experimental approach may be used to derive probabilities. An example would be using meteorological records to estimate the probability of rain on the 30th June. Again this is a form of objective probability, but based on the relative frequency in a large number of experiments, i.e. 'empirical probability'.

(c) **Subjective probability**

These are estimates made by individuals of the relative likelihood of events occurring. Thus an individual may estimate that the likelihood of the Conservative Party winning the next British election is 0.4. This is a personal view, though it may be based on the individual's own predictive model of the political future. It cannot be confirmed by either a priori reasoning or experimentation, i.e. it is 'subjective probability'.

Some statisticians would say that this type of probability is invalid, but many business problems are of this nature, and it is difficult to find any other method of quantifying the relative likelihood of forecasts. Irrespective of the theoretical arguments, subjective probability forecasts are widely used.

Subjective probabilities are assumed to follow the same laws as objective probabilities. This is why we study the behaviour of dice, coin tossing, etc; not because we are interested in such problems for themselves, but because the mathematical laws derived from them are applied to subjective probabilities which are of much greater importance in business.

Finally, it should be noted that the categories of probability are not absolute. Very often business forecasts will combine elements of all three types of probability.

Activity 1

A batch of electronic components had the following composition:

Type of component	Total quantity	Number defective
A	1,000	20
B	500	15
Total	1,500	35

If a component is selected at random, state the probability of each of the following.

(a) It is of type A.

(b) It is defective.

(c) It is of type A or defective.

(d) It is of type A and defective.

(e) It is of type A if defective.

(f) It is defective if of type A.

Feedback to this activity is at the end of the chapter.

1.3 Venn diagrams

Venn diagrams are a pictorial method used in mathematics and other fields to show the relationship between different sets, or groups, of objects. In probability theory these sets can be used to represent events and the resulting diagrams are a useful way of seeing key theories and for solving some problems.

For example, suppose we are looking at the different possible outcomes of rolling a die.

Let A = rolling an even number = {2,4,6}

Let B = rolling a multiple of 3 = {3,6}

This can be shown in the following diagram:

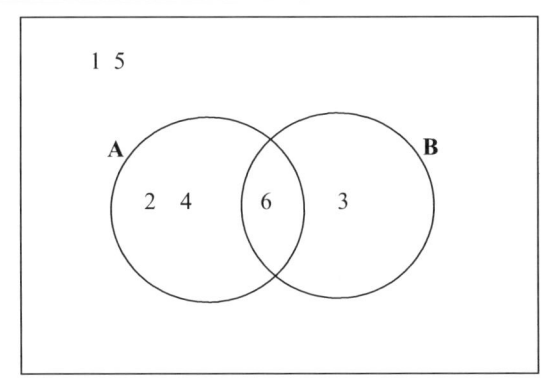

The diagram can be interpreted as follows:

- All possible outcomes are contained within the box – so, for example, the outcomes '1' and '5' are within the box, even though they are not included within events 'A' or 'B'.

- 'A' and 'B' are shown as circles with each possible outcome contained within them.

- If asked to consider the probability of 'A or B' happening (in this case being the likelihood of the outcomes {2,3,4,6} occurring), then you need to look at the area shown by adding the two circles together.

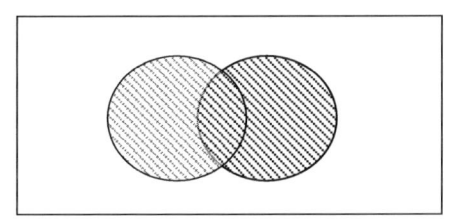

- If asked to consider the probability of 'A and B' occurring (here just getting a six), then on the diagram this is represented by the overlap of A and B:

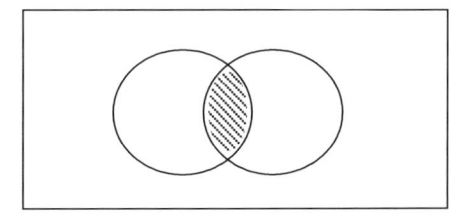

2 Laws of probability

2.1 Addition law for mutually exclusive events

Two or more events are said to be mutually exclusive if the occurrence of any one of them precludes the occurrences of all the others, i.e. only one can happen. For example, when a dice is thrown once, it can only show one score. If that score is 6 (say), then all the other possible outcomes (1, 2, 3, 4 or 5) will not have occurred. Hence the six possible outcomes are all mutually exclusive. On the other hand, the outcomes 'score 6', and 'score an even number' are not mutually exclusive because both outcomes could result from one throw.

Mutually exclusive events may be written in symbols as:

$$P(A \text{ and } B) = 0$$

The probability of a 6 and a 1 in a single throw of one dice is clearly zero.

In terms of the Venn diagram, mutual exclusivity is when the circles for A and B do not overlap.

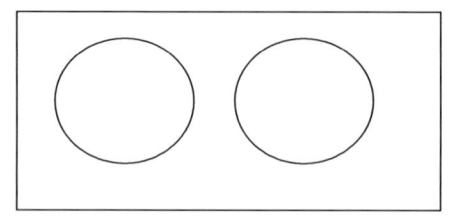

If A and B are two mutually exclusive events, then the probability that either A or B occurs in a given experiment is equal to the sum of the separate probabilities of A and B occurring, i.e.

$$P(A \text{ or } B) = P(A) + P(B)$$

This is obvious from the diagram as we are just adding the different circles together.

This law can cover any number of events, as long as they are mutually exclusive:

$$P(A \text{ or } B \text{ or } C \text{ or } D \text{ or } \ldots) = P(A) + P(B) + P(C) + P(D) + \ldots$$

Example 1

A bag contains four red, six blue and 10 black balls. What is the probability of selecting either a red or a black ball when one ball is drawn from the bag?

Clearly, the events are mutually exclusive, since if the ball is red, it cannot be black, and vice versa.

∴ P(red) = 4/20   P(black) = 10/20

∴ P(red or black) = P(red) + P(black)
                   = 4/20 + 10/20
                   = 14/20 (or 0.7)

Example 2

The probability of drawing an ace or king, when one card is drawn from a pack of 52 playing cards is calculated as follows:

∴ P(ace) = 4/52   P(king) = 4/52

∴ P(ace or king)   = P(ace) + P(king)
                   = 4/52 + 4/52
                   = 8/52 (or 0.15)

2.2 Addition law for non-mutually exclusive events

KEY POINT

Addition law states:

P(A or B) = P(A) + P(B) − P(A and B)

which becomes:

P(A or B) = P(A) + P(B) when A and B are mutually exclusive.

Two events are not mutually exclusive if they can occur at the same time. This is sometimes regarded as an 'overlap situation' as the two circles in the Venn diagram do now overlap.

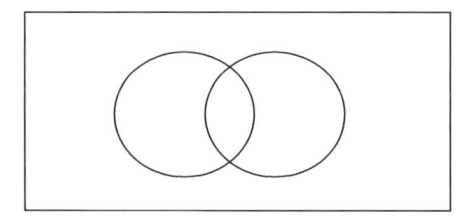

If A and B are two non-mutually exclusive events, then the probability that either A or B occurs in a given experiment is equal to the sum of the separate probabilities minus the probability that they both occur.

i.e.   P (A or B) = P (A) + P (B) − P (A and B)

This can be seen from the diagram because if we add the two circles together, then we have double counted the overlap or intersection.

The term P(A and B) must be subtracted to avoid double counting as simply adding the two circles together means that the overlap has been covered twice. This is best illustrated by an example.

Example 1

What is the probability of selecting a heart or a queen, when one card is drawn at random from a pack of playing cards?

The probability of selecting a heart or a queen is an overlap situation, as the Queen of Hearts would be included in both events. To avoid including this probability twice, it must be subtracted once.

P(any heart) = 13/52   P(any queen) = 4/52   P(queen of hearts) = 1/52

∴ P(heart or queen) =   P(heart) + P(queen) − P(queen of hearts)
                      =   13/52 + 4/52 − 1/52
                      =   16/52 (or 0.31)

Example 2

Twenty identical discs are marked 1 to 20 and placed in a large box. One is drawn at random from a box. The following probabilities will be calculated; that the number on the disc is:

(a)   a multiple of 2

(b)   a multiple of 5

(c)   a multiple of 2 or 5

Solution 2

(a) P(multiple of 2)   = P(2 or 4 or 6 ... 20)

                               = 10/20 (or 0.5) i.e. all even numbers

(b) P(multiple of 5)   = P(5, 10, 15, or 20) = 4/20 (or 0.2)

(c) P(multiple of 2 and 5) = P(10 or 20) = 2/20 (or 0.1)

∴ P(multiple of 2 or 5) = P(multiple of 2) + P(multiple of 5) − P(multiple of 2 and 5)

                               = 10/20 + 4/20 − 2/20

                               = 12/20 (or 0.6)

This is easily verified from the fact that there will be 12 such discs (2, 4, 5, 6, 8, 10, 12, 14, 15, 16, 18, 20).

2.3 Multiplication law: independent events

Two or more events are said to be **independent** if the occurrence or non-occurrence of one event does not affect the occurrence or non-occurrence of the other.

For example, consider the events:

    A = 'I will be successful in the examination.'
    B = 'I will undergo a course of study for the examination.'
    C = 'I have blue eyes.'

Clearly A will have a higher probability if B occurs than if it does not occur. A is therefore dependent on B. But the colour of one's eyes has no known effect on the ability to pass examinations or vice versa, hence A and C are independent.

If any two events, A and B, are independent, then the probability of both A and B occurring is the **product** of the separate probabilities.

$$P(A \text{ and } B) = P(A) \times P(B)$$

Example 1

The probability of drawing an ace from a pack of cards and throwing a six with an unbiased dice is calculated as follows:

P(ace) = 4/52   P(6) = 1/6

∴ P(ace and 6)   = P(ace) × P(6)

                     = 1/13 × 1/6

                     = 1/78 (or 0.013)

The two events are independent because which card is drawn from the pack will have no influence on which score will be given by the dice and vice versa.

Example 2

A case contains 12 valves of which four are defective and the rest are non-defective. The probability of picking out two non-defective valves, if the first valve is **replaced** before the second one is selected, is calculated as follows.

Since four are defective then the remaining eight are non-defective.

So P(defective) = 4/12, P(non-defective) = 8/12

∴ P(valve 1 non-defective) = 8/12 = 2/3,

P(valve 2 non-defective) = 8/12 = 2/3

P(valves 1 and 2 non-defective) = P(valve 1 non-defective) × P(valve 2 non-defective)

$= 2/3 \times 2/3$

$= 4/9$ (or 0.44 or 44%)

2.4 Multiplication law: dependent events

KEY POINT

Multiplication law states:

P(A and B) = P(A) × P(B|A) which becomes:

P(A and B) = P(A) × P(B) when A and B are independent.

Two or more events are said to be **dependent** when the probability of the second event occurring is conditional upon the first event having taken place.

If A and B are two events such that B is conditional upon A, then the probability of A and B occurring is the product of the probability of A and the conditional probability of B occurring.

Thus, P(A and B) = P(A) × P(B given that A has occurred).

The probability that event B occurs given that A occurs is denoted by the symbol P(B|A). The '|' is read as 'given' or 'if'.

Example 1

Two cards are drawn from a pack, the first card is **not replaced** before the second is drawn. The probability that they are both aces is calculated as follows:

P(first card is an ace) = 4/52

This is not replaced, therefore three aces remain, out of 51 cards.

P(second card is an ace, given that the first card is an ace) = 3/51.

∴ P(both aces) = P(first card is an ace) × P(second card is an ace, given that first card is an ace)

= 4/52 × 3/51

= 12/2,652 (or 0.0045)

Using the $\boxed{a^{b/c}}$ button on your calculator you can simplify the fraction to 1/221.

Example 2

A bag contains three black, four red and 13 blue marbles. The probability that if three are selected without replacement then they will be red, blue, black in that order is calculated as follows:

P(first red) = 4/20

P(second blue given first red) = 13/19

P(third black, given that the first two were red and blue) = 3/18

P(red, blue, black) = $\frac{4}{20} \times \frac{13}{19} \times \frac{3}{18}$ = 156/6,840   = 13/570 (or 0.023)

2.5 Complementary probabilities: two possible outcomes

When a single event has **only two possible outcomes**, usually denoted as success and failure, then, if p and q are the probabilities of success and failure respectively, it follows that:

p = 1 – q

This is because p + q = 1, since they are the only possible outcomes of the event.

Example 1

When an unbiased dice is thrown, a six is regarded as success and any other number as failure.

∴ p = P(success) = 1/6
and q = P(failure) = 1 – 1/6 = 5/6

Example 2

The probability that a job will be finished on time is 0.8. Therefore the probability that it will **not** be finished on time is 0.2 because:

p = P(success) = 0.8
q = P(failure) = 1 – 0.8 = 0.2

The event 'A does **not** occur' is called the **negation** of A and is denoted by $\overline{A}$ or A'. Hence:

$P(\overline{A}) = 1 - P(A)$

$P(\overline{A})$ is called the **complement** of P(A).

In a Venn diagram, the complement is shown as the rest of the diagram – if A is represented by a circle as usual, then $\overline{A}$ is shown by the shaded area:

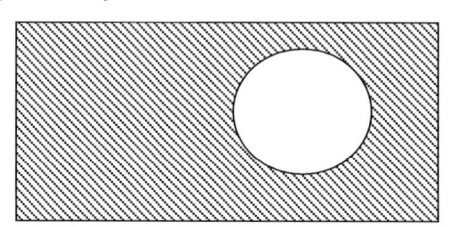

2.6 Complementary probabilities: at least one occurs

When several events are being considered then the probability that **at least one of them occurs** is given by:

P (at least one) = 1 – P (none of them)

This is because either none of the events occurs or at least one of them does, therefore:

P(none of them) + P(at least one) = 1

> **KEY POINT**
>
> When several events are possible, the probability that at least one of them occurs is given by:
>
> P(at least one) = 1 – P(none of them).

Example 1

If three dice are thrown together, then the probability of obtaining at least one six is calculated as follows:

P(at least one six) = 1 − P(no sixes)

Assuming independence then:

P(no sixes) = P(not six on first dice and not six on second dice and not six on third dice)

$= 5/6 \times 5/6 \times 5/6$

$= \dfrac{125}{216}$

P(at least one six) = 1 − 125/216

$= \dfrac{216}{216} - \dfrac{125}{216}$

$= \dfrac{91}{216}$ (or 0.42)

Example 2

If a coin is tossed five times then the probability of obtaining at least one head is calculated as follows:

$P(head) = \dfrac{1}{2}$ and $P(tail) = \dfrac{1}{2}$

P(at least one head) = 1 − P(no heads)

$= 1 - (\dfrac{1}{2} \times \dfrac{1}{2} \times \dfrac{1}{2} \times \dfrac{1}{2} \times \dfrac{1}{2})$

= 1 − 1/32

= 31/32 (or 0.97)

2.7 Combination of addition and multiplication laws

The examples given so far in this section have been kept simple in order to illustrate the basic laws. When it comes to solving more complex problems it is important to work out and write down the outcomes that are favourable to a particular situation and then calculate the corresponding probabilities.

Example

A bag contains five white, four red and three blue balls. Three balls are drawn without replacement.

Events A, B, C and D are defined as follows:

- A   at least one white ball is drawn
- B   exactly two white balls are drawn
- C   one ball of each colour is drawn
- D   the third ball is white.

(a) Which two events are mutually exclusive?

(b) Calculate the probabilities of A, B, C and D respectively.

Solution

(a) B and C are mutually exclusive because if only three balls are drawn the probability of drawing two whites excludes the possibility of drawing one of each colour (and vice versa). No other combination is mutually exclusive.

(b) (i) P(A) = P(at least one white)

= 1 − P(no whites)

The bag contains five white and seven non-white balls i.e. the red and blue can be grouped together as non-white.

∴ P(non-white on first ball) = 7/12

∴ P(A) = 1 − (7/12 × 6/11 × 5/10)

= $1 - \dfrac{210}{1{,}320}$

= $\dfrac{1{,}110}{1{,}320}$

= $\dfrac{37}{44}$ (or 0.84)

(ii) P(B) = P(exactly two whites)

Exactly two whites can be drawn in any one of three possible ways:

Possibility	First ball	Second ball	Third ball
1	White	White	Non-white
2	White	Non-white	White
3	Non-white	White	White

P(1) = 5/12 × 4/11 × 7/10 = $\dfrac{140}{1{,}320}$

P(2) = 5/12 × 7/11 × 4/10 = $\dfrac{140}{1{,}320}$

P(3) = 7/12 × 5/11 × 4/10 = $\dfrac{140}{1{,}320}$

∴ P(exactly two whites) = P(1 or 2 or 3)

= $\dfrac{140}{1{,}320} + \dfrac{140}{1{,}320} + \dfrac{140}{1{,}320}$

= $\dfrac{420}{1{,}320}$

= $\dfrac{7}{22}$ (or 0.32)

Note: the table showing the various ways of achieving the desired result, exactly two white balls, is an essential working for this type of probability problem.

(iii) P(C) = P(one ball of each colour)

One of each colour can be drawn in any one of six possible ways.

Possibility	First ball	Second ball	Third Ball
1	Red	Blue	White
2	Red	White	Blue
3	Blue	Red	White
4	Blue	White	Red
5	White	Red	Blue
6	White	Blue	Red

P(1) = 4/12 × 3/11 × 5/10 = $\dfrac{60}{1,320}$

P(2) = 4/12 × 5/11 × 3/10 = $\dfrac{60}{1,320}$

P(3) = 3/12 × 4/11 × 5/10 = $\dfrac{60}{1,320}$

P(4) = 3/12 × 5/11 × 4/10 = $\dfrac{60}{1,320}$

P(5) = 5/12 × 4/11 × 3/10 = $\dfrac{60}{1,320}$

P(6) = 5/12 × 3/11 × 4/10 = $\dfrac{60}{1,320}$

P(one of each colour) = P(1 or 2 or 3 or 4 or 5 or 6)

= 60/1,320 + 60/1,320 + 60/1,320 + 60/1,320 + 60/1,320 + 60/1,320

= 6 × 60/1,320 = 360/1,320

= 3/11 (or 0.27)

Note: work out the probability of achieving the required result in **one particular** order (60/1,320); then find the **number of orders** (6); then multiply the two.

(iv) P(D) = P(third ball is white)

There are now four possibilities to consider:

Possibility	First	Second	Third
1	Not white	Not white	White
2	Not white	White	White
3	White	Not white	White
4	White	White	White

P(1) = 7/12 × 6/11 × 5/10 = $\dfrac{210}{1,320}$

P(2) = 7/12 × 5/11 × 4/10 = $\dfrac{140}{1,320}$

P(3) = 5/12 × 7/11 × 4/10 = $\dfrac{140}{1,320}$

P(4) = 5/12 × 4/11 × 3/10 = $\dfrac{60}{1,320}$

P(third ball is white)

$$= \text{P(1 or 2 or 3 or 4)}$$
$$= 210/1{,}320 + 140/1{,}320 + 140/1{,}320 + 60/1{,}320$$
$$= 550/1{,}320$$
$$= 5/12 \text{ (or 0.42)}$$

Note: a fatal mistake to make here is to say, 'it doesn't matter what the first ball is, therefore the probability is 1'. This makes it impossible to think clearly about the various ways of achieving the desired result (**third** ball white).

3 Conditional probability

3.1 Introduction

DEFINITION

Conditional probability – the probability of an event whose calculation is based on the knowledge that some other event has occurred.

Conditional probability is the probability of an event whose calculation is based on the knowledge that some other event has occurred.

This topic was considered earlier in the chapter when discussing dependent events, and the calculation of the probability of them both occurring. Remember that the symbol P(A|B) is read as 'the probability of A occurring given that B has already occurred' and we can say that:

P (A and B) = P (A|B) × P (B)

This formula can be rewritten in a variety of ways, depending on what you are trying to find out.

P(A and B) = P(B|A) × P(A)

P(A|B) × P(B) = P(B|A) × P(A)

$$P(A|B) = \frac{P(A \text{ and } B)}{P(B)}$$

$$P(B|A) = \frac{P(B \text{ and } A)}{P(A)}$$

However, this can get a bit mind-boggling! Much the easiest way to deal with this sort of problem is to use what is known as a contingency table.

3.2 Contingency tables

Contingency tables are created by taking the given probabilities, multiplying by some convenient number, typically 100 or 1,000 (to make the numbers easy to work with), then drawing a table to show the various combinations of factors which may exist.

Some examples should make this clear.

Example 1

40% of the output of a factory is produced in workshop A and 60% in workshop B. Fourteen out of every 1,000 components from A are defective and six out of every 1,000 components from B are defective. After the outputs from A and B have been thoroughly mixed, a component drawn at random is found to be defective.

Calculate the probability that it came from workshop B.

Solution 1

The problem will be solved by drawing a contingency table, showing defective and non-defective components and output from workshops A and B.

Consider 10,000 components, we know that of these 4,000 (40%) will be from workshop A and 6,000 (60%) from workshop B.

	Workshop A	Workshop B	Total
Defective			
Non-defective			
Total	4,000	6,000	10,000

Of the 4,000 from workshop A, 14/1,000 – that is 56 – will be defective, and from workshop B 6/1,000 – that is 36 – will be defective.

Hence the table can be completed so far:

	Workshop A	Workshop B	Total
Defective	56	36	
Non-defective			
Total	4,000	6,000	10,000

All the remaining figures can be competed as **balancing figures**, and the final contingency table looks like this.

	Workshop A	Workshop B	Total
Defective	56	36	92
Non-defective	3,944	5,964	9,908
Total	4,000	6,000	10,000

The problem was: what is the probability that a component came from workshop B, given that it is defective?

Given that it is defective, we know that we are dealing with one of the 92 components in the top row of the table. We can see that of these 92 components, 36 come from workshop B.

Hence P(came from workshop B given that it is defective) $= \dfrac{36}{92}$

$= 0.39$

There are other ways of solving such problems but the contingency table method is much the easiest and quickest way.

Activity 2

30% of the new cars of a particular model are supplied from a factory X, the other 70% from factory Y. 10% of factory X's production has a major fault, 12% of factory Y's production has such a fault.

A purchaser's new car has a major fault: what is the probability that it was made at factory Y?

Feedback to this activity is at the end of the chapter.

Example 2

A product is manufactured in a two-stage process, the stages being designated A and B. Each process has two machines, named A_1 and A_2 for process A, and B_1 and B_2 for process B.

Each unit of finished product must pass through either one of the two machines in process A, and then through either one of the two machines in process B. (50% go through A_1 and 50% through A_2. Similarly for B_1 and B_2.)

(a) How many different ways may a product be manufactured?

(b) If the probabilities of a defective product from each machine are as follows:

2% for A^1, 6% for A^2, 4% for B^1, 2% for B^2.

and the defectives are thrown out as they occur, what is the probability of a perfect item being produced?

(c) The total production is 10,000 items started pa, the loss on each defective item is £10, and the profit on each item is £80. Calculate the expected net profit.

Solution 2

(a) The product can be manufactured in four mutually exclusive ways.

$A_1 \to B_1$

$A_1 \to B_2$

$A_2 \to B_1$

$A_2 \to B_2$

(b) The probability of a perfect item being produced can be quickly solved with contingency tables. The first three columns are completed as illustrated previously, then the probabilities of producing a perfect item by each method are extracted and multiplied.

Contingency tables　　　　　　　　　　　　　　　　*Manufacturing method*

	A_1	A_2	Total	A_1B_1	A_1B_2	A_2B_1	A_2B_2
Defective (2%, 6%)	10	30	40				
Perfect	490	470	960	490/1000	490/1000	470/1000	470/1000
	500	500	1000				

	B_1	B_2	Total				
Defective (4%, 2%)	20	10	30				
Perfect	480	490	970	480/1000	490/1000	480/1000	490/1000
	500	500	1000				

Probability of a perfect item (e.g. 490/1000 × 480/1000)　　0.2352　　0.2401　　0.2256　　0.2303

$$\therefore \text{P (Perfect item)} = \text{P}(A_1B_1 \text{ or } A_1B_2 \text{ or } A_2B_1 \text{ or } A_2B_2)$$
$$= \text{P}(A_1B_1) + \text{P}(A_1B_2) + \text{P}(A_2B_1) + \text{P}(A_2B_2)$$
$$= 0.2352 + 0.2401 + 0.2256 + 0.2303$$
$$= 0.9312$$

(c) Since the total production is 10,000 items pa, the expected number of perfect items is $0.9312 \times 10,000 = 9,312$.

The profit on each of these is £80, therefore the expected profit on the perfect items is $9,312 \times £80 = £744,960$.

P(perfect item) $= 0.9312$

∴ P(defective item) $= 1 - 0.9312 = 0.0688$

∴ expected number of defects is $0.0688 \times 10,000 = 688$. The loss on each of these is £10, therefore the expected loss on the defective items is $688 \times £10 = £6,880$.

The expected net profit $= £744,960 - £6,880$

$= £738,080$.

This is the average profit that the company might expect to make per annum.

3.3 Probability trees

Another useful way of breaking down complex problems is to use a probability tree – a diagram that sets out all the possibilities. You will study the technique in more detail in your later studies. For now just look at a tricky example

Example 3

A mad professor has invented and produced a revolutionary new two-stage rocket to take his wife to Mars. Problems have, however, developed in its ignition system. The ultimate failure of either stage to ignite means that the rocket blows up.

Three attempts at ignition of the first stage are possible. The first attempt has a probability of successful ignition of 60%, the second attempt 40% and the third attempt 20%. If all three attempts fail, the rocket blows up.

To ignite the second stage three attempts are also possible. The probability of success of the first attempt at igniting the second stage depends on whether the first stage ignited at the first attempt or not. If the first stage ignited at the first attempt then the probability of the second stage igniting at the first attempt is 65%. If not the probability is only 50%.

The probability of successful ignition at the second attempt is 30% and at the third attempt 25% irrespective of whether the first stage ignited at the first attempt or not.

What is the probability of the professor's wife surviving ignition?

Solution 3

Here is the probability tree diagram.

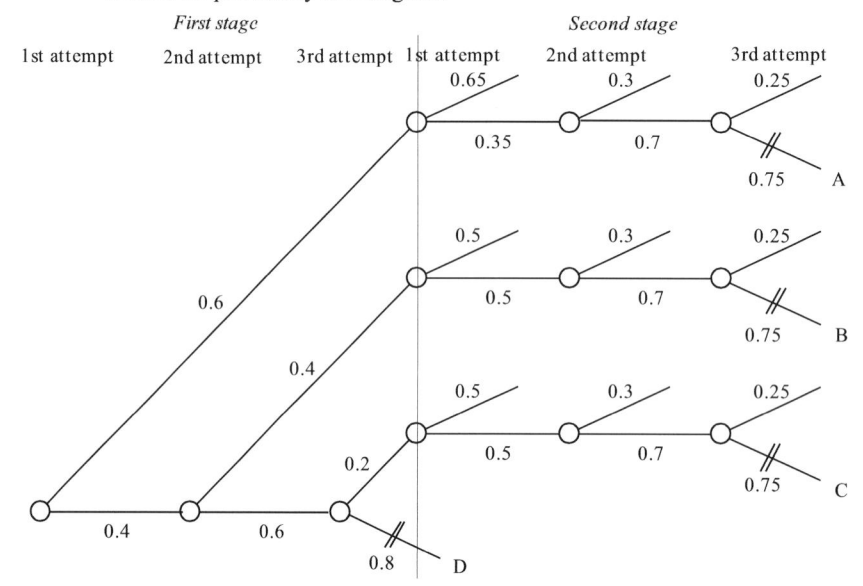

```
            First stage                          Second stage
1st attempt   2nd attempt  3rd attempt  1st attempt  2nd attempt  3rd attempt
                                          0.65          0.3          0.25
                                         ○────────────○────────────○
                                              0.35         0.7      ╫ 0.75   A

                                           0.5          0.3          0.25
                                         ○────────────○────────────○
                               0.6            0.5         0.7      ╫ 0.75   B

                                     0.4
                                           0.5          0.3          0.25
                                         ○────────────○────────────○
                                    0.2       0.5         0.7      ╫ 0.75   C

    ○────────○────────○
   0.4      0.6        ╫  D
                      0.8
```

Each path that ends in failure has been labelled, A, B, C, D. The paths are then evaluated by working from **right to left**.

Failure route		Probability								
A	0.75 × 0.7 × 0.35					×	0.6	=	0.1103
B	0.75 × 0.7 × 0.5		×	0.4	×	0.4	=	0.0420
C	0.75 × 0.7 × 0.5	×	0.2	×	0.6	×	0.4	=	0.0126
D				0.8	×	0.6	×	0.4	=	0.1920

Probability of **failing** to survive 0.3569
Probability of surviving = 1 − 0.3569 = 0.6431

You could check this final answer by tracing the 9 survival routes.

Incidentally, this is a good example of a problem where repeated trials are not feasible, unless the mad professor has an unlimited supply of wives.

Summary

The basic laws of probability have been outlined with many detailed examples to show the methods of calculation.

When solving complex problems, it is very important to decide on the possible outcomes and then calculate the corresponding probabilities.

Answers may be left in fractional or decimal form: in the latter case give two or three decimal places.

Self-test questions

1 Probability is measured on a scale from 0 to 1. What do these figures represent? (1.1)

2 Why might subjective probability be important? (1.2)

3 What are mutually exclusive events? (2.1)

4 Explain the addition law. (2.1 & 2.2)

5 Define a dependent event. (2.4)

6 Summarise the multiplication law. (2.4)

7 What is a contingency table used for? (3.2)

Practice questions

Question 1

A company uses any one of three machines to produce 'identical' hinges. The output of hinges from the three machines is in the ratio 6:3:1. The percentage of defects is 5, 20 and 10 respectively. The overall percentage of defects is closest to:

A 8
B 9
C 10
D 11

Question 2

A company recommends its employees to have free influenza vaccinations but only 50% do so. The effectiveness of the vaccine is known to be 90%. The probability of any non-vaccinated employee getting influenza by chance is 0.3. An employee catches influenza. What is the probability that she was vaccinated?

A 0.05
B 0.10
C 0.20
D 0.25

Question 3

Next year sales may rise, fall or remain the same as this year, with the following respective probabilities: 0.56, 0.23 and 0.21.

The probability of sales remaining the same or falling is:

A 0.05
B 0.12
C 0.13
D 0.44

Question 4

A sample of 100 companies has been analysed by size and whether they pay invoices promptly. The sample has been cross-tabulated into LARGE/SMALL against FAST PAYERS/SLOW PAYERS. 60 of the companies are classified as LARGE of which 40 are SLOW PAYERS. In total, 30 of all the companies are FAST PAYERS.

The probability that a company chosen at random is a FAST PAYING SMALL COMPANY is:

A   0.10

B   0.20

C   0.30

D   0.40

Question 5

Invoices produced within a firm are known to contain errors: 3% contain a very serious error, 6% a serious error and 12% a minor error.

The probability that a randomly-chosen invoice will have a serious error or a minor error is:

A   0.06

B   0.09

C   0.18

D   0.21

For the answers to these questions, see the 'Answers' section at the end of the book.

Additional question

Red, blue and yellow beads

A box contains 4 red beads, 1 blue bead and 2 yellow beads. Three beads are selected at random.

If there is no replacement between each selection find the probability of selecting:

(a)   one of each colour

(b)   three of the same colour.

For the answer to this question, see the 'Answers' section at the end of the book.

Feedback to activities

Activity 1

$$\text{Probability} = \frac{\text{number of times a particular event occurs}}{\text{number of tests for that event}} = \frac{n}{m}$$

(a) $n = 1{,}000$, $m = 1{,}500$, $P(A) = \dfrac{1{,}000}{1{,}500} = \dfrac{2}{3}$ or 0.667

(b) $n = 35$, $m = 1{,}500$, $P(D) = \dfrac{35}{1{,}500} = 0.023$

(c) n = 1,000 + 15 = 1,015 (do not count defective As twice)

m = 1,500

$$P(A \text{ or } D) = \frac{1,015}{1,500} = 0.677$$

(d) n = 20, m = 1,500, $P(A \text{ and } D) = \frac{20}{1,500} = 0.013$

(e) The effect of the condition 'defective' is to limit the population, and hence the value of m, to those fulfilling that condition.

n = 20, m = 35, $P(A \text{ if } D) = \frac{20}{35} = 0.571$

(f) n = 20, m = 1,000, $P(D \text{ if } A) = \frac{20}{1,000} = 0.020$

Activity 2

Using 1,000 as a suitable multiple, i.e. considering 1,000 cars are manufactured, the contingency table is:

	Made at factory X	Y	Total
Has major fault	30	84	114
No major fault	270	616	886
Total	300	700	1,000

Hence $P(\text{made at factory Y}|\text{major fault exists}) = \frac{84}{114}$

$= 0.737$

12

EXPECTED VALUE AND DECISIONS

Contents

1. Expected value (EV)
2. Decision analysis

1 Expected value (EV)

1.1 Introduction

DEFINITION

The expected value of a particular action is the sum of the values of the possible outcomes each multiplied by their respective probabilities.

The expected value of a particular action is the sum of the values of the possible outcomes each multiplied by their respective probabilities.

If the probability of winning £x is p then the expectation (or expected value) is p × £x.

This is rather a mathematical (or theoretical) concept as will be seen from the following example.

KEY POINT

Where there is more than one possible outcome, each with a probability attached, the expected value of the outcome E(x) will be the sum of the expected values of the individual outcomes.

Thus $E(x) = \Sigma px$.

Example

On the throw of a dice £5 is to be paid for a six, £4 for a five, £3 for a four and nothing for a 1, 2 or 3. The expectation is calculated as follows:

P(6)	=	1/6	∴	expectation = 1/6 × £5	=	£0.83
P(5)	=	1/6	∴	expectation = 1/6 × £4	=	£0.67
P(4)	=	1/6	∴	expectation = 1/6 × £3	=	£0.50
P(1, 2 or 3)	=	3/6	∴	expectation = 3/6 × £0	=	£0.00
				Total		£2.00

The expectation is £2.

In fact a person playing a game of this type will either win £5 or £4 or £3 or nothing. They cannot actually win £2. The expectation is the amount they can expect to win per game, on average, over a long series of games. It is also a fair price to pay for playing the game.

This same approach can be applied to decision making. Two or more possible courses of action may be open to a firm and the only basis on which they can make a decision is that of expected profits.

When using expected values to assess projects, accept projects only if the EV is positive; if the EV is negative (i.e. an expected loss) the project should be rejected. If deciding between projects which all have positive EVs then the project with the highest expected value should be chosen.

Activity 1

A supermarket is opening a new store and two sites are available to them: A or B. From past experience, they calculate that the probability of success on Site A is 0.8 with an annual profit of £500,000. If not successful, the annual loss is estimated at £80,000.

For Site B the corresponding figures are 0.6 for the probability of success with an annual profit of £600,000, or an annual loss of £120,000.

Where should the branch be located in order to maximise expected profits?

Feedback to this activity is at the end of the chapter.

2 Decision analysis

A decision is a choice between two or more alternatives.

2.1 Certainty or uncertainty?

Decisions may be taken under conditions of certainty, e.g.

I have received an offer to sell my car for £5,000. Should I accept the offer?

The decision has a simple yes/no choice which can be evaluated:

Accept – receive £5,000 and have no car.

Reject – keep a car but do not receive £5,000.

Alternatively the decision may involve:

(a) keeping the car

(b) **trying** to sell it privately for £5,000

(c) **trying** to sell it at auction for £4,800.

Clearly the outcome of (b) and (c) is uncertain; the car may not be sold at all, and if it is sold the proceeds may not be for the sums suggested.

2.2 Decisions made under uncertainty

Most decisions which a company's management has to make can be described as **decisions made under uncertainty**. The essential features of making a decision under uncertain conditions are:

- the decision maker is faced with a choice between several alternative courses of action

- each course of action may have several possible outcomes, dependent on a number of uncertain factors, i.e. even when a decision has been made the outcome is by no means certain

- which choice is made will depend upon the criteria used by the decision maker in judging between the outcomes of the possible courses of action.

2.3 Risk and uncertainty

Risk refers to the possibility that actual results, events or outcomes in the future will be different from what is expected.

The term 'risk' is often associated with the chance of something 'bad' happening, and that a future outcome will be adverse. This type of risk is called **'down-side' risk** or **pure risk**, which is a risk involving the possibility of loss, with no chance of gain.

Examples of pure risk are the risk of disruption to business from a severe power cut, or the risk of losses from theft or fraud, the risk of damage to assets from a fire or accident, and risks to the health and safety of employees at work.

Not all risks are pure risks or down-side risks. In many cases, risk is two-way, and actual outcomes might be either better or worse than expected. **Two-way risk** is sometimes called **speculative risk**. For many business decisions, there is an element of speculative risk and management are aware that actual results could be better or worse than forecast.

For example, a new product launch might be more or less successful than planned, and the savings from an investment in labour-saving equipment might be higher or lower than anticipated.

In everyday speech most people use the terms 'risk' and 'uncertainty' as though they were interchangeable. As far as your studies are concerned, however, there is a distinction.

The term 'risk' is used to describe a scenario when we know the different possible outcomes and can estimate their associated probabilities. This is the context for using expected values, for example.

The term 'uncertainty' is used when we do not know the possible outcomes and/or their associated probabilities – uncertainty is essentially a matter of ignorance. The future cannot be predicted because there is insufficient information about what the future outcomes might be. Decisions under conditions of uncertainty are often a matter of guesswork.

2.4 Maximisation of expected value

In order to have a **rational** basis for decision making it is necessary to have some estimate of the probabilities of the various outcomes and then to use them in a decision criterion. One such criterion is the **maximisation of expected value**, which consists in choosing the option giving the maximum expect return.

The expected value $\bar{x}$ of a particular action is defined as the **sum of the values of the possible outcomes, each multiplied by their respective probabilities** (it is analogous to the arithmetic mean), $\bar{x} = \sum px$.

> **KEY POINT**
>
> The expected value (EV) criterion of decision making consists in choosing the option giving the maximum expected return.

Example 1

Using the following data, apply the criteria of **maximisation of expected value** to decide the best course of action for the company, assuming the following probabilities:

P (low demand)	0.1
P (medium demand)	0.6
P (high demand)	0.3
	1.0

A company has three new products A, B and C, of which it can introduce only one. The level of demand for **each** course of action might be low, medium or high. If the company decides to introduce product A, the net income that would result from the levels of demand possible are estimated at £20, £40 and £50 respectively. Similarly, if product B is chosen, net income is estimated at £80, £70 and –£10, and for product C, £10, £100 and £40, respectively.

The expected value of the decision to introduce product A is given by the following summation:

$$0.1 \times £20 + 0.6 \times £40 + 0.3 \times £50 \quad = \quad £41$$

(i.e. on 10% of all occasions demand will be low and net income £20, on 60% of all occasions demand will be medium and net income £40 and on 30% of all occasions demand will be high and net income £50. Thus, on average, net income will be the weighted average of all three net incomes, weighted by their respective probabilities.)

Solution 1

The expected value of all the products may be calculated by means of a pay-off table:

KEY POINT

A pay-off table (or contribution table) is a method of setting out financial returns when faced with choosing between a number of options with a number of outcomes that are not dependent on the option chosen.

Table of expected values

State of the world (demand)	Prob of state of the world	Product A Income	A Income × Prob	B Income	B Income × Prob	C Income	C Income × Prob
		£	£	£	£	£	£
Low	0.1	20	2	80	8	10	1
Medium	0.6	40	24	70	42	100	60
High	0.3	50	15	(10)	(3)	40	12
Total	1.0		41		47		73

Thus, if the criterion is to maximise the expected value, it means that the product with the highest expected value will be chosen, in this case product C.

Example 2

A grocer buys fresh tomatoes, which have to be sold on the date purchased or thrown away. Each tomato costs 10p to buy and sells for 15p. The levels of demand per day and their associated probabilities are as follows:

Demand per day	Probability
200	0.2
220	0.2
240	0.3
260	0.2
280	0.1
	1.0

How many tomatoes should the grocer buy?

Solution 2

Pay-off table

Demand	Purchased per day				
	200	220	240	260	280
200	(W1) £10	(W4) £8	£6	£4	£2
220	(W2) £10	£11	£9	£7	£5
240	(W3) £10	£11	£12	£10	£8
260	£10	£11	£12	£13	£11
280	£10	£11	£12	£13	£14

W1 = The grocer purchased 200 tomatoes and sold 200 tomatoes, and on each tomato made 5p profit (i.e. 15p – 10p).

Therefore the total profit is 5p × 200 = £10.

W2 = The grocer purchases 200 tomatoes, and although demand is 220, there are still only 200 tomatoes.

Therefore the total profit is 5p × 200 = £10.

W3 = The grocer purchases 200 tomatoes and although demand is 240, there are still only 200 tomatoes.

Therefore the total profit is 5p × 200 = £10.

W4 = If the grocer buys 220 tomatoes the cost = 220 × 10p = £22

If only 200 tomatoes are sold the revenue = 200 × 15p = £30

Hence profit = 30 − 22 = £8.

The rest of the above table can be filled in using the same process.

To calculate the Expected Value (EV):

Production per day

Demand per day	Probability	200	220	240	260	280
200	0.2	(W1) 2.0	1.6	1.2	0.8	0.4
220	0.2	2.0	2.2	1.8	1.4	1.0
240	0.3	(W2) 3.0	3.3	3.6	3.0	2.4
260	0.2	2.0	2.2	2.4	2.6	2.2
280	0.1	1.0	1.1	1.2	1.3	1.4
EV		10.0	10.4	10.2	9.1	7.4

W1 = Using the pay-off table value of £10, this is multiplied by the probability of 0.2, i.e. £10 × 0.2 = 2.

W2 = Using the pay-off table value of £10, this is multiplied by the probability of 0.3, i.e. £10 × 0.3 = 3.

All the values are calculated by multiplying the pay-off table value by its respective probability.

Therefore, the grocer should buy 220 tomatoes per day, giving an expected profit of £10.40.

2.5 Applicability and limitations of expected values

The criterion of expected value is only valid where the decision being made is either:

(a) one that is repeated regularly over a period of time; or

(b) a **one-off** decision, but where its size is fairly small in relation to the total assets of the firm and it is one of many, in terms of the sums of money involved, that face the firm over a period of time.

In other words, the **law of averages** will apply in the long run, but clearly the result of any single action must, by definition, be one of the specified outcomes. Thus, in Example 1, while the expected value of introducing product C is £73, each actual outcome will result in either £10, £100 or £40 net income, and it is only if a whole series of product introductions were involved that the **average** over a period of time would approach £73, so long as the expected value criterion was applied consistently to all the decisions.

Therefore, it is quite acceptable to adopt the expected value as the decision-making criterion for the company in the example, so long as it has several other products and the same sort of marketing decision arises fairly regularly.

To illustrate the distinction being made, consider someone insuring their house against fire damage for a year.

- Suppose the house is worth £50,000 and the probability of the house being burnt down is 0.0001 (the only other outcome being that the house is not burnt down with a probability of 0.9999). They would be quite prepared to pay, say, £15 pa to insure their house even though the expected value if they did not (or expected cost in this case) is only 0.0001 × £50,000 + 0.9999 × 0 = £5. They cannot afford to pay £50,000 out more than once in their lifetime and therefore cannot afford to play the averages by using expected value as their decision criterion (if so they would refuse to pay a premium greater than £5).

- However, to the insurance company, £50,000 is not a large sum, most of their transactions being for similar or greater amounts and therefore expected value would be appropriate as a decision criterion for them. In fact, the expected value of the insurance company's decision to insure the house at £15 pa is:

    0.0001 × (−£49,985) + 0.9999 × £15

    or   −£4.9985 + £14.9985   =   £10

    and any positive expected value would, in theory, have made it worth their while to insure.

Another problem is that expected values fail to incorporate the risks of the projects being considered. For example, suppose we are choosing between the following two projects:

State of the world	Probability	A outcome	B outcome
I	0.5	Win £2million	Win £0.5 million
II	0.5	Lose £1million	Win £0.5 million

The expected value for project A = 0.5×2 + 0.5×(-1) = +£0.5 million

Project B gives a certain gain of £0.5 million.

Both projects have the same expected value but they are not equivalent in the minds of potential investors. Project B has no risk whereas project A has considerable upside and downside risk. Most rational investors are risk-averse and will only accept higher risks if they believe that they will receive higher returns. In this case most rational investors would prefer project B.

Activity 2

If the three possible outcomes of a decision are profits of £10, £50 and £80 with probabilities of 0.3, 0.3 and 0.4 respectively, what is the expected profit?

Feedback to this activity is at the end of the chapter.

2.6 Other decision criteria

Whilst expected value is the most commonly used measure of outcomes used to evaluate decisions made under conditions of uncertainty, it is not the only technique.

Expected value takes an average position; other factors which influence the decisions are the risk attitudes of the decision maker – the pessimist would look to maximise the benefit from the worst possible outcome whereas the optimist would seek to maximise the benefit from the best possible outcome.

Summary

This chapter has considered the nature of a decision and distinguished between decisions made under conditions of certainty and those made under conditions of uncertainty.

The technique of expected value has then been used to show how decisions made under conditions of uncertainty may be evaluated.

Self-test questions

1. What is an expected value? (1)
2. What is a decision? (2)
3. How do conditions of uncertainty differ from conditions of certainty? (2.1, 2.3)
4. What is the difference between risk and uncertainty (2.3)
5. The criterion of expected value is only valid under certain conditions. What are they? (2.5)

Practice questions

Question 1

A company is deciding which of four products (W, X, Y or Z) to launch. The expected payoff from each of the products is shown below in £000s.

Demand	Probability	W	X	Y	Z
High	0.5	30	50	40	20
Medium	0.3	30	0	20	30
Low	0.2	30	(50)	0	40

If the company wants to maximise the expected profits, which product should be launched?

A W
B X
C Y
D Z

Question 2

Three sales representatives – J, K and L – rate their (independent) chances of achieving certain levels of sales as follows:

	Possible sales	£10,000	£20,000	£30,000
J	Probability	0.3	0.5	0.2
K	Probability	0.3	0.4	0.3
L	Probability	0.2	0.6	0.2

(For example, J rates her chances of selling £20,000 worth of business as 'fifty-fifty' and K has a 30% chance of selling £30,000 worth.)

On this evidence, the highest expected sales will be from:

A   J alone

B   K alone

C   L alone

D   K and L

Question 3

A company is bidding for three contracts which are awarded independently of each other. The Board estimates its chances of winning contract X as 50%, of winning contract Y as 1 in 3, and of winning contract Z as 1 in 5. The profits from X, Y and Z are estimated to be £50,000, £90,000 and £100,000 respectively.

The **expected value** to the company of the profits from all three contracts will be closest to (£000):

A   50

B   75

C   90

D   100

For the answers to these questions, see the 'Answers' section at the end of the book.

Feedback to activities

Activity 1

To answer this it is necessary to calculate the expected profit on each site, and then choose the site giving the higher figure.

Site A

P(success) = 0.8 ∴ expectation = £(0.8 × 500,000)

P(failure) = 0.2 ∴ expectation = £(0.2 × (−80,000))

∴ The expectation is £400,000 − £16,000 = £384,000 pa

Site B

P(success) = 0.6 ∴ expectation = £(0.6 × 600,000)

P(failure) = 0.4 ∴ expectation = £(0.4 × (−120,000))

∴ The expectation is £360,000 − £48,000 = £312,000 pa

Note: it has been assumed that the only outcomes are profit or loss. Break-even (resulting in zero profit) has been ignored. It has also been assumed that the probability of profit or loss remains constant each year.

On the basis of these calculations, the new store should be located on Site A, because of the higher expected profit, i.e. on average, the profits are expected to be £384,000 pa over a number of years.

Activity 2

Expected profit = 0.3 × £10 + 0.3 × £50 + 0.4 × £80   =   £50

13

NORMAL DISTRIBUTION

Contents

1 Properties of normal distribution
2 Combined normal distributions

1 Properties of normal distribution

1.1 Introduction

As we saw in Chapters 6 and 9, when continuous data has been collected and a frequency distribution formed, it is often shown diagrammatically in a histogram, where the total frequency of the distribution is represented by the total area of the rectangles.

A particular type of histogram that is commonly met is the bell-shaped diagram (Figure 1), i.e. the highest column is in the centre of the histogram with decreasing columns spread symmetrically on either side of this peak.

Figure 1

If the class intervals are very small, the histogram becomes a frequency curve, as in Figure 2.

Figure 2

> **DEFINITION**
>
> Normal distribution is a continuous probability distribution which is symmetrical and bell-shaped, and is exactly specified by just its mean and standard deviation.

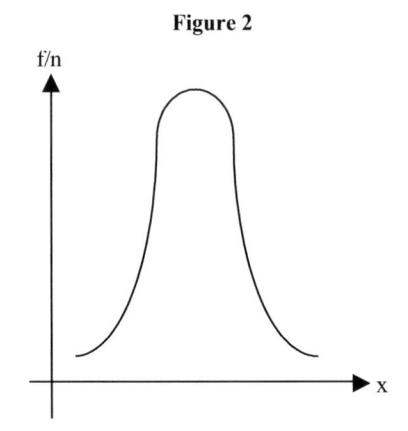

The **normal distribution** curve is a theoretical relative frequency curve which has a shape as in Figure 2.

1.2 Features of the normal curve

KEY POINT

Area under the normal curve represents probability – so total area is one unit.

(a) It is a mathematical curve, calculated from a complex equation, but which closely fits many naturally occurring distributions, such as heights of people.

(b) It is symmetrical and bell-shaped.

(c) Both tails of the distribution approach, but never meet, the x-axis. This is its chief difference from naturally occurring distributions. No person, for example, has an infinite height (or a negative height).

(d) The mean, median and mode lie together on the axis of symmetry of the curve.

(e) The area under the curve is considered to be **one unit of area** and, by symmetry, the area to the left of the mean equals the area to the right of the mean (0.5 units of area each).

1.3 Normal distribution table and z variables

Since the total area under the curve is one unit, the probability that a value of a variable lies between certain limits will be the corresponding proportion of the total area.

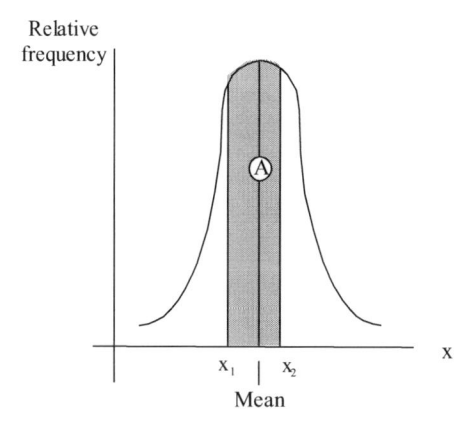

So, the probability that a (randomly picked) value x lies between x_1 and x_2 is the area A (shaded).

or $P(x_1 < x < x_2) = A$

The proportion of the whole area that this shaded area represents can be found by using the 'normal distribution table'. This can be found at the front of this book and it is usually issued in an exam. It is the one entitled 'Area under the normal curve'. Have a look now and read the explanation at the top of the table.

KEY POINT

Variable is transformed to standard variable z using the formula:

$$z = \frac{x - \mu}{\sigma}$$

In order to use the table it is necessary to know the mean (μ) and the standard deviation (σ) of the distribution being studied. Knowing these, the values (x_1 and x_2) of the variable can be **'standardised'**, i.e. they can be expressed in terms of the **number of standard deviations** by which they differ from the mean.

The formula for calculating the standardised variables (usually given the letter z to distinguish them from the original data) is:

$$z = \frac{x - \mu}{\sigma}$$

The z values are then looked up in the table, as we shall see in a moment.

1.4 Calculating probabilities

The normal distribution has many applications in life; e.g. height, weight, intelligence of the population and many other matters have this type of distribution. We'll look at some practical applications later in this chapter, but first let's make sure you understand the theory and how to use the table.

Example 1

> **KEY POINT**
>
> In solving problems it is **always** advisable to **draw a sketch** of the distribution to ensure that the correct area is being calculated.

Suppose a normal distribution has a mean of 68 and a standard deviation of 3. What is the probability that a randomly chosen member of the population described by the distribution will have a value that lies between 68 and 74?

The probability is given by the area under the curve between the mean and 74. To get a better understanding a rough diagram can be sketched and the required area shaded. It need not be to scale.

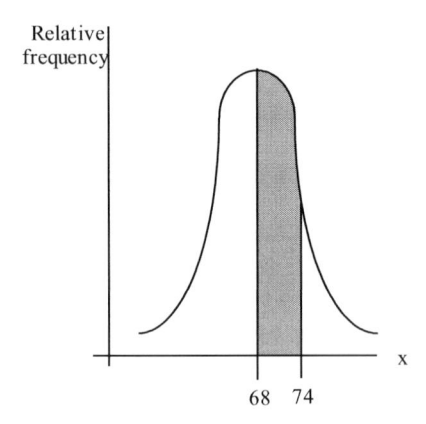

In order to find the **area** between 68 (x_1) and 74 (x_2) it is necessary to standardise the values of the variables using the formula.

For $x_1 = 68$ and with μ also $= 68$ and $\sigma = 3$

$$z_1 = \frac{68 - 68}{3} = 0$$

For $x_2 = 74$ and $\mu = 68$ and $\sigma = 3$

$$z_2 = \frac{74 - 68}{3} = 2$$

> **KEY POINT**
>
> z measures the number of standard deviations between the variable and the mean and enables one set of standard normal distribution tables to be used.

z_1 and z_2 measure the number of standard deviations between each value of the variable (i.e. 68 and 74) and the mean, so 68 is zero standard deviations from the mean, since it is the mean, and 74 is two standard deviations above the mean (i.e. $2 \times 3 = 6$ and $68 + 6 = 74$).

Now we turn to the table and look up these values by finding the relevant row and column. For the value 2.00 for instance find the 2.0 row and the 0.00 column. (If we had been looking up 2.55 we'd look in the 2.5 row and the 0.05 column.)

Look at the table now and confirm the following:

$z_1 = 0$ gives an area of 0.0000, and

$z_2 = 2$ gives an area of 0.4772

Note: the total proportion of area to the right of the mean is 0.5000.

Therefore the probability that x lies between 68 and 74 is (0.4772 – 0.0000) = 0.4772, since that proportion of the area is enclosed between these limits. This is the shaded area in the rough sketch above.

$$\therefore P(68 < x < 74) = 0.4772$$

(As a rule you wouldn't bother to standardise a value that was the same as the mean because it will always result in a zero. We only did so in this first example for the purposes of your initial understanding: in the remaining examples it will be taken as understood.)

Example 2

Suppose a normal distribution has a mean of 12, and a standard deviation of 3. The probability that a randomly chosen value of x lies between the values of 6 and 15 is calculated as follows.

Again, the curve is drawn and the appropriate area shaded.

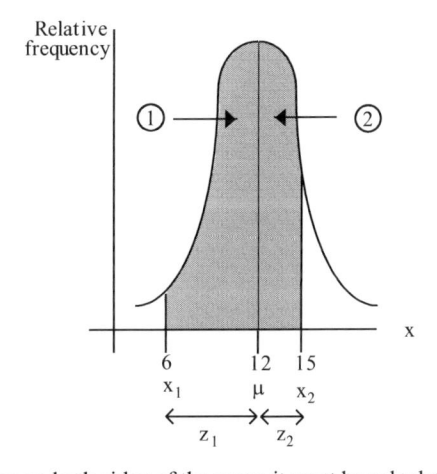

Since the area lies on both sides of the mean it must be calculated in two steps.

Step 1

The area from 6 to the mean of 12 will be found.

Step 2

The area from the mean of 12 to 15 will be found.

(a) $\quad z_1 = \dfrac{6-12}{3} = \dfrac{-6}{3} = -2$

The **minus sign** merely indicates that 6 is 2 standard deviations **below** the mean. It can be ignored for the purposes of the calculation, since the distribution is symmetrical, and the area for $z = -2$ is therefore the same as for $z = +2$.

(b) $z_2 = \dfrac{15-12}{3} = \dfrac{3}{3} = 1$

From tables:

$z_2 = 1$ gives an area of 0.3413

$z_1 = 2$ gives an area of 0.4772

∴ total area 0.8185

∴ Probability that a randomly chosen value of x lies between the values of 6 and 15 is 0.8185

or P (6 < x < 15) = 0.8185 or 81.85%

1.5 Practical applications

Now consider how this theory could be used in, say, quality control of a manufacturing process.

Example 3

Jam is packed in tins that are supposed to weigh 1,000g. The actual weight of jam delivered to a tin by the filling machine is normally distributed about the set weight with a standard deviation of 12g.

If the set, or average, filling of jam is 1,000g, calculate the proportion of tins containing:

(a) less than 985g

(b) more than 1,030g

(c) between 985g and 1,030g.

Solution 3

(a) Less than 985g, i.e. P (x < 985)

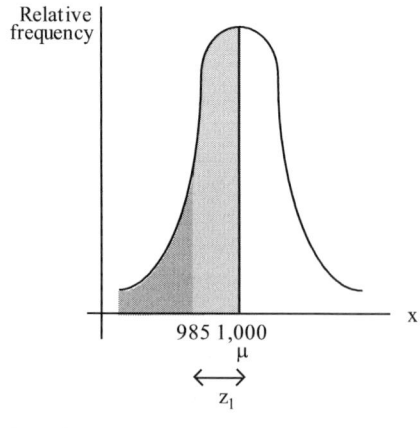

In order to calculate the proportion of tins containing less than 985g it is necessary to find the area between 985 and 1,000 (lightly shaded) and subtract this from the area under half the curve, i.e. 0.5.

∴ $z_1 = \dfrac{985 - 1{,}000}{12} = -1.25$

(again the minus sign can be ignored)

From the table $z_1 = 1.25$ gives an area of 0.3944, found in the row labelled 1.2 and the column headed 0.05.

∴ Area of darker shaded part of diagram = 0.5 − 0.3944 = 0.1056

So P (x < 985) = 0.1056

∴ Proportion of tins is 0.1056 (or 10.56%).

(b) More than 1,030g, i.e. P (x > 1,030)

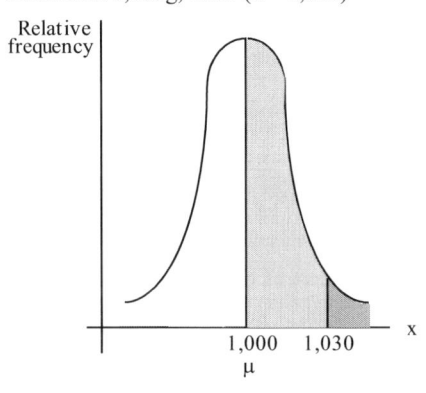

This is calculated in a similar way to part (a) i.e. area under half the curve less area with light shading is the required area (shaded darkly).

$$z_2 = \frac{1,030 - 1,000}{12} = 2.5$$

From the table $z_2 = 2.5$ gives an area of 0.4938

∴ Area of dark shaded part of diagram = 0.5 − 0.4938

so P (x > 1,030) = 0.0062

∴ Proportion of tins is 0.0062 (or 0.62%).

(c) Between 985g and 1,030g, i.e. P (985 < x < 1,030)

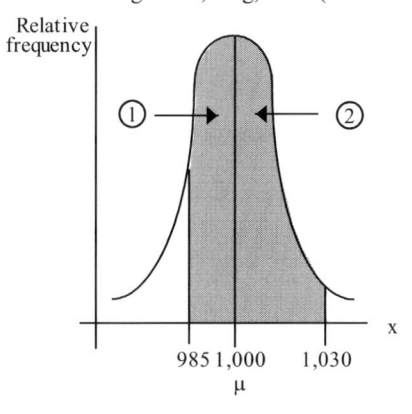

The area will again be calculated in two steps:

(i) the area between the mean and 985

(ii) the area between the mean and 1,030.

These areas have already been calculated in (a) and (b).

$$\text{Area 1 is } 0.3944$$
$$\text{Area 2 is } 0.4938$$
$$\text{So } P(985 < x < 1{,}030) = 0.3944 + 0.4938 = 0.8882$$

∴ Proportion of tins is 0.8882 (or 88.82%).

1.6 Quality control

To bring home the implications of the above, we will convert from percentages to physical objects and look at the expected frequency of the occurrence of each category of tin.

Example

Considering the data of the previous example with jam tins, if 50,000 tins a week pass through the filling machine the number of tins expected to contain:

(a)   less than 985g

(b)   more than 1,030g, and

(c)   between 985g and 1,030g,

is calculated as follows:

(a)	$P(x < 985)$	=	0.1056
	∴ expected number of tins	=	$50{,}000 \times 0.1056$
		=	5,280
(b)	$P(x > 1{,}030)$	=	0.0062
	∴ expected number of tins	=	$50{,}000 \times 0.0062$
		=	310
(c)	$P(985 < x < 1{,}030)$	=	0.8882
	∴ expected number of tins	=	$50{,}000 \times 0.8882$
		=	44,410
	(Check: 5,280 + 310 + 44,410	= 50,000)	

This indicates that more than 5,000 customers aren't getting all the jam they pay for: the process is under-filling a fairly large number of tins. The machinery probably needs to be adjusted: perhaps some pipes have got clogged up and need cleaning.

Although we have kept the example very simple this is exactly how quality procedures work – perhaps on a second-by-second basis – in a modern factory with computerised, statistically-controlled machines.

2 Combined normal distributions

2.1 Introduction

Many circumstances exist where two or more normal distributions are combined together. When this happens the resulting distribution will again be normal and therefore probabilities may be determined in the usual way once values have been obtained for the mean and standard deviation of the combined distribution.

2.2 Mean and standard deviation

The mean of the combined distribution is arrived at by simply adding together the means of the distributions that are combining.

In general terms:

Mean (A + B) = Mean A + Mean B

The same is not true of the standard deviation, although it is true for the variance of a distribution. Remember the variance of a distribution is the square of its standard deviation.

Variance = σ^2

Variance (A + B) = Variance A + Variance B

∴ standard deviation is given by

$\sigma(A + B) = \sqrt{\sigma_A^2 + \sigma_B^2}$

Example

Over a period of time, a certain branch of Richquick Bank has analysed its daily note issue and found that demands for five pound, ten pound and twenty pound notes on any day of the week have approximately normal distributions with the following parameters:

	Number of notes	
Denominations	Mean	Standard deviation
£5	1,200	250
£10	600	100
£20	50	5

The demand for the three denominations are independent of one another.

What is the probability that the demand for cash exceeds £15,000 on any one day?

Mean daily demand (£) = 1,200 × £5 + 600 × £10 + 50 × £20

= 6,000 + 6,000 + 1,000

= £13,000

Standard deviation of demand = $\sqrt{(250 \times £5)^2 + (100 \times £10)^2 + (5 \times £20)^2}$ (£)

= $\sqrt{1{,}250^2 + 1{,}000^2 + 100^2}$ (£)

= $\sqrt{2{,}572{,}500}$ (£)

= £1,603.90

$$z = \frac{15{,}000 - 13{,}000}{1{,}603.90} = 1.25$$

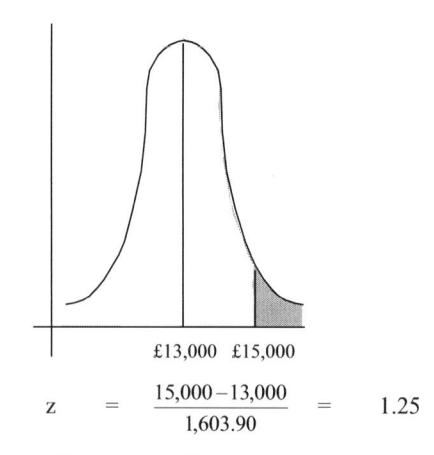

(*Note*: Since normal distribution tables are only produced for values of z to 2 decimal places, there is no point in calculating z more accurately, although σ should be found to several decimal places to avoid rounding.)

Area of tail (from tables) = 0.3944

Probability that demand is greater than £15,000 is 0.5 − 0.3944 = 0.1056 = 10.56%.

One day in every ten the bank will run out of money if it is 'mean' enough only to keep £15,000 in its safe!

Summary

This chapter demonstrated how the normal distribution can be used to calculate simple probabilities which can be applied to practical situations.

Self-test questions

1   What are the features of the normal curve? (1.2)

2   What is the formula for the value of z? (1.3)

3   What are the formulae for the mean and standard deviation of combined normal distributions? (2.2)

Practice questions

Question 1

A normal distribution is to be split into four equal areas, two to the right of Z = 0 and two to the left of Z = 0 (Z = 0 at the mean). Using tables, the Z value that splits the area in this way is closest to:

A   0.1915

B   0.3333

C   0.5000

D   0.6750

Question 2

A normal distribution has a mean of 150, and a standard deviation of 20. 80% of the distribution is below (approximately):

A   158

B   170

C   161

D   167

For the answers to these questions, see the 'Answers' section at the end of the book.

Additional question

Workers' weekly wages

A group of workers has a weekly wage which is normally distributed with mean £120 and standard deviation £15.

Find the probability of a worker earning:

(a)   more than £110

(b)   less than £85

(c)   more than £150

(d)   between £110 and £135

(e)   between £125 and £135.

Find the limits which enclose the middle:

(f)   95%

(g)   98%

For the answer to this question, see the 'Answers' section at the end of the book.

14

CORRELATION AND REGRESSION

Contents

1 Scatter diagrams
2 Regression
3 Correlation
4 Conclusions and illustration
5 Forecasting using correlation and regression

1 Scatter diagrams

1.1 Introduction

Information about two variables that are considered to be related in some way can be plotted on a scatter diagram, each axis representing one variable. For example, the amount of rainfall and the crop yield per acre could be plotted against each other, or the level of advertising expenditure against sales revenue of a product.

It is important, however, to decide which variable can be used to predict the other – i.e. which is the **independent** and which the **dependent variable**. In many cases it is quite clear, e.g. the amount of rainfall obviously causes a particular crop yield, and not vice-versa. Here, rainfall is the independent variable and crop yield the dependent variable (i.e. yield depends on the amount of rainfall). Some relationships have classic 'chicken and egg' characteristics; for example, advertising and sales revenue. Whether a given level of advertising causes a particular level of sales or whether a particular level of sales provokes a certain level of advertising is not quite so clear. In fact, advertising tends to **directly** affect sales levels whereas sales only have an indirect influence on decisions about advertising expenditure and therefore sales tends to be regarded as the dependent variable and advertising expenditure the independent variable.

> **KEY POINT**
>
> The independent variable is usually marked along the horizontal (x) axis and the dependent variable along the vertical (y) axis. It is convenient to think in terms of the x-axis being the cause, and the y-axis the effect.

The independent variable is usually marked along the horizontal (x) axis and the dependent variable up the vertical (y) axis.

Students are advised to think in terms of the x-axis being the cause, and the y-axis the effect.

The values of the two variables are plotted together so that the diagram consists of a number of points. The way in which these are scattered or dispersed indicates if any link is likely to exist between the variables.

For example:

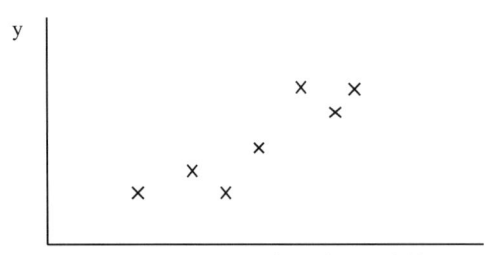

1.2 Correlation

> **DEFINITION**
>
> Correlation is a measure of how strong the connection is between the two variables.

Correlation is a measure of how strong the connection is between the two variables.

One advantage of a scatter diagram is that it is possible to see quite easily if the points indicate that a relationship exists between the variables, i.e. to see if any correlation exists between them.

It is not possible to establish how strong the relationship is (to measure the degree of correlation) from a scatter diagram. However, as will be seen later, there are methods of calculating a numerical value for this.

1.3 Types of correlation

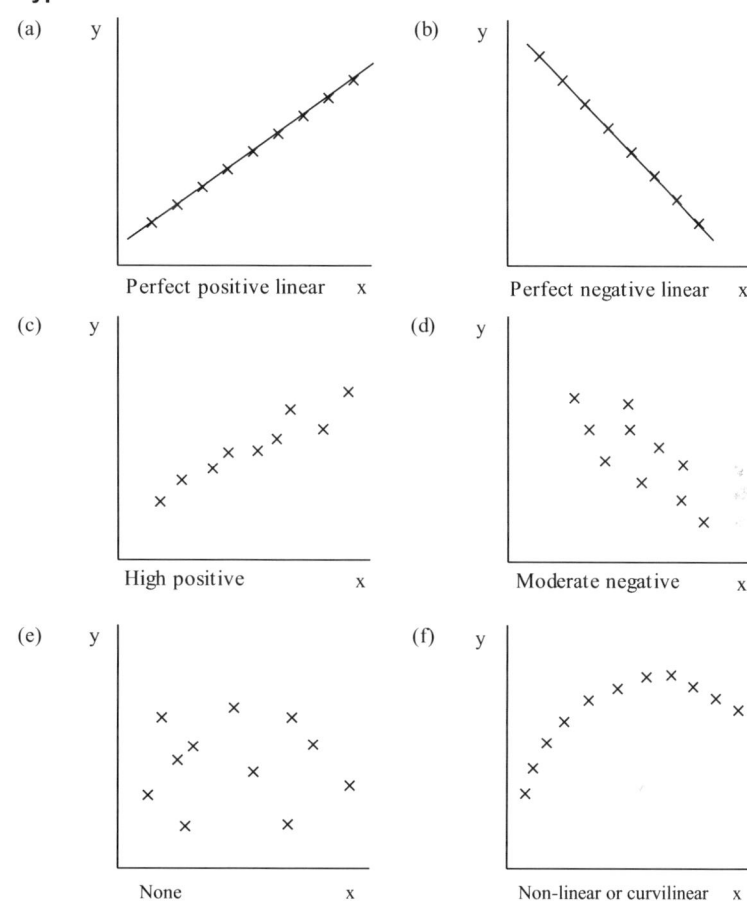

(a) Perfect positive linear
(b) Perfect negative linear
(c) High positive
(d) Moderate negative
(e) None
(f) Non-linear or curvilinear

These six scatter diagrams illustrate some of the different types of correlation. Scatter graphs of non-linear correlation can assume many different types of curve.

> **KEY POINT**
>
> Positive correlation exists where the values of the variables increase together (direct relationship). Negative correlation exists where one variable increases as the other decreases in value (inverse relationship).

If the points lie exactly on a straight line, then the correlation is said to be perfect linear correlation. In practice this rarely occurs and it is more usual for the points to be scattered in a band; the narrower the band the higher the degree of correlation.

Positive correlation exists where the values of the variables increase together. Negative correlation exists where one variable increases as the other decreases in value.

Thus, considering the six diagrams:

(a) This is an example of perfect positive linear correlation since the points lie exactly on a straight line and as x increases so y increases.

(b) This is an example of perfect negative linear correlation since the points again lie on a straight line, but as the x values increase so the y values decrease.

(c) In this diagram, the points lie in a narrow band rather than on a straight line, but x and y still tend to increase together, therefore a high degree of positive correlation is evident.

(d) This time the points lie in a much wider band and, as x increases, y tends to decrease, so this is an example of negative correlation where, because of the wider spread of the points than those in (c), the correlation is only moderate.

(e) When the points are scattered all over the diagram, as in this case, then little or no correlation exists between the two variables.

(f) Here the points lie on an obvious curve. there is a relationship between x and y, but it is not a straight line relationship.

2 Regression

2.1 Linear correlation

When the points on a scatter diagram tend to lie in a narrow band, there is a strong correlation between the variables. This band may be curved or straight. For example:

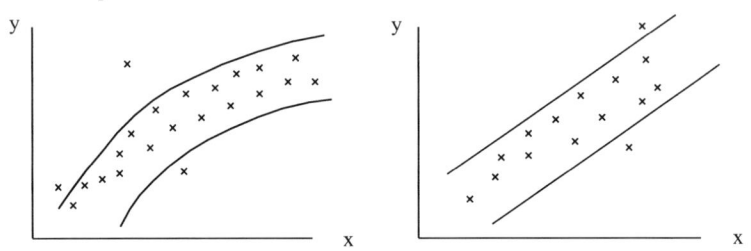

When the band is straight the correlation is linear and the relationship between the variables can be expressed in terms of the equation of a straight line. It is this type of correlation that will be studied throughout this chapter.

2.2 Line of best fit

To obtain a description of the relationship between two variables in the form of an equation in order to forecast values, it is necessary to fit a straight line through the points on the scatter diagram which best represents all of the plotted points. There are several ways of accomplishing this.

2.3 Establishing trend lines by eye

One method which can be used to fit a straight line through the points, is to fit it 'by eye'. To do this a line must be drawn, going directly through the centre of all the points. Obviously, the more correlated the points, the easier the line will be to draw. However this method does have the disadvantage that if there is a large amount of scatter, no two people's lines will coincide and it is, therefore, only suitable where the amount of scatter is only small.

2.4 Equation of a straight line

The equation for any straight line is of the form:

$$y = a + bx$$

where x and y are the variables and a and b are constants for the particular line in question.

a is called the **intercept** on the y-axis and measures the point at which the line will cut the y-axis.

b is called the **gradient** of the line and measures its degree of slope.

a and b can take any value, including zero, and may be positive or negative.

In order to locate any particular line, it is therefore necessary to determine the values of a and b for that line.

2.5 Parameters of a regression line by inspection

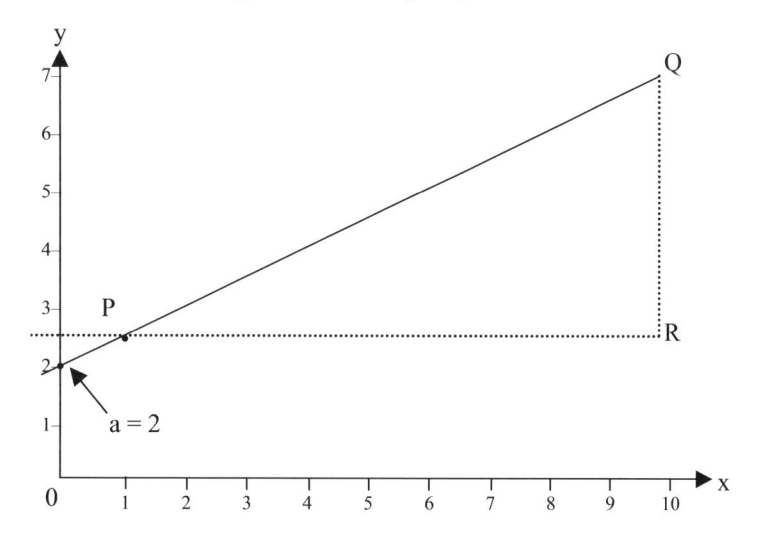

The diagram shows a line which has been fitted to a scatter graph by eye. The points of the scatter graph have been omitted for clarity. It is required to find the values of a and b for this line in the general equation y = a + bx.

Method

a is the intercept on the y-axis, i.e. the value of y at which the line cuts the y-axis. Hence a = 2.

To find the slope, b, take any two points (P and Q) on the line.

The further apart P and Q are, the more accurate will be the result.

Draw horizontal and vertical lines through P and Q to meet at R.

The length of PR **as measured on the x-scale**   =   9 units

The length of RQ **as measured on the y-axis**   =   4.5 units

The slope = $\dfrac{RQ}{PR} = \dfrac{4.5}{9} = 0.5$, hence b = 0.5

The equation is therefore:

y   =   2 + 0.5x

Note: for this method, no part of the x-scale can be omitted, otherwise the vertical axis is not the true y-axis and the intercept will not be correct.

An alternative method which can be used if part of the x-scale needs to be omitted is to read off from the graph the values of x and y at P and Q, substitute these values into the general equation and solve the resulting simultaneous equations for a and b.

$$y = a + bx$$

at P, $x = 1$, $y = 2.5$, hence:

$$2.5 = a + b \times 1$$

i.e. $a + b = 2.5$ .... (1)

at Q, $x = 10$, $y = 7$, hence:

$$7 = a + b \times 10$$

i.e. $a + 10b = 7$ .... (2)

Subtract (1) from (2) to eliminate a:

$$a + 10b = 7$$
$$a + b = 2.5$$
$$9b = 4.5$$
$$b = \frac{4.5}{9} = 0.5$$

Substitute in (1) to find a:

$$a + 0.5 = 2.5$$
$$a = 2.5 - 0.5$$
$$\therefore a = 2.0$$

Hence $a = 2.0$ and $b = 0.5$ as before.

2.6 Least squares linear regression

> **KEY POINT**
>
> The method of least squares regression is the most mathematically acceptable method of fitting a line to a set of data. Instead of relying on our eyes to draw the line of best fit, mathematical techniques are used to derive the equation.

The method of least squares regression is the most mathematically acceptable method of fitting a line to a set of data. Instead of relying on our eyes to draw the line of best fit, mathematical techniques are used to derive the equation. This sounds horrible and looks very complicated at first sight, but actually it is just a matter of plugging numbers into a formula which is always given in exams.

It is possible to calculate two different regression lines for a set of data, depending on whether the horizontal deviations or the vertical deviations of the points from the line are considered. It is the sum of the **squares** of these deviations which is minimised; this overcomes problems that might arise because some deviations would be positive and some negative, depending on whether the point was above or below the line (squaring a negative number gives a positive number). It is not necessary to go into the theory of this method any more deeply at this level.

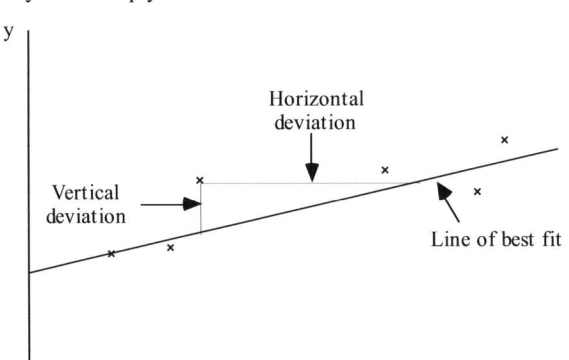

The regression line of y on x must be used when an estimate of y is required for a given value of x. This line minimises the sum of the squares of the vertical distances of the points from the line. The regression line of x on y must be used when an estimate of x is required for a known value of y. This line minimises the sum of the squares of the horizontal distances of the points from the line.

The scatter diagram has the following appearance when the regression lines are graphed:

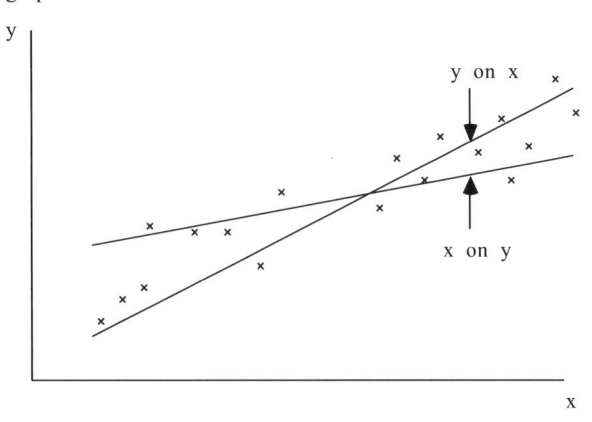

The two lines will intersect at the point $(\bar{x}, \bar{y})$, i.e. the mean of the x-values and the mean of the y-values.

2.7 The regression line of y on x

Assuming that the equation of the regression line of y on x is:

$$y = a + bx$$

it is necessary to calculate the values of a and b so that the equation can be completely determined.

The following formulae may be used; a knowledge of their derivation is not necessary. They do not need to be memorised since they are always supplied in exams (using upper case X and Y).

$$a = \bar{y} - b\bar{x} = \frac{\Sigma y}{n} - \frac{b\Sigma x}{n}$$

$$b = \frac{n\Sigma xy - \Sigma x \Sigma y}{n\Sigma x^2 - (\Sigma x)^2}$$

n is the number of pairs of x, y values, i.e. the number of points on the scatter graph.

The value of b must be calculated first as it is needed to calculate a.

Example

The following table shows the amount of fertiliser applied to identical fields, and their resulting yields:

Fertiliser (kg/hectare)	Yield (tonnes/hectare)
100	40
200	45
300	50
400	65
500	70
600	70
700	80

Calculate the regression line for y on x.

Solution

Step 1

Tabulate the data and determine which is the dependent variable, y, and which the independent, x.

Step 2

Calculate Σx, Σy, Σx^2, Σxy (leave room for a column for Σy^2 which may well be needed subsequently.

Step 3

Substitute in the formulae in order to find b and a in that order.

Step 4

Substitute a and b in the regression equation.

The calculation is set out as follows, where x is the amount of fertiliser in units of **hundreds** of kg/hectare and y is the yield in tonnes/hectare.

	x	y	xy	x^2
	1	40	40	1
	2	45	90	4
	3	50	150	9
	4	65	260	16
	5	70	350	25
	6	70	420	36
	7	80	560	49
Σ	28	420	1,870	140

n = 7

$$b = \frac{n\Sigma xy - \Sigma x \Sigma y}{n\Sigma x^2 - (\Sigma x)^2}$$

(Try to avoid rounding at this stage since, although $n\Sigma xy$ and $\Sigma x \Sigma y$ are large, their difference is much smaller.)

$$= \frac{(7 \times 1{,}870) - (28 \times 420)}{(7 \times 140) - (28 \times 28)}$$

$$= \frac{13{,}090 - 11{,}760}{980 - 784}$$

$$= \frac{1{,}330}{196}$$

$$= 6.79$$

(Ensure you make a note of this fraction in your workings. It may help later.)

$$a = \frac{\Sigma y}{n} - \frac{b\Sigma x}{n}$$

$$= \frac{420}{7} - 6.79 \times \frac{28}{7}$$

$$= 60 - 27.16$$

$$= 32.84$$

∴ the regression line for y on x is:

y   =   32.84 + 6.79x   (x in hundreds of kg per hectare
                         y in tonnes per hectare)

(Always specify the units for x and y very carefully.)

This line would be used to estimate the yield corresponding to a given amount of fertiliser. If, say, 250 kg/hectare of fertiliser is available, it is possible to predict the expected yield by using the regression line with = 2.5:

y   =   32.84 + 6.79 × 2.5

    =   32.84 + 16.975

    =   49.815

∴ y = 50 tonnes/hectare (rounding to whole numbers in line with original data)

Activity 1

If $\Sigma x = 560$, $\Sigma y = 85$, $\Sigma x^2 = 62{,}500$, $\Sigma xy = 14{,}200$ and $n = 12$, find the regression line of y on x (the line of best fit).

Feedback to this activity is at the end of the chapter.

2.8 The regression line of x on y

If asked to find a line of best fit the calculations just shown are what is required. This second regression line is less likely to be needed in an exam, but it may be requested, and it gives some insight into correlation.

The method of finding the regression line is the same as for the regression line of y on x, but with x and y interchanged. Thus the equation is:

x   =   a' + b'y

where   a'   = $\bar{x} - b'\bar{y}$ = $\frac{\Sigma x}{n} - \frac{b'\Sigma y}{n}$

$$b' = \frac{n\Sigma xy - \Sigma x \Sigma y}{n\Sigma y^2 - (\Sigma y)^2}$$

To calculate the equation for the data in the previous example, Σy^2 is required.

y^2
1,600
2,025
2,500
4,225
4,900
4,900
6,400

Σy^2 = 26,550

$$b' = \frac{n\Sigma xy - \Sigma x \Sigma y}{n\Sigma y^2 - (\Sigma y)^2}$$

$$= \frac{1,330}{7 \times 26,550 - (420)^2}$$

(1,330 and 420 come from the previous calculation)

$$= \frac{1,330}{9,450} = 0.141$$

$$a' = \frac{\Sigma x}{n} - \frac{b'\Sigma y}{n}$$

$$= \frac{28}{7} - \frac{0.141 \times 420}{7}$$

$$= -4.46$$

∴ The regression line of x on y is:

x = −4.46 + 0.141y

This equation would be used to estimate the amount of fertiliser that had resulted in a given yield. For example, if the yield was 60 tonnes/hectare, the estimated amount of fertiliser would be given by:

x = −4.46 + 0.141 × 60

= 4.0 (hundreds of kg/hectare)

∴ 400 kg/hectare of fertiliser would have been used to give a yield of 60 tonnes/hectare.

2.9 Regression and correlation

The angle between the two regression lines y on x and x on y decreases as the correlation between the variables increases.

In the case of perfect correlation the angle between the lines is zero, i.e. the two lines coincide and become one.

At the other extreme, the angle between the lines becomes 90° when there is no correlation between the variables. In this case one line is parallel to the x-axis and the other parallel to the y-axis.

Measures of correlation are discussed later in this book.

2.10 Interpolation and extrapolation

As has been shown, regression lines can be used to calculate intermediate values of variables, i.e. values within the known range. This is known as **interpolation** and it is one of the main uses of regression lines.

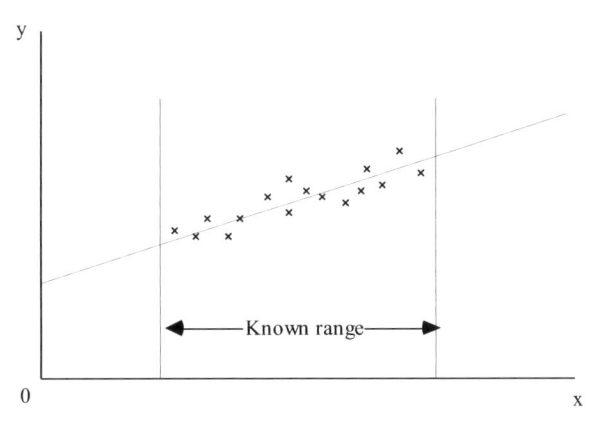

It is also possible to extend regression lines beyond the range of values used in their calculation. It is then possible to calculate values of the variables that are outside the limits of the original data; this is known as **extrapolation**.

The problem with extrapolation is that it assumes that the relationship already calculated is still valid. This may or may not be so.

For example, if the fertiliser was increased outside the given range there would come a point where it had an adverse effect on the yield. The seed might actually be damaged by too much fertiliser.

The resultant diagram could be of this form:

KEY POINT

Generally speaking, extrapolation must be treated with caution, since once outside the range of known values other factors may influence the situation, and the relationship which has been approximated as linear over a limited range may not be linear outside that range. Nevertheless, extrapolation of a time series is a valuable and widely used technique for forecasting.

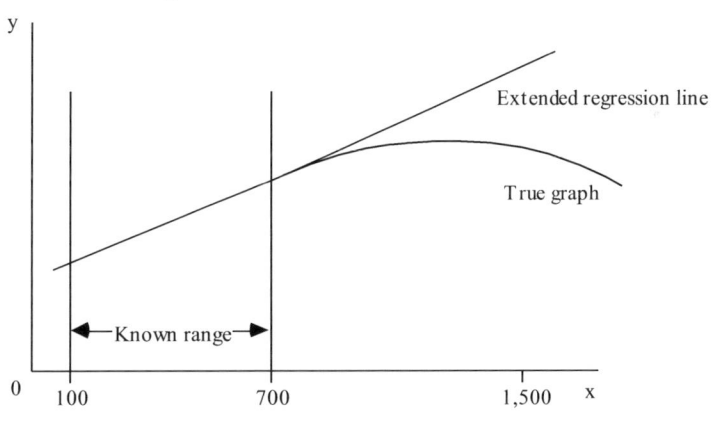

Therefore the yield from using 1,500 kg/hectare of fertiliser as estimated from the regression line may be very different from that actually achieved in practice.

Generally speaking, extrapolation must be treated with caution, since once outside the range of known values other factors may influence the situation, and the relationship which has been approximated as linear over a limited range may not be linear outside that range. Nevertheless, extrapolation of a time series is a valuable and widely used technique for forecasting.

3 Correlation

3.1 Introduction

Through regression analysis it is possible to derive a linear relationship between two variables and hence estimate unknown values. However, this does not measure the **degree of correlation** between the variables, i.e. how strong the connection is between the two variables. It is possible to find a line of best fit through any assortment of data points; this doesn't mean that we are justified in using the equation of that line.

3.2 Correlation coefficient, r

Pearson's correlation coefficient, r, is defined as:

$$r = \frac{n\Sigma xy - \Sigma x \Sigma y}{\sqrt{(n\Sigma x^2 - (\Sigma x)^2)(n\Sigma y^2 - (\Sigma y)^2)}}$$

where x and y represent pairs of data for two variables x and y, and n is the number of pairs of data used in the analysis.

This formula does not have to be memorised, since it is also supplied in the exam, but practice is needed at applying it to data and interpreting the result.

Example

Using the data of the example in the previous section relating to fertiliser and crop yield calculate the correlation coefficient.

The totals required are:

$\Sigma x = 28$, $\Sigma y = 420$, $\Sigma xy = 1,870$, $\Sigma x^2 = 140$, $\Sigma y^2 = 26,550$, $n = 7$

Solution

$$\text{Thus } r = \frac{(7 \times 1,870) - (28 \times 420)}{\sqrt{((7 \times 140) - (28 \times 28))((7 \times 26,550) - (420 \times 420))}}$$

$$= \frac{13,090 - 11,760}{\sqrt{(980 - 784)(185,850 - 176,400)}}$$

$$= \frac{1,330}{\sqrt{(196 \times 9,450)}}$$

$$= 0.98$$

(If you look at your calculations for b and b' in Sections 2.7 & 2.8 you will notice that you've already found the terms in this section.)

3.3 Interpretation of coefficient of correlation

Having calculated the value of r, it is necessary to interpret this result. Does r = 0.98 mean that there is high correlation, low correlation or no correlation?

> **DEFINITION**
>
> The coefficient of linear correlation (r) is a numerical measure of the degree of linear correlation between two variables. It has a range of values between –1 and +1.

r varies between +1 and –1 where:

r	=	+1	means perfect positive linear correlation
r	=	0	means no correlation, and
r	=	–1	means perfect negative linear correlation

So in this case the value of 0.98 indicates a high degree of positive correlation between the variables.

In general, the closer that r is to +1 (or −1) the higher the degree of linear correlation. This will usually be confirmed by the scatter diagram where the points will lie in a narrow band for such values.

KEY POINT

The closer r is to +1 (or −1) the higher the degree of linear correlation.

It must be realised that r only measures the amount of linear correlation, i.e. the tendency to a straight line relationship. It is quite possible to have strong non-linear correlation and yet have a value of r close to zero.

The more data points the farther r may be from 1 and still indicate good correlation. If there are few data points, as here, we would wish to see r very close to 1 (clearly if there are only 2 points they will lie exactly on the line of best fit).

3.4 Coefficient of determination, r^2

DEFINITION

The coefficient of determination (r^2) is a measure of the explanatory power of a regression model, i.e. how much of the variation in the dependent variable can be explained by variation in the independent variable.

The coefficient of determination is the square of the coefficient of correlation, and so is denoted by r^2 (or $100r^2$ if it is expressed as a percentage). The advantage of knowing the coefficient of determination is that it is a measure of how much of the variation in the dependent variable is 'explained' by the variation of the independent variable. The variation not accounted for by variations in the independent variable will be due to random fluctuations, or to other specific factors which have not been identified in considering the two-variable problem.

In the example on fertiliser and yield, r had a value of 0.98 and so $r^2 = 0.96$.

Thus, variations in the amount of fertiliser applied account for 96% of the variation in the yield obtained.

3.5 Spurious correlation

KEY POINT

Spurious or accidental correlation may result between two variables when there is no direct casual relationship. A hidden third variable could be present.

Students should be aware of the big danger involved in correlation analysis. Two variables, when compared, may show a high degree of correlation but they may still have no direct connection. Such correlation is termed **spurious** or **nonsense** correlation and unless two variables can reasonably be assumed to have some direct connection the correlation coefficient found will be meaningless, however high it may be.

The following are examples of variables between which there is high but spurious correlation:

- Salaries of school teachers and consumption of alcohol.
- Number of television licences and the number of admissions to mental hospitals.

Such examples clearly have no direct **causal** relationship. However, there may be some other variable which is a causal factor common to both of the original variables. For example, the general rise in living standards and real incomes is responsible both for the increase in teachers' salaries and for the increase in the consumption of alcohol.

Activity 2

If r = 0.42, how much of the variation in the dependent variable is explained by the variation of the independent variable?

Feedback to this activity is at the end of the chapter.

4 Conclusions and illustration

4.1 Conclusions

This chapter has been concerned so far with 'bivariate distributions', i.e. the distributions of two variables. The three methods used to investigate the interrelationship of two distributions are:

- scatter diagrams
- regression analysis
- correlation coefficients.

A number of formulae have been used; these must be well practised so that calculations can be made quickly and accurately.

(It is worth finding out whether your calculator has regression functions and learning how to use them, using the examples in this book.)

Illustration

The following figures show the power to the nearest kilowatt and the top speeds to the nearest mile per hour of 12 racing cars:

Power (kw)   70 63 72 60 66 70 74 65 62 67 65 68

Top speed (mph)   155 150 180 135 156 168 178 160 132 145 139 152

(a) Plot the information on a scatter diagram, showing top speed as the dependent variable.

(b) Calculate the line of regression of y on x.

(c) Estimate the top speed of a car with a power rating of 71 kw.

(d) From the calculations carried out so far, is it possible to estimate the power rating of a car which has a top speed of 175 mph? Give reasons.

(e) What would be the problems involved in estimating a top speed for a car with a power rating of 95 kw?

Solution

(a) Since top speed is the dependent variable it is plotted on the vertical y-axis. Power is therefore plotted on the x-axis.

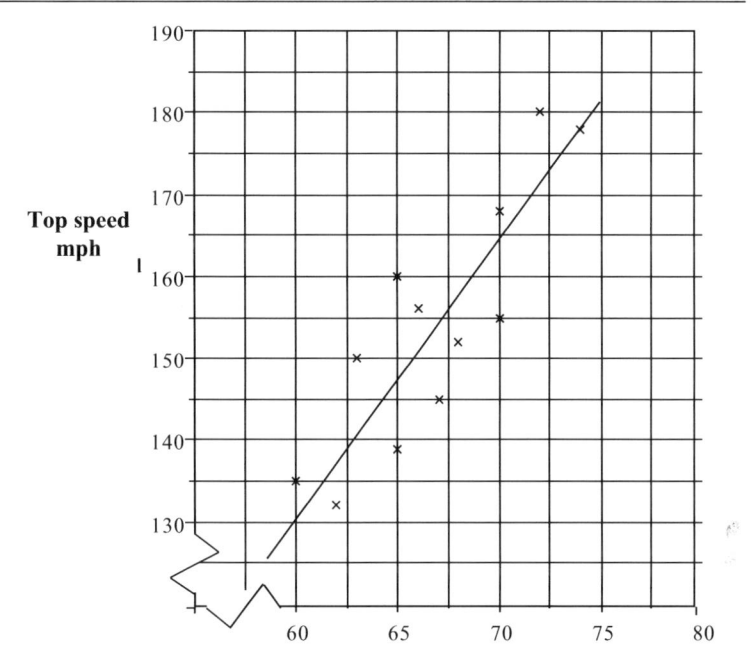

(b)

[Scatter plot showing Top speed (mph) vs Power (kw), with data points and a line of best fit. X-axis: Power (kw) from 60 to 80. Y-axis: Top speed mph from 130 to 190.]

Power (kw) x	Top speed (mph) y	xy	x^2
70	155	10,850	4,900
63	150	9,450	3,969
72	180	12,960	5,184
60	135	8,100	3,600
66	156	10,296	4,356
70	168	11,760	4,900
74	178	13,172	5,476
65	160	10,400	4,225
62	132	8,184	3,844
67	145	9,715	4,489
65	139	9,035	4,225
68	152	10,336	4,624
$\Sigma x = 802$	$\Sigma y = 1,850$	$\Sigma xy = 124,258$	$\Sigma x^2 = 53,792$

$$y = a + bx$$

Using $\quad b = \dfrac{n\Sigma xy - \Sigma x \Sigma y}{n\Sigma x^2 - (\Sigma x)^2}, \text{ and } a = \dfrac{\Sigma y}{n} - \dfrac{b\Sigma x}{n}$

$$b = \dfrac{(12 \times 124{,}258) - (802 \times 1{,}850)}{(12 \times 53{,}792) - (802 \times 802)}$$

$$= \dfrac{1{,}491{,}096 - 1{,}483{,}700}{645{,}504 - 643{,}204}$$

$$= \dfrac{7{,}396}{2{,}300}$$

∴ $\quad b = 3.22$ (to 3sf)

$$a = \frac{1{,}850}{12} - 3.22 \times \frac{802}{12}$$

$$= 154.2 - 215.2$$

$$\therefore \quad a = -61.0$$

So the regression line is: $y = -61.0 + 3.22x$

(c) If power rating is 71 kw then replacing $x = 71$ in equation gives:

$$y = -61.0 + 3.22 \times 71$$
$$= -61.0 + 228.62$$
$$\therefore \quad y = 168 \text{ mph (to nearest whole number)}$$

(d) Strictly speaking, it is not possible to estimate power rating for a given top speed without working out the line of regression of x on y, which has not yet been done.

(e) As soon as a regression line is used to predict values of y for given values of x outside the observed range, there is an immediate risk of error which continues to increase the further away one goes from the observed values.

There is no reason why a particular relationship should remain linear for higher (or lower) values of the variables (in fact the reverse is often more likely as saturation point is reached).

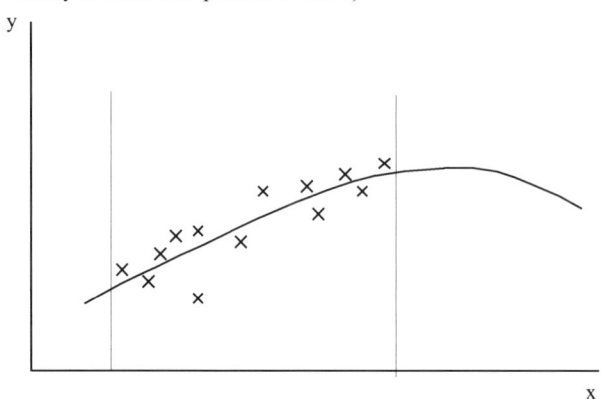

Thus, since 95 kw is a power rating well outside the present observed range, it would be unreliable to extrapolate in order to obtain an estimate of top speed for that rating.

5 Forecasting using correlation and regression

5.1 Causal forecasting

This is used where there is a causal relationship between the variable whose value is to be forecast and another variable whose value can be ascertained for the period for which the forecast is to be made. If, for example, there is correlation between the demand for sun roofs in a given year and the sales of new cars in the previous year, then this year's car sales could be used to predict sun roof demand for next year.

Example

Hi-Fi Videos plc has obtained the relationship between net profit (y) and number of sales outlets (x) as:

$$y = 0.25x - 1.9$$

where y = net profit in £m.

It plans to increase sales outlets next year to 18. The forecast of net profit for next year will therefore be:

Net profit = $0.25 \times 18 - 1.9$
= £2.6m

This is subject to the limitations of extrapolation already discussed.

5.2 Trend extrapolation

The trend is the smoothed-out line through the data when plotted against a time scale. The time scale is taken as the x variable, and the trend is the line of best fit.

Example

Year	Sales (£000)
20X3	12.0
20X4	11.5
20X5	15.8
20X6	15.0
20X7	18.5

To forecast sales for 20X8:

The sales in £000 units are taken as the y values. Year 20X3 is taken as x = 1, 20X4 as x = 2, 20X5 as x = 3, etc, in which case the forecast for year 20X8 will be the value of y when x = 6.

The least squares regression line of y on x (the line of best fit) for this data is:

$$y = 9.61 + 1.65x$$

(check this for themselves.)

Hence, the forecast of sales for year 20X8 is obtained by putting x = 6 in this equation, giving:

y = $9.61 + 1.65 \times 6$
= 19.51 (£000)
= £19,510

Notes:

(a) Any consecutive numbers could be used for the year values; there are computational advantages in taking 20X3 as –2, 20X4 as –1, 20X5 as 0, etc, as this makes $\Sigma x = 0$. In this case the forecast for 20X8 would be obtained when x = 3, and the regression line would be y = 14.56 + 1.65x.

(b) To forecast future demands, previous demands should be used, not previous sales. These are not the same as there may have been unfulfilled demand due to stock-outs.

Summary

Regression analysis is used to describe a linear relationship between two variables in the form of an equation. The coefficient of correlation gives us a measure of the strength of that relationship. These tools can be used to predict values of variables for forecasting purposes as long as their limitations are borne in mind.

Self-test questions

1   What is a scatter diagram? (1.1)

2   What is the difference between perfect positive linear correlation and perfect negative linear correlation? (1.3)

3   What is a 'line of best fit'? (2.2)

4   What is the equation of a straight line? (2.4)

5   What is the difference between interpolation and extrapolation? (2.10)

6   What is Pearson's correlation coefficient? (3.2)

Practice questions

Question 1

A company's weekly costs (£C) were plotted against production level (P) for the last 50 weeks and a regression line calculated to be C = 1,000 + 250P. Which statement about the breakdown of weekly costs is true?

A	Fixed costs are £1,000	Variable costs per unit are £5
B	Fixed costs are £250	Variable costs per unit are £1,000
C	Fixed costs are £1,000	Variable costs per unit are £250
D	Fixed costs are £20	Variable costs per unit are £5

Question 2

A company's management accountant is analysing the reject rates achieved by 100 factory operatives working in identical conditions. Reject rates, y%, are found to be related to months of experience, x, by this regression equation: y = 20 – 0.25x. (The correlation coefficient was r = –0.9.)

Using the equation, the predicted reject rate for an operative with 12 months' experience is closest to:

A   17%

B   19%

C   20%

D   23%

Question 3

In a forecasting model based on Y = a + bX, the intercept is £234. If the value of Y is £491 when X is 20, then the value of the slope, to two decimal places, is:

A −24.55

B −12.85

C 12.85

D 24.85

Question 4

Management accountants often need to predict future costs, revenues and other factors. The variable to be predicted (e.g. costs) is known as the:

A dependent variable

B statistical variable

C independent variable

D high-low variable

Question 5

The coefficient of determination (r^2) explains the:

A percentage variation in the coefficient of correlation

B percentage variation in the dependent variable which is explained by the independent variable

C percentage variation in the independent variable which is explained by the dependent variable

D extent of the causal relationship between two variables

For the answers to these questions, see the 'Answers' section at the end of the book.

Additional question

D & E Ltd

D & E Ltd produces brakes for the motor industry. Its management accountant is investigating the relationship between electricity costs and volume of production. The following data for the last ten quarters has been derived, the cost figures having been adjusted (i.e. deflated) to take into account price changes.

Quarter	1	2	3	4	5	6	7	8	9	10
Production, X, (000 units)	30	20	10	60	40	25	13	50	44	28
Electricity costs, Y, (£000)	10	11	6	18	13	10	10	20	17	15

(Source: Internal company records of D & E Ltd.)

$\Sigma X^2 = 12{,}614$, $\Sigma Y^2 = 1{,}864$, $\Sigma XY = 4{,}728$

You are required:

(a) to draw a scatter diagram of the data on squared paper

(b) to find the least squares regression line for electricity costs on production and explain this result

(c) to predict the electricity costs of D & E Ltd for the next two quarters (time periods 11 and 12) in which production is planned to be 15,000 and 55,000 standard units respectively

(d) to assess the likely reliability of these forecasts.

For the answer to this question, see the 'Answers' section at the end of the book.

Feedback to activities

Activity 1

Equation of line is: $y = a + bx$

$$b = \frac{12 \times 14{,}200 - 560 \times 85}{12 \times 62{,}500 - 560 \times 560} = \frac{122{,}800}{436{,}400} = 0.281$$

$$a = \frac{85}{12} - 0.281 \times \frac{560}{12} = -6.03$$

Regression line is: $y = -6.03 + 0.281x$

Activity 2

If $r = 0.42$, then $r^2 = 0.1764$, so about 17.6% of the variation is explained by variations in the independent variable (poor correlation).

15

TIME SERIES

Contents

1 Time series
2 Analysis of a time series

1 Time series

1.1 Introduction

DEFINITION

A time series is the name given to a set of observations taken at equal intervals of time, e.g. daily, weekly, monthly, etc. The observations can be plotted against time to give an overall picture of what is happening. **The horizontal axis is always the time axis.**

A time series is the name given to a set of observations taken at equal intervals of time, e.g. daily, weekly, monthly, etc. The observations can be plotted against time to give an overall picture of what is happening. **The horizontal axis is always the time axis**.

Examples of time series are total annual exports, monthly unemployment figures, daily average temperatures, etc.

Example

The following data relates to the production (in tonnes) of floggels by the North West Engineering Co. These are the quarterly totals taken over four years from 20X2 to 20X5.

	1st Qtr	2nd Qtr	3rd Qtr	4th Qtr
20X2	91	90	94	93
20X3	98	99	97	95
20X4	107	102	106	110
20X5	123	131	128	130

This time series will now be graphed so that an overall picture can be gained of what is happening to the company's production figures.

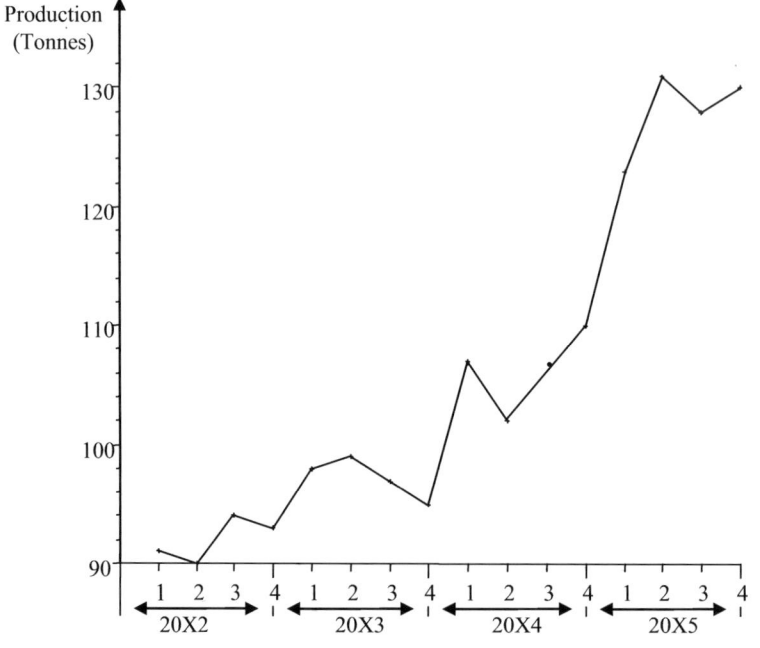

Note: each point must be plotted at the **end** of the relevant quarter.

The graph shows clearly how the production of floggels has increased over the four-year time period. This is particularly true during the last year considered.

1.2 Variations in observations

A time series is influenced by a number of factors, the most important of these being:

(a) **Long-term trends**

This is the way in which the graph of a time series appears to be moving over a long interval of time when the short-term fluctuations have been smoothed out. The rise or fall is due to factors which only change slowly, e.g.

    (i)   increase or decrease in population

    (ii)   technological improvements

    (iii) competition from abroad.

(b) **Cyclical variations**

This is the wave-like appearance of a time series graph when taken over a number of years. Generally, it is due to the influence of booms and slumps in industry. The distance in time from one peak to the next is often approximately five to seven years.

(c) **Seasonal variations**

This is a regular rise and fall over specified intervals of time. The interval of time can be any length – hours, days, weeks, etc, and the variations are of a periodic type with a fairly definite period, e.g.:

    (i)   rises in the number of goods sold before Christmas and at sale times

    (ii)   rises in the demand for gas and electricity at certain times during the day

    (iii) rises in the number of customers using a restaurant at lunch time and dinner time.

These are referred to under the general heading of 'seasonal' variations, as a common example is the steady rise and fall of, for example, sales over the four seasons of the year.

However, as can be seen from the examples, the term is also used to cover regular variations over other short periods of time.

They should not be confused with cyclical variations (paragraph b) which are long-term fluctuations with an interval between successive peaks greater than one year.

(d) **Residual or random variations**

This covers any other variation which cannot be ascribed to (a), (b) or (c) above. This is taken as happening entirely at random due to unpredictable causes, e.g.:

    (i)   strikes

    (ii)   fires

    (iii) sudden changes in taxes.

Not all time series will contain all four elements. For example, not all sales figures show seasonal variations.

1.3 A time series graph

The graph in the example covered the quarterly production of floggels over a four-year time period.

The long-term trend (a) and seasonal (quarterly) variation (c) were obvious from the graph. However, in order to be able to observe any cyclical variations it is usually necessary to have data covering a much wider time-span, say 10 – 15 years minimum.

The following graph shows the production (in tonnes) of widgets for each quarter of the 18 years from 20X1 to 20Y8.

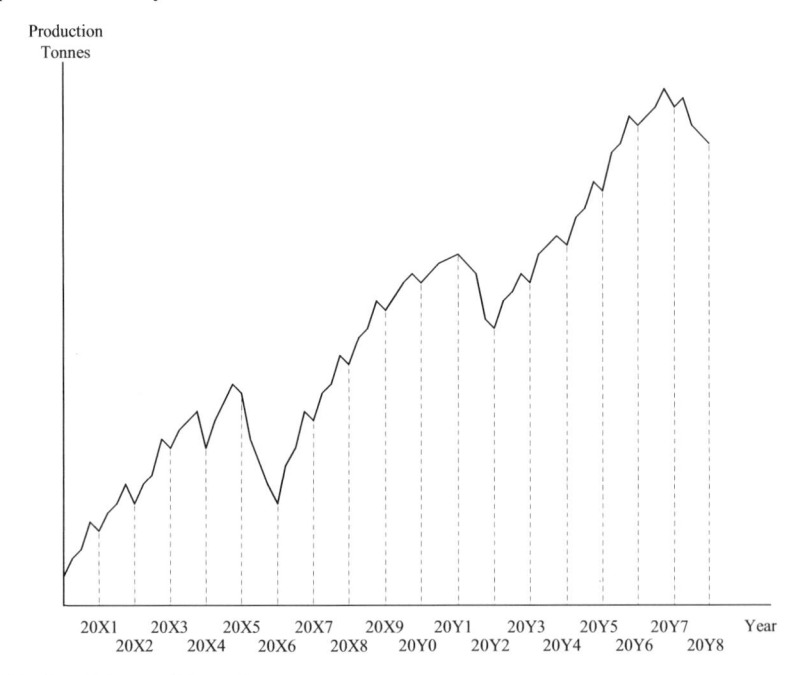

This time it is possible to detect:

(a) **The long-term trend** – upwards in this case.

(b) **Cyclical variations** – the wave like appearance of the graph shows that the business cycle spans six years, i.e. the distance in time between successive peaks (and successive troughs) is six years.

(c) **Seasonal variation** – since these are quarterly production figures this is sometimes called quarterly variation. These are the small steps in each year which are evident on the first graph. They occur because some parts of the year are busier than others and the actual pattern will depend very much on the type of industry, e.g. the building industry tends to be slack during the winter months because of the weather, whereas an engineering company may be quietest during the summer months due to holidays.

(d) **Residual variation** – this is simply the difference between the actual figure and that predicted – taking into account trends, cyclical variations and seasonal variations. By its nature it cannot be fully explained.

1.4 Analysis of a time series

It is essential to be able to disentangle these various influences and measure each one separately. The main reasons for analysing a time series in this way are:

- to be able to predict future values of the variable, i.e. to make forecasts
- to attempt to control future events
- to 'seasonally adjust' or 'deseasonalise' a set of data; that is to remove the seasonal effect. For example, seasonally adjusted unemployment values are more useful than actual unemployment values in studying the effects of the national economy and Government policies on unemployment.

2 Analysis of a time series

2.1 Additive and multiplicative models

KEY POINT

Additive time series is a model of a time series where the overall series is obtained by **adding** the separate trend, seasonal, cyclical and random components. Used when fluctuations about the trend are constant.

To analyse a time series, it is necessary to make an assumption about how the four components described combine to give the total effect. The simplest method is to assume that the components are added together, i.e. if:

A   =   actual value for the period
T   =   trend component
C   =   cyclical component
S   =   seasonal component
R   =   residual component

Then $A = T + C + S + R$ This is called an **additive model**.

Another method is to assume the components are multiplied together, i.e.:

$A = T \times C \times S \times R$ This is called a **multiplicative model**.

KEY POINT

Multiplicative time series is a model of a time series where the overall series is obtained by **multiplying** the separate trend, seasonal, cyclical and random components. Used when fluctuations about the trend increase as the trend increases.

The additive model is the simplest, and is satisfactory when the fluctuations about the trend are within a constant band width. If, as is more usual, the fluctuations about the trend increase as the trend increases, the multiplicative model is used. Illustrated diagrammatically:

(a)

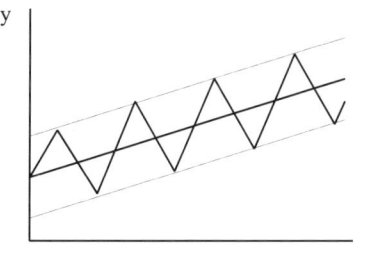

Constant band width.
Use additive model.

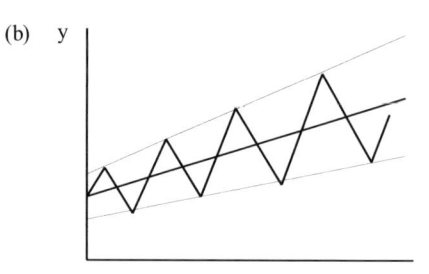

(b)

Band width proportional to trend.
Use multiplicative model.

2.2 Trend

> **KEY POINT**
>
> Trend can be estimated by using a graph, by using linear regression or by smoothing out the fluctuations using **moving averages**.

The trend can be obtained by using regression to obtain the line of best fit through the points on the graph, taking x as the year numbers (1, 2, 3. . ., etc) and y as the vertical variable. It is not necessary for the trend to be a straight line, as non-linear regression can be used, but for this method it is necessary to assume an appropriate mathematical form for the trend, such as parabola, hyperbola, exponential, etc. If the trend does not conform to any of these, the method cannot be used.

An alternative, which requires no assumption to be made about the nature of the curve, is to smooth out the fluctuations by **moving averages**.

The simplest way to explain the method is by means of an example.

Example

The following are the sales figures for Bloggs Brothers Engineering Ltd for the 14 years from 20X1 to 20Y4.

Year	Sales (£000)
20X1	491
20X2	519
20X3	407
20X4	452
20X5	607
20X6	681
20X7	764
20X8	696
20X9	751
20Y0	802
20Y1	970
20Y2	1,026
20Y3	903
20Y4	998

Using the method of moving averages the general trend of sales will be established.

Solution

Step 1

First, it is advisable to draw a graph of the time series so that an overall picture can be gained and the cyclical movements seen.

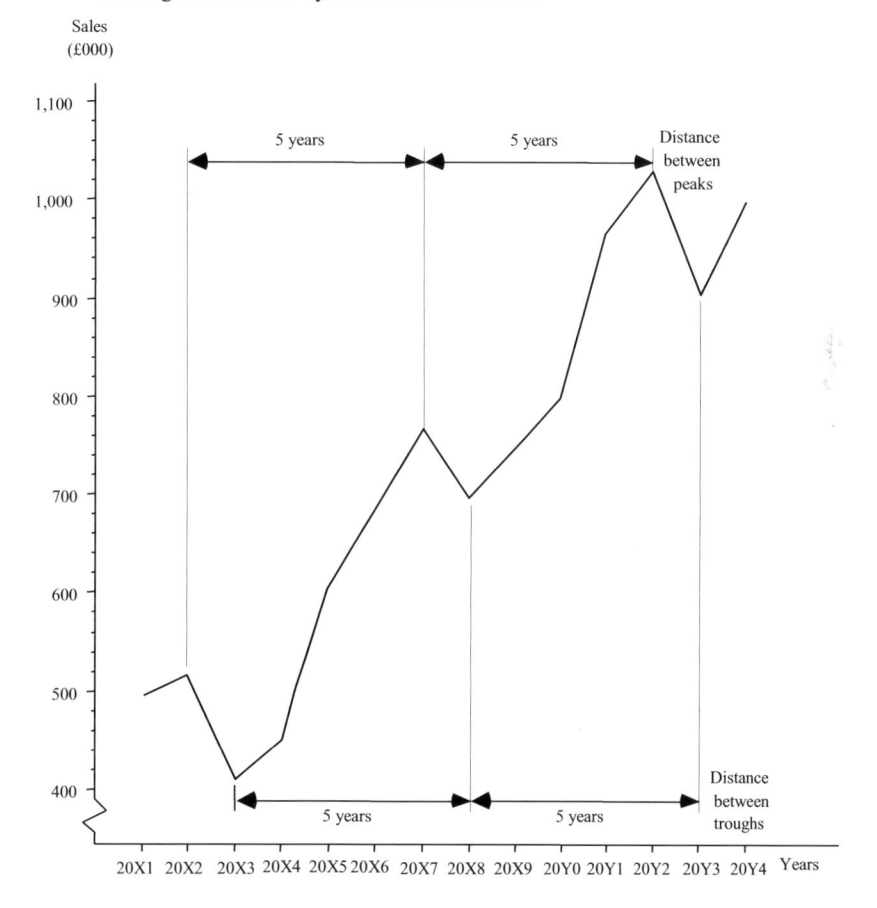

In order to calculate the trend figures it is necessary to establish the span of the cycle. From the graph it can easily be seen that the distance in time between successive peaks (and successive troughs) is five years; therefore a five point moving average must be calculated.

Step 2

A table of the following form is now drawn up:

Year	Sales (£000)	5 yearly moving total	5 yearly moving average
20X1	491	–	–
20X2	519	–	–
20X3	407	2,476	495
20X4	452	2,666	533
20X5	607	2,911	582
20X6	681	3,200	640
20X7	764	3,499	700
20X8	696	3,694	739
20X9	751	3,983	797
20Y0	802	4,245	849
20Y1	970	4,452	890
20Y2	1,026	4,699	940
20Y3	903	–	–
20Y4	998	–	–

Notes on the calculation

(a) As the name implies, the five yearly moving total is the sum of successive groups of five years' sales, i.e.

491 + 519 + 407 + 452 + 607 =   2,476

Then, advancing by one year:

519 + 407 + 452 + 607 + 681 =   2,666

| |
| |
| |
| |

802 + 970 + 1,026 + 903 + 998 =   4,699

(b) These moving totals are simply divided by 5 to give the moving averages, i.e.

2,476 ÷ 5   =   495
2,666 ÷ 5   =   533
|
|
|
|

4,699 ÷ 5   =   940

(c) Averages are always plotted in the middle of the time period, i.e. 495 is the average of the figures for 20X1, 20X2, 20X3, 20X4 and 20X5 and so it is plotted at the end of 20X3, this being the mid-point of the time interval from the end of 20X1 to the end of 20X5. Similarly, 533 is plotted at the end of 20X4, and 940 is plotted at the end of 20Y2.

Step 3

A second graph is now drawn showing the original figures again and the trend figures, i.e. the five yearly moving averages.

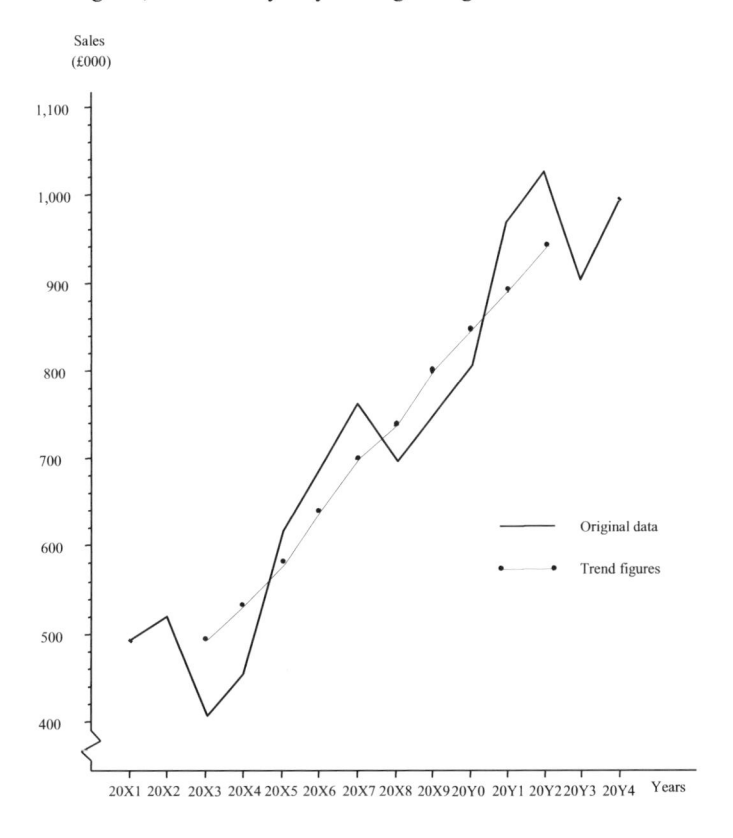

Sales (£000)

[Graph showing original data and trend figures from 20X1 to 20Y4, with sales ranging from 400 to 1,100]

2.3 Cyclical variation

KEY POINT

The cyclical variation is the **long term** variation about the trend.

The cyclical variation is the **long term** variation about the trend. Having calculated the trend figures it is a simple matter to work out the cyclical variations.

For annual data, there cannot be a seasonal component. Hence, using the additive model,

$$A = T + C + R$$

Subtracting T from both sides,

$$A - T = C + R$$

So, by subtracting the trend values from the actual values, the combined cyclical and residual variation will be obtained.

If the multiplicative model is used, A must be divided by T,

$$A = T \times C \times R$$

$$\frac{A}{T} = C \times R$$

As before, this will be explained by way of an example.

Example

Using the same data, establish the cyclical variation, using the additive model.

Solution

Step 1

A table of the following type is drawn up:

Year	Period of moving averages	Sales (£000) (A)	Trend figures (T)	Cyclical + Residual variation (=A − T)
20X1	1	491	–	–
20X2	2	519	–	–
20X3	3	407	495	−88
20X4	4	452	533	−81
20X5	5	607	582	25
20X6	1	681	640	41
20X7	2	764	700	64
20X8	3	696	739	−43
20X9	4	751	797	−46
20Y0	5	802	849	−47
20Y1	1	970	890	80
20Y2	2	1,026	940	86
20Y3	3	903	–	–
20Y4	4	998	–	–

Notes on the calculation

The figures in the last column for the cyclical variation are just the differences between the actual sales and the trend figures, i.e.:

$$407 - 495 = -88$$
$$452 - 533 = -81$$
$$1{,}026 - 940 = 86$$

The '+' and '−' signs are important since they show whether the actual figures are above or below the trend figures.

Step 2

Summarise the variations as follows and calculate the average variation for each period.

	Period				
	1	2	3	4	5
	–	–	−88	−81	25
	41	64	−43	−46	−47
	80	86	–	–	–
Total	121	150	−131	−127	−22
Average	61	75	−66	−64	−11

The individual variations have been averaged out for each year of the cycle, i.e.

Year 1 of each cycle $= \dfrac{41+80}{2} = \dfrac{121}{2} = 60.5,$ rounded to 61

Year 2 of each cycle $= \dfrac{64+86}{2} = \dfrac{150}{2} = 75$

etc.

Step 3

One more step is necessary because the cyclical variation should total to zero, and $61 + 75 + (-66) + (-64) + (-11) = -5$.

The adjustment is made by dividing the excess (– 5 in this case) by the number of years in the cycle (5 in this case) and subtracting the result from each of the cyclical variations.

Adjustment is $-5 \div 5 = -1$

Cyclical variations within each cycle are:

Year 1	$61 - (-1)$	=	$61 + 1$	=	62
Year 2	$75 - (-1)$	=	$75 + 1$	=	76
Year 3	$-66 - (-1)$	=	$-66 + 1$	=	-65
Year 4	$-64 - (-1)$	=	$-64 + 1$	=	-63
Year 5	$-11 - (-1)$	=	$-11 + 1$	=	-10

(and just as a check, the revised cyclical variations do total zero: $62 + 76 - 65 - 63 - 10 = 0$)

2.4 Seasonal variations

> **KEY POINT**
>
> For data covering only a few years, the cyclical component can be ignored and the seasonal component can be identified. Seasonal component is the **short term** variation about the trend.

When figures are available for a considerable number of years as in the examples above, it is possible to establish the trend and the cyclical variations.

Usually, however, monthly or quarterly figures are only available for a few years, three or four, say. In this case, it is possible to establish the trend by means of a moving average over an annual cycle by a method very similar to that used above. The span of the data is insufficient to find cyclical variations, but average seasonal variations can be found.

Example

The following table gives the takings (£000) of a shopkeeper in each quarter of four successive years.

Qtrs	*1*	*2*	*3*	*4*
20X1	13	22	58	23
20X2	16	28	61	25
20X3	17	29	61	26
20X4	18	30	65	29

Calculate the trend figures and quarterly variations, and draw a graph to show the overall trend and the original data.

Solution

Again the additive model will be used, but as the data is now over too short a time for any cyclical component to be apparent, the model becomes:

$$A = T + S + R$$

Step 1

It is necessary to draw up a table as follows:

Year and quarter		Takings (£'000) A	4 quarterly moving average	Centred value T	Quarterly + Residual variation S + R (= A− T)
20X1	1	13	–	–	–
	2	22		–	–
			29		
	3	58		30	28
			30		
	4	23		31	−8
			31		
20X2	1	16		32	−16
			32		
	2	28		33	−5
			33		
	3	61		33	28
			33		
	4	25		33	−8
			33		
20X3	1	17		33	−16
			33		
	2	29		33	−4
			33		
	3	61		34	27
			34		
	4	26		34	−8
			34		
20X4	1	18		35	−17
			35		
	2	30		36	−6
			36		
	3	65		–	–
	4	29		–	–

Notes on the calculation

Column 3

To smooth out quarterly fluctuations, it is necessary to calculate a 4-point moving average, since there are four quarters (or seasons) in a year.

i.e. $\frac{13 + 22 + 58 + 23}{4} = \frac{116}{4} = 29$

then, advancing by one quarter:

$\frac{22 + 58 + 23 + 16}{4} = \frac{119}{4} = 30$ (rounding to nearest whole number)

$\frac{18 + 30 + 65 + 29}{4} = \frac{142}{4} = 36$ (rounding to nearest whole number)

29 is the average of the figures for the four quarters of 20X1 and so, if plotted, would be at the mid-point of the interval from the end of the first quarter to the end of the fourth quarter, i.e. half-way through the third quarter of 20X1.

Step 2

Column 4

In order to subsequently find A – T, it is essential that A and T both relate to the same point in time. The four-quarterly moving averages do not correspond with any of the A values, the first coming between the second and third A values and so on down. To overcome this, the moving averages are 'centred', i.e. averaged in twos. The first centred average will coincide with the third A value and so on.

Note: this is necessary because the cycle has an even number of values (4) per cycle. Where there is an odd number of values per cycle, as in the previous example, the moving averages themselves correspond in time with A values, and centring should not be done.

The centring is as follows:

i.e. $\dfrac{29+30}{2} =$ 30   (rounding up)

$\dfrac{30+31}{2} =$ 31   (rounding up)

$\vdots$

$\dfrac{35+36}{2} =$ 36   (rounding up)

The first average now corresponds in time with the original value for the 3rd quarter, and so on.

These are the trend values.

Step 3

Column 5

A – T = S + R, hence the figures for the quarterly + residual variations are the differences between the actual figures and the centred values.

i.e. 58 – 30 =   28

23 – 31 =   –8

$\vdots$

30 – 36 =   –6

Step 4

In order to establish the quarterly variation another table must be drawn up (as in example 6 on cyclical variation) to remove the residual variation R.

	Quarter 1	Quarter 2	Quarter 3	Quarter 4
	–	–	28	–8
	–16	–5	28	–8
	–16	–4	27	–8
	–17	–6	–	–
Totals	–49	–15	83	–24
Seasonal variation	–16	–5	28	–8

248 BUSINESS MATHS

The individual variations have been averaged out for each quarter of the cycle:

i.e. Quarter 1 $\quad \dfrac{-16+(-16)+(-17)}{3} \quad = \quad \dfrac{-49}{3} \quad = \quad -16$

Quarter 2 $\quad \dfrac{-5+(-4)+(-6)}{3} \quad = \quad \dfrac{-15}{3} \quad = \quad -5$

Step 5

> **KEY POINT**
>
> Using the additive model, the seasonal variations are given by (Actual Data – Trend) and when averaged should sum to zero.

The quarterly variations should total to zero again, but $-16 + (-5) + 28 + (-8) = -1$. However, the adjustment would only be $-1 \div 4$, i.e. -0.25 which means using a spurious accuracy of two decimal places. To avoid this, one value only need be adjusted, choosing the greatest value as this will give the lowest relative adjustment error.

```
1st   Quarter  =              -16
2nd   Quarter  =               -5
3rd   Quarter  =  28 + 1  =    29
4th   Quarter  =               -8
                                0
```

Step 6

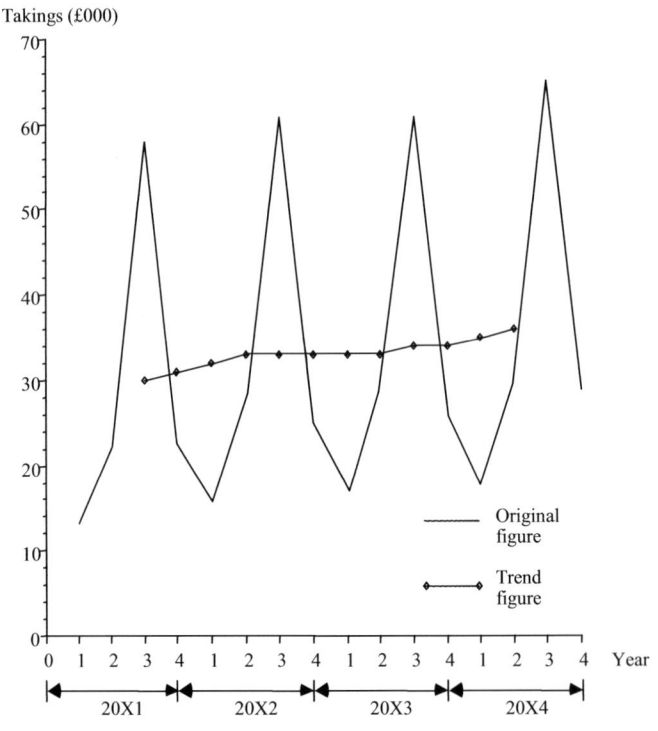

Takings (£000)

[Graph showing Original figure and Trend figure plotted against Year, across years 20X1, 20X2, 20X3, 20X4]

Step 7

Comment

As can be seen from the calculations and the graph, the takings show a slight upward trend and the seasonal (quarterly) variations are considerable.

2.5 Seasonally adjusted figures

DEFINITION

Deseasonalisation is the process of removing the effect of seasonal variation from a time series.

A popular way of presenting a time series is to give the seasonally adjusted or deseasonalised figures. Deseasonalisation is the process of removing the effect of seasonal variation from a time series.

This is a very simple process once the seasonal variations are known.

For the additive model:

$$\text{Seasonally adjusted data} = \text{Original data} - \text{Seasonal variation} = A - S$$

For the multiplicative model:

$$\text{Seasonally adjusted data} = \text{Original data} \div \text{Seasonal indices} = A \div S$$

The main purpose in calculating seasonally adjusted figures is to remove the seasonal influence from the original data so that non-seasonal influences can be seen more clearly.

Example 1

The same shopkeeper found the takings for the four quarters of 20X5 were £19,000, £32,000, £65,000 and £30,000 respectively. Has the upward trend continued?

Solution 1

Deseasonalising the figures gives:

Seasonally adjusted figures (£000)

Quarter 1	19 – (–16) =	35
Quarter 2	32 – (–5) =	37
Quarter 3	65 – 29 =	36
Quarter 4	30 – (–8) =	38

So, as can be seen from comparing the seasonally adjusted figures with the trend figures calculated earlier, the takings are indeed still increasing, i.e. there is an upward trend.

Example 2 (Multiplicative model)

Having mentioned a multiplication model (or proportional model) this now needs illustrating.

The following data will be seasonally adjusted using 'seasonal indices.'

	Quarter			
	1	2	3	4
Sales (£000)	59	50	61	92
Seasonal Variation	–2%	–21%	–9%	+30%

If $A = T \times S \times R$, the deseasonalised data is A/S.

> **KEY POINT**
>
> Using the multiplicative model, the seasonal factors are given by (Actual Data ÷ Trend) and when averaged should sum to 4. Note: a seasonal factor of 0.98 means a decrease of 2%, i.e. −2%.

A decrease of −2% means a factor of 0.98. Similarly, an increase of 30% means a factor of 1.3. Hence the seasonal factors are 0.98, 0.79, 0.91, 1.30 respectively. The actual data, A, must be **divided** by these values to remove the seasonal effect. Hence:

A	Seasonal factor (S)	Seasonally adjusted figure (= A/S)
59	0.98	60
50	0.79	63
61	0.91	67
92	1.30	71

While actual sales are lowest in summer and highest in winter, the seasonally adjusted values show a fairly steady increase throughout the year.

2.6 Forecasting using time series

It has been shown in the above section how data can be deseasonalised in order to identify the underlying trend. However, it is often the case that predictions are required to be made about the future, but taking into account seasonal factors.

This can be done in two ways:

(a) by fitting a line of best fit (straight or curved) by eye (preferably through the trend found by moving averages), and

(b) by using linear regression. This will be considered below.

The line is then extended to the right in order to estimate future trend values. This 'trend' value is then adjusted in order to take account of the seasonal factors.

Hence, the forecast = $T_e + S$, where T_e = extrapolated or estimated trend.

Residual variations are by nature random and therefore unforecastable.

> **KEY POINT**
>
> Forecasting – using additive model:
>
> Forecast = Estimated Trend + Seasonal Variation.

Example 1 (continued)

Using the data from the shopkeeper, predict the takings of the shop for the first and second quarters of 20X5.

Solution

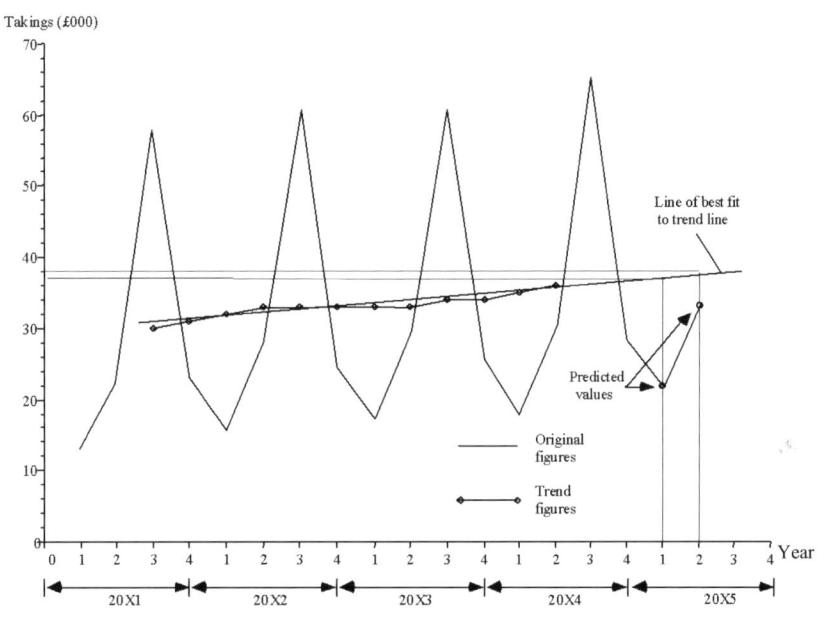

Takings (£000)

[Graph showing quarterly takings from 20X1 to 20X5 with original figures, trend figures, line of best fit to trend line, and predicted values marked]

From the graph it can be seen that the trend line predicts values as follows:

Quarter in 20X5	(i) Trend value	(ii) Seasonal variation	(i) + (ii) Final prediction
1	37,000	−16,000	21,000
2	38,000	−5,000	33,000

The predicted values of £21,000 and £33,000 have been plotted on the graph.

For the multiplicative model, the extrapolated trend must be **multiplied** by the appropriate seasonal factor. Thus in example 2, if the predicted trend value for the first quarter of the following year was £65,000, the appropriate seasonal factor for this quarter being 0.98, the forecast of actual sales would be £65,000 × 0.98 = £64,000 (to the nearest £000).

KEY POINT

Forecasting – using multiplicative model:

Forecast = Estimated Trend x Seasonal Variation.

2.7 Time series applied to forecasting models – alternative method

An alternative method for making predictions is to use linear regression in order to establish the trend line in the first place (rather than using the method of moving averages), and then on the basis of this regression line it is possible to predict the figures for the underlying trend. These are then used to estimate seasonal variations and the extrapolated trend values are calculated from the regression equation.

2.8 Conclusion

It is important to appreciate that although the various methods which have been used to identify seasonal (and cyclical) factors and hence predict future values of a particular variable will give different results, it is often not possible to say that any one answer is more valid than another. All methods essentially assume that whatever has caused fluctuations and trends to occur in the past will continue similarly into the future. Clearly this is often not the case and therefore any value forecast by any of the methods should be treated with due caution.

Summary

A time series can be analysed into an underlying trend and variations of different types around that trend. Once these have been identified, they can be used for forecasting purposes.

Self-test questions

1   What is time series analysis? (1.1)

2   What is a seasonal variation? (1.2)

3   What is the formula for an additive time series model? (2.1)

Practice questions

Question 1

A product has a constant (flat) trend in its sales, and is subject to quarterly seasonal variations as follows:

Quarter	Q_1	Q_2	Q_3	Q_4
Seasonality	+50%	+50%	−50%	−50%

Sales last quarter, Q_2, were 240 units.

Assuming a multiplicative model for the time series, predicted unit sales for the next quarter, Q_3, will be closest to:

A   60

B   80

C   120

D   160

Question 2

Based on the last 15 periods the underlying trend of sales is y = 345.12 – 1.35x. If the 16th period has a seasonal factor of – 23.62, assuming an additive forecasting model, then the forecast for that period, in whole units, is:

A   300

B   343

C   347

D   390

Question 3

Over an 18-month period, sales have been found to have an underlying linear trend of y = 7.112 + 3.949x, where y is the number of items sold and x represents the month. Monthly deviations from trend have been calculated and month 19 is expected to be 1.12 times the trend value.

The forecast number of items to be sold in month 19 is approximately:

A   91

B   92

C   93

D   94

For the answers to these questions, see the 'Answers' section at the end of the book.

Additional question

Report on sales

As the result of a takeover, the performance of three brands – A, B and C is being reviewed. The unit sales for the last nine quarters are shown below. Contribution is 10 pence per unit.

Quarterly sales (thousand units)

Brand	20X0 Q_1	Q_2	Q_3	Q_4	20X1 Q_1	Q_2	Q_3	Q_4	20X2 Q_1
A	40	33	60	104	56	45	80	136	72
B	78	63	101	158	81	59	98	162	80
C	400	290	460	700	335	240	380	575	270

You are required to analyse this data and to write a management report of your main findings, including at least five clear points.

Note: no technical statistical analysis is required but graphs, diagrams or simple tables may be included as necessary.

For the answer to this question, see the 'Answers' section at the end of the book.

16

SPREADSHEETS

Contents

1. Features and functions of commonly-used spreadsheet software
2. Advantages and disadvantages of spreadsheet software
3. Applications – The use of spreadsheet software in day-to-day work

1 Features and functions of commonly-used spreadsheet software

1.1 Introduction

> Note: it is not the purpose of this chapter to provide a full working manual on how to set up and use spreadsheets. Instead it highlights selected features of relevance to your studies. You are advised to ensure that you are reasonably competent in the use of Microsoft Excel or a similar package by working through the online tutorials provided at, for example,
>
> http://office.microsoft.com/en-us/training/CR061831141033.aspx

Much of the data of a company is likely to be held on a number of spreadsheets. They are a convenient way of setting up all sorts of charts, records and tables, including:

- profit and loss accounts
- sales forecasting
- budgeting and cash flow forecasts
- breakeven analysis
- stock valuation
- discounted cashflow analysis

Spreadsheets can be used for anything with a **rows and columns format** and normally have the following elements:

- Worksheet: a worksheet or spreadsheet is the basis of all the work you do. It could be considered to be the electronic equivalent of an accountant's ledger.

- Workbook: is a collection of worksheets. The workbook is simply a folder that binds together your worksheets. When you open a new workbook, it automatically contains 16 worksheets.

- Cells: the worksheet is divided into columns and rows. The intersection of a column and a row is known as a 'cell'. To refer to a particular cell, use its column and row location. This is called a 'cell address', for example A1, B22, etc.

- Columns: each column is referenced by one or two letters in the column heading. The whole worksheet consists of 256 columns, labelled A through IV.

- Rows: each row is referenced by the row number shown in the row heading to the left of a row. There are 65,536 rows in Excel.

- Data: each cell can contain numbers, text or a formula. Formulae are not visible when you are entering data but reside in the background. A formula normally involves a mathematical calculation on the content of other cells, the result being inserted in the cell containing the formula. This allows the spreadsheet to automatically update itself when data is altered.

1.2 Spreadsheet formulae

Spreadsheet packages can incorporate most formulae. All start by inputting '=' into the cell but some formulae have to be entered in a particular way to work:

- Addition: addition can be performed within a formula

  e.g. typing '=4+10' into a cell formula would display '14' in the cell

  The addition function is more useful when used to sum the values in different cells

  For example, suppose we want to sum the figures in a column from cell C2 down to C11. This can be done simply as '=SUM(C2:C11)'

- Multiplication: spreadsheet multiplication uses the symbol * instead of ×

- Division: spreadsheet division uses the symbol / instead of ÷

- Powers: to raise to a power the easiest approach is use the ^ symbol

- For example, to calculate 35, we can use '=3^5'

- An alternative is to input '=POWER(3,5)'

Note that formulae can be copied across cells. For example suppose you want to multiply two columns of figures together as follows:

	A	B	C	D
1	Correlation			
2				
3		Advertising	Sales	
4		£000	£m	
5		x	y	xy
6		50	6	
7		60	7	
8		45	5	
9		35	5	
10		50	7	
11		70	9	

In cell D6 the formula =B6*C6 can be entered manually. If this cell is left highlighted, then it can be seen to have a box round it with a small square in the bottom right-hand corner

	A	B	C	D
1	Correlation			
2				
3		Advertising	Sales	
4		£000	£m	
5		x	y	xy
6		50	6	300
7		60	7	
8		45	5	
9		35	5	
10		50	7	
11		70	9	
12				

If you left click and drag the small square down it will automatically input the formula into the cells D7, D8 and so on, updating the row reference. For example the formula in D7 will be =B7*C7.

1.3 Formatting

Row heights and column widths can be set as follows:

- Highlight the relevant column(s) and right click to bring up a menu
- Click on **Column Width**
- Set as required

To format a cell, highlight it and then right-click to bring up a menu. The formatting option can then be chosen.

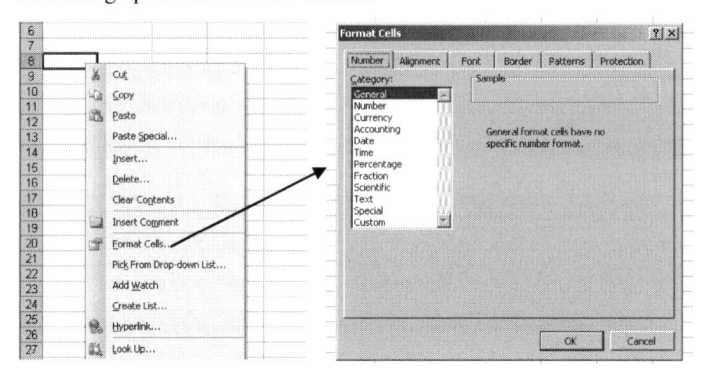

The main aspects of formatting cells to make a spreadsheet easier to read are as follows:

- Text options, such as changing the font, size and colour of text.
- Setting number specifications – e.g. working to 2 decimal places prevents figures running across the worksheet.
- Setting the alignment of information – e.g. at the top of cells
- Wrapping text – if more text has been put into a cell than can fit, then it will normally be seen reading across the spreadsheet. However, if the cell to the right of the original one contains anything, then the contents of the first cell will be hidden. To reveal it the text wrap box in the alignment section can be ticked.

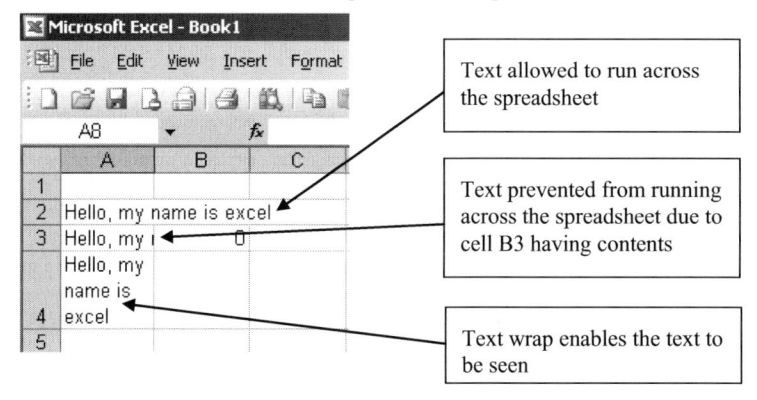

1.4 Graphics

A major advantage of using a spreadsheet package is the ease with which graphs and charts can be generated.

For example, suppose we want to present the following information about customer invoices graphically:

DC Carers Ltd	£58.68
F Browns Ltd	£32.31
J Cables Ltd	£134.68
J Hoggs Ltd	£271.43
L Quick Ltd	£1,098.63

The easiest way to do this is to use the chart wizard, with the icon:

With the two columns in the spreadsheet selected, you can click on the Chart Wizard and select the type of chart or graph that you prefer and experiment with changing the data labels and percentages. Two examples are shown below.

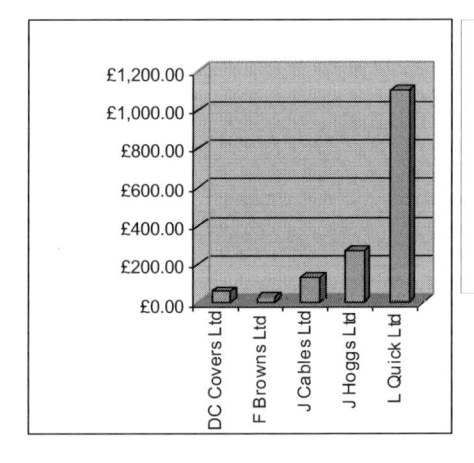

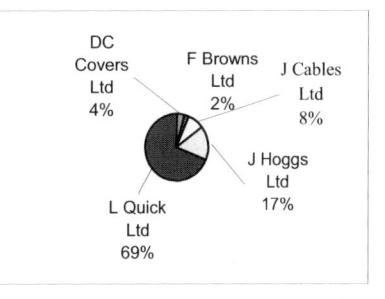

1.5 Macros

If there is a process that you wish to repeat, such as reformatting financial statements to reflect International Accounting Standards, then one way of doing this is to use the macro function. This acts like a mini tape recorder and will record all of the actions specified. This can then be replayed to implement the actions on a new selection of cells, say the financial statements on other worksheets.

To set up a macro involves the following steps:

1. On the **Tools** menu, point to **Macro**, and then click **Record New Macro**.
   - In the **Macro name** box, enter a name for the macro.
2. If you want to run the macro by pressing a keyboard shortcut key, enter a letter in the **Shortcut key** box.
3. In the **Store macro in** box, click the location where you want to store the macro.
4. Click **OK**.

5. If you want the macro to run *relative* to the position of the active cell, record it using relative cell references. On the **Stop Recording** toolbar, click **Relative Reference** so that it is selected. If this is not selected, then the macro will repeat the actions only on the original cell locations specified on each new sheet.

6. Carry out the actions you want to record.

7. On the **Stop Recording** toolbar, click **Stop Recording**.

To run the macro involves the following steps:

1. On the **Tools** menu, point to **Macro**, and then click **Macros**.

2. Highlight the macro you wish to run and click **Run**.

2 Advantages and disadvantages of spreadsheet software

2.1 Spreadsheet software compared to manual analysis

Compared to performing similar tasks manually, spreadsheet software has the following advantages and disadvantages:

Advantages

- Speed
- Accuracy
- Legibility
- Management reporting – spreadsheets can generate graphs and diagrams as specified above. Along with the data in the spreadsheet itself, these can be copied into other applications to generate reports.

Disadvantages

- Security – a computer –based approach exposes the firm to threats from viruses, hackers and general system failure. Each of these can be managed using appropriate e-security software and by the use of back-ups.

2.2 Spreadsheet software compared to other software applications

Many users use spreadsheets to store data, even though the data could be better managed in a database. There is a lot of confusion concerning the differences between spreadsheets and databases. The confusion stems from the basic similarity that the key function of both spreadsheets and databases is to store and manipulate data. However, there are some distinct advantages and disadvantages to both spreadsheets and databases that define their usefulness as a data management tool.

Spreadsheets

Spreadsheets are designed to analyze data and sort list items, not for long-term storage of raw data. A spreadsheet should be used for 'crunching' numbers and storage of single list items. They also include graphing functions that allow for quick reporting and analysis of data.

Advantages	Disadvantages
• Spreadsheet programs are relatively easy to use, • require little training to get started and • most data managers are familiar with them.	• You have to re-copy data over and over again to maintain it in separate data files. • Inability to efficiently identify data errors. • Spreadsheets lack detailed sorting and querying abilities. • There can be sharing violations among users wishing to view or change data at the same time. • Additionally, spreadsheets are restricted to a finite number of records, and can require a large amount of hard-drive space for data storage.

Databases

To store large amounts of raw data, it is best to use a database. This is especially true in circumstances where two or more users share the information.

Advantages	Disadvantages
• The most important benefit gained by using a database is the ease of reporting and sharing data. • Databases require little or no duplication of data between information tables. • Changes made to the data do not corrupt the programming (like at the cell level of a spreadsheet where calculations are running). • Databases offer better security to restrict users from accessing privileged information, and from changing coded information in the programming.	• Requires the user to learn a new system. • Requires a greater investment in training and software. • The initial time and cost of migrating all of the data into a new database system.

For optimal effectiveness, spreadsheets and databases should be used in conjunction with one another. The database should be used to store and protect all of the data. This includes when the data is initially entered, checked for errors, and verified. Since almost all databases easily import and export data to and from spreadsheet programs, the data can then be shared with a spreadsheet program to analyze the data, run calculations, and create tables and graphs.

3 Applications

3.1 Budgeting and forecasting

Preparing budgets and forecasts are classic applications of spreadsheets, as they allow estimates to be changed without having to recalculate everything manually. For example, here is an extract from a cashflow forecast.

	A	B	C	D	E
1	Revised cashflow forecast for 05/06				
2	£000	Jul-05	Aug-05	Sep-05	Oct-05
3					
4	Sales receipts	1867	1828	1893	1939
5					
6	Payments				
7	Purchases	1691	1644	1701	1798
8	Overheads	57	57	57	57
9	Capex	50	50	50	25
10	Bank loan	12	12	12	12
11	VAT	160			171
12	CT				
13	Bank o/d interest	2	2	2	1
14		1972	1765	1822	2064
15					
16	Net cash in/out flow	-105	63	71	-125
17					
18	Bal b/f *	-134	-239	-176	-105
19	Bal c/f	-239	-176	-105	-230
20					

Apart from the formatting to make the forecast easy to read, the key formulae are as follows:

Total payments:	e.g. B14:	=SUM(B7:B13)
Net cashflow:	e.g. B16:	=+B4-B14
Bal c/f:	e.g. B19:	=+B18+B16

3.2 Reporting performance

Performance appraisal usually involves calculating ratios, possible involving comparatives between companies and from one year to the next. A neat way of doing this is to input the raw data, such as financial statements on one sheet and calculate the ratios on another. For example, here is an extract from the five years results for a company called Parkland, input on a sheet titled 'historic data':

	A	Formula Bar	D	E	
1					
2				Rutwater	
3	£000	2005	2004	2003	
4					
5	Revenue	319,361	316,197	309,119	30
6	Cost of sales	-81,428	-84,627	-83,039	-8
7	Gross profit	237,933	231,570	226,080	22
8					
9	EBITDA	157,105	151,003	145,010	14

Here are some ratios set up on a separate sheet (titled 'current and historic ratios') in the same workbook:

	A	B	C	D	E
1					
2	Historic ratio analysis				Rutwater
3			2005	2004	2003
4					
5	RoC		11.7%	12.5%	12.5%
6	Margin		27.8%	27.8%	26.8%
7	Asset turnover		£0.42	£0.45	£0.47
8	Gross margin		74.5%	73.2%	73.1%
9	EBITDA margin		49.2%	48.1%	47.2%
10					

Don't worry about the detail of the ratios – you will encounter them at some stage in your studies. Taking just one as an example, gross margin - this is calculated as gross profit divided by revenue. The answer has been formatted to show as a percentage to one decimal place and the formula for cell C8 is as follows:

='Historic data'!C7/'Historic data'!C5

The 'historic data'! part indicates which worksheet the information came from. While this looks complex, setting up the formula was simply a matter of clicking on the correct cells in the first place:

- On the sheet 'current and historic ratios' click on cell C8 and press '='
- Switch to sheet 'historic data' and click on cell C7
- Type '/'
- Click on cell C5 while still on sheet 'historic data'
- Press enter and you will automatically return to the 'current and historic ratios' sheet.

3.3 Variance analysis

Variance analysis involves management comparing actual results with budget and then investigating the differences. A relatively simple statement could be along the lines of the following:

264 BUSINESS MATHS

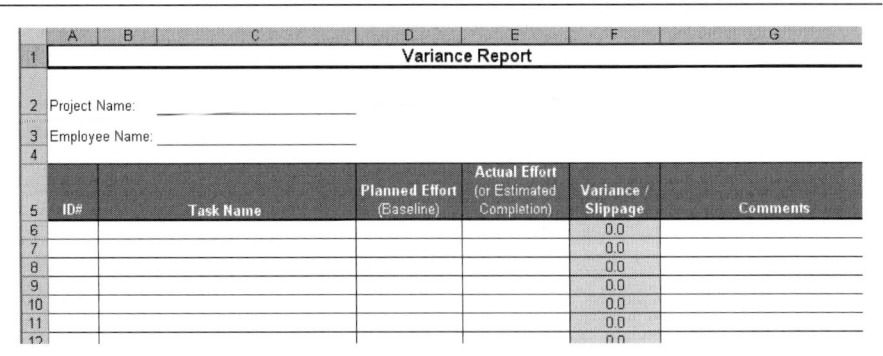

[Variance Report spreadsheet template showing columns: ID#, Task Name, Planned Effort (Baseline), Actual Effort (or Estimated Completion), Variance / Slippage, Comments]

While a spreadsheet can be used to perform the calculations it can also be used to highlight significant variances.

The tool that could be used here is conditional formatting. This is accessed by clicking on **Format** on the top toolbar and then **Conditional Formatting**, giving the following menu:

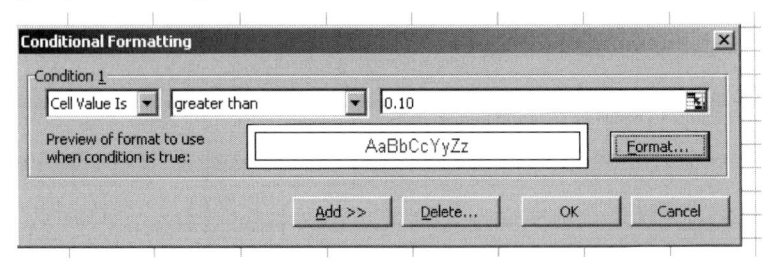

[Conditional Formatting dialog box: Condition 1 — Cell Value Is greater than 0.10; Preview of format to use when condition is true: AaBbCcYyZz; buttons: Add>>, Delete..., OK, Cancel]

The above set-up will examine the variance to see if it exceeds 10%. If it does, then the answer is displayed as red with a black box round it. If not, then the answer is displayed as usual. This will enable management to see at a glance which variances are significant.

3.4 Discounted cashflow calculations

A NPV calculation can be set up using formulae with any layout you choose. For example:

	A	B	C	D	E	F
1	NPV calculation					
2	Discount rate		10.00%			
3						
4	Time	Narrative		CF	DF	PV
5	0	Invest		-10,000	1	-10,000
6	1	Returns		4,000	0.909091	3,636
7	2	Returns		5,000	0.826446	4,132
8	3	Returns		3,000	0.751315	2,254
9	4	Returns		2,000	0.683013	1,366
10		NPV				**1,389**

Examples of formulae used:

Discount factors: E6:   =(1+C2)^(-1*A6)

Present values: F6:   =D6*E6

NPV: F10: =SUM(F5:F9)

To get the IRR it is relatively simple to change the discount rate in cell C2 until the NPV is zero – this occurs when the rate is approximately 17%. Other sensitivity or 'what-if' analysis can also be performed, such as varying the cashflow in year four and seeing the results.

However, Excel does have the capability to calculate NPVs and IRRs if you set out the spreadsheet in an appropriate way.

The function is **NPV(rate,value1**,value2, ...), where

- **rate** = discount rate
- **value1** = cashflow at end of the first year
- value2 = cashflow at the end of the second year, etc

Note that the cashflow at time zero is not included here so must be included separately.

The NPV could thus be calculated by the formula:

=NPV(C2,D6:D9)+D5

Likewise the IRR can be calculated using **IRR(values**,guess), where

- **values** are the cashflows in order (including now time zero if required) and
- guess is your first guess at the IRR

The IRR for our example could thus be calculated as 17.07%, using

=IRR(D5:D9,C2)

These functions can save a great deal of time – all you have to do is calculate the annual cashflows in the correct order.

Self-test questions

1   What are the main features of a spreadsheet? (1.1)

2   What are the advantages of a spreadsheet compared to a database programme? (2.2)

3   How can you calculate NPV and IRR using a spreadsheet? (3.4)

Practice questions

Question 1

Mike has produced the following spreadsheet to calculate the correlation coefficient between sales and advertising:

	A	B	C	D	E	F
1	Correlation					
2						
3		Advertising	Sales			
4		£000	£m			
5		x	y	xy	x^2	y^2
6		50	6	300	2500	36
7		60	7	420	3600	49
8		45	5	225	2025	25
9		35	5	175	1225	25
10		50	7	350	2500	49
11		70	9	630	4900	81
12						
13	Totals	310	39	2100	16750	265
14						
15	Correlation coefficient =					
16						

What formula is required in cell D15?

Question 2

Petra has been asked to calculate the NPV of the following cashflows at a rate of 10%.

	A	B	C	D	E	F
1	NPV					
2						
3	Time	0	1	2	3	4
4	CF	-105	24	35	64	45

She has suggested using the following formula for this

=NPV(0.10,B4:F4)

What should the formula be?

For the answers to these questions, see the 'Answers' section at the end of the book.

17

ANSWERS TO END OF CHAPTER QUESTIONS

Chapter 1

PRACTICE QUESTIONS

1   C

$$10^{-2} = \frac{1}{10^2} = \frac{1}{100}$$

2   C

$2 < 4 > 0$

3   D

$$\frac{X^{10}}{X^5} = X^{10} \times X^{-5} = X^{(10-5)} = X^5$$

4   B

When one power is raised to another, the powers are multiplied.

5   C

$(x^2)^3 = x^6$

$$\Rightarrow \frac{(x^2)^3}{x^5} = \frac{x^6}{x^5} = x$$

6   B

$$\frac{x^5}{x^6} = x^5 \times x^{-6} = x^{(5-6)} = x^{-1}$$

7   C

$$\frac{(5^3)^3}{5^7} = \frac{(125)^3}{78,125} = \frac{1,953,125}{78,125} = 25$$

$$\text{or} = \frac{5^9}{5^7} = 5^{9-7} = 5^2 = 25$$

Chapter 2

PRACTICE QUESTIONS

1 D

$$X\% \text{ of } 200 = \frac{X}{100} \times 200 = \frac{200X}{100} = 2X$$

(check by letting $X = 10$ then 10% of $200 = 2 \times 10 = 20$)

2 B

First calculate the increase in price, which here is £8. Express this as a percentage of the original price, which here is £45.99. This gives an answer of 17.3951%. Now 0.3951 is closer to 0.40 than to 0.39, so to two decimal places the answer is 17.40%.

3 B

$$\text{Ex-VAT price} = \frac{84p}{1.125} = 74.67p$$

With VAT at $17.5\% = 74.67 \times 1.175 = 87.73$

i.e. **88p** to nearest penny

4 B

$$\frac{£298}{117.5} \times 100 = £253.62$$

5 A

Time	t–3	t–2	t–1	t0
Price	£27.50 × 1.05 =	£28.875 × 1.06 =	£30.6075	29.69

↑ Change in 3rd year

$$= \frac{29.69 - 30.6075}{30.6075} \times 100\% = -3\%$$

6 A

$$\text{Price before sales tax} = £90.68 \times \frac{1}{1.19} \times 0.8$$

$$= £60.96$$

Chapter 3

PRACTICE QUESTION

1 B

$$\frac{56.99 - 52.49}{56.99} \times 100 = 7.896\%$$

then to 2dp the percentage reduction in price is 7.89%

Chapter 4

PRACTICE QUESTIONS

1 C

$$100 = \sqrt{\frac{2D \times 10}{6 \times 0.2}}$$

So $10{,}000 = \frac{20D}{1.2}$

So $D = \frac{10{,}000 \times 1.2}{20} = 600$

2 B

(A is X = 2, C is Y = ½X, D is Y = 2)

3 B

Volume = length × height × depth

Volume = 2a × a × a

$1{,}458 = 2a^3$

$729 = a^3$

$\sqrt[3]{729} = a$

$9 = a$

ADDITIONAL QUESTION 1

Exercises in solving equations

(a) $3x - 2 = 4x - 4$

   $3x - 4x = -4 + 2$

   $-x = -2$

   $\therefore x = 2$

(b) $4 - 5x = 14 + 12x$

   $-12x - 5x = 14 - 4$

   $-17x = 10$

   $x = -0.588$

(c) $\frac{12 - 3x}{4x + 5} = 4$ (cross multiply by (4x + 5))

   $12 - 3x = 4(4x + 5)$ (multiply out bracket)

   $12 - 3x = 16x + 20$ (subtract 16x and 12 from both sides)

   $-19x = 8$

   $x = -0.421$

(d) Add equations

$12x + 2y = 4$ (1)

$\underline{x - 2y = 9}$ (2)

$13x = 13$

$\therefore x = 1$

Substitute $x = 1$ into either equation (for example equation 2)

$x - 2y = 9$

$1 - 2y = 9$

$-2y = 8$

$y = -4$

Check in other equation (i.e. equation 1)

$12 \times 1 + 2 \times (-4) = 12 - 8$

$= 4$

which is correct.

Hence $(x, y) = (1, -4)$

(e)

$10x + 5y = 3 - 2x$

rearrange to $12x + 5y = 3$ (1)

$4x + 10y = 8 - 3x$

rearrange to $7x + 10y = 8$ (2)

Multiply equation (1) by 2

$24x + 10y = 6$ (1) × 2

Subtract $\underline{7x + 10y = 8}$ (2)

$17x = -2$

$\therefore x = \dfrac{-2}{17} = -0.118$

Substitute value of x into equation (2)

$(7 \times -\tfrac{2}{17}) + 10y = 8$

$10y = 8 + 0.823529$

$y = \dfrac{8.823529}{10}$

$y = 0.882$

Check in equation (1) in its original form,

$10x + 5y = 3 - 2x$

$10 \times (-0.118) + 5 \times 0.882 = 3 - 2 \times (-0.118)$

$-1.18 + 4.41 = 3 + 0.236$

$3.23 = 3.236$

The difference is due to rounding errors (which wouldn't occur if fractions were consistently used).

(f) $(2x + 5)(x + 1) = 5$
$2x^2 + 5x + 2x + 5 = 5$ (multiply out brackets)
$2x^2 + 7x = 0$ (rearrange)
$x(2x + 7) = 0$ (factorise)
$x = 0$ or $(2x + 7) = 0$
$x = 0$ or $x = -7/2$

(g) $6x^2 + 12x = 4(5x + 2)$ (multiply out brackets)
$6x^2 + 12x = 20x + 8$ (rearrange)
$6x^2 - 8x - 8 = 0$ (solve by formula)

$$x = \frac{-(-8) \pm \sqrt{(-8)^2 - (4 \times 6 \times (-8))}}{2 \times 6}$$

$$= \frac{8 \pm \sqrt{64 + 192}}{12}$$

$$= \frac{8}{12} \pm \frac{16}{12}$$

$x = \frac{-2}{3}$ or $x = 2$

(h) $3x^2 - 2x + 7 = 0$

Solve by formula:

$$x = \frac{-(-2) \pm \sqrt{(-2)^2 - (4 \times 3 \times 7)}}{2 \times 3}$$

$$= \frac{2 \pm \sqrt{(-80)}}{6}$$

There are no real roots to this equation, since the square root of (–80) cannot be found.

(i) $2x^2 - 5x + 4xy = 60$ (1)
$3x - y = 9$ (2)
From equation (2), $y = 3x - 9$ (3)
Substitute into (1) to get:
$2x^2 - 5x + 4x(3x - 9) = 60$ (multiply out bracket)
$2x^2 - 5x + 12x^2 - 36x = 60$ (rearrange)
$14x^2 - 41x - 60 = 0$ (solve by formula)

$$x = \frac{41 \pm \sqrt{(41 \times 41) - (4 \times 14 \times -60)}}{2 \times 14}$$

$$= \frac{41 \pm \sqrt{5{,}041}}{28} = \frac{41}{28} \pm \frac{71}{28}$$

$x = 4$, or $x = \frac{-30}{28}$ $(= -1.07)$

Substitute into (3) to give:

y = (3 × 4 − 9) = 3, or y = (3 × $^{-30}/_{28}$ − 9) = −12$^{6}/_{28}$ (or − 12.21)

Hence (x, y) = (4, 3) or (x, y) = (−1.07, −12.21)

Chapter 5

PRACTICE QUESTIONS

1   **B**

Let r be the monthly compound interest rate.

$(1 + r)^{12}$ = 1.3

$1 + r$ = $\sqrt[12]{1.3}$ = 1.0221

So r = 2.21%

2   **D**

£1,000 (1 + cumulative factor for Year 4 at 8%)

= £1,000 (1 + 3.312)

= £4,312

3   **C**

Year beginning	Rent £	Discount Factor
1	1,000	1
2	1,000	1.08^{-1}
3	1,000	1.08^{-2}
.	.	.
.	.	.
.	.	.
10	1,000	1.08^{-9}

Using the tables: 8% for 9 years:

Annuity factor = 6.247

NPV = 1,000 (6.247 + 1)

NPV = 1,000 × 7.247

NPV = £7,247

4   **C**

$£2,500(1.08)^3$ = £3,149.28

5   **D**

1,200/1.12 = £1,071

$1,400/(1.12)^2$ = £1,116

$1,600/(1.12)^3$ = £1,139

$1,800/(1.12)^4$ = £1,144

ANSWERS TO END OF CHAPTER QUESTIONS   273

ADDITIONAL QUESTION 1

Sum of a series

Sum of series

(a) 20th term $= a + 19d$ where $a = 20; d = -2.5$
    $= 20 + 19 \times (-2.5)$
    $= -27.5$

$S_{20} = \frac{n}{2}[2a + (n-1)d]$ where $n = 20$

$= \frac{20}{2}[2 \times 20 + 19 \times (-2.5)]$

$= -75$

(b) Using the S_n formula,

$420 = \frac{n}{2}[2 \times 2 + (n-1) \times 6]$

multiplying by 2 and multiplying out the inner bracket:

$840 = n[4 + 6n - 6]$
$= 4n + 6n^2 - 6n$
$= 6n^2 - 2n$

$\therefore 6n^2 - 2n - 840 = 0$

Solving by the quadratic formula:

$n = \frac{+2 \pm \sqrt{2^2 - 4 \times 6 \times (-840)}}{2 \times 6}$

$= \frac{2 \pm \sqrt{4 + 20{,}160}}{12} = \frac{2 \pm 142}{12}$

$= 12$ or -11.67

As a fractional or negative number of terms is not admissible, the number of terms is 12.

(c) 10th term $= AR^9$ where $A = 3; R = 0.4$
    $= 3 \times (0.4)^9$
    $= 0.0007864$

$S_{10} = \frac{A(1 - R^{10})}{1 - R}$

$= \frac{3 \times (1 - 0.4^{10})}{1 - 0.4}$

$= 4.999$

$S_\infty = \frac{A}{1 - R}$

$= \frac{3}{1 - 0.4}$

$= 5$

ADDITIONAL QUESTION 2

Cash flows for projects A and B

(a)

Project A

Rate	Time 1 - 4	Factor		Time 0	NPV
0.1	10	3.170	31.70	-25	6.70
0.2	10	2.589	25.89	-25	0.89
0.3	10	2.166	21.66	-25	-3.34
0.4	10	1.849	18.49	-25	-6.51

Project B

Time	Cash flow	D.F (0.1)	£	D.F (0.2)	£	D.F (0.3)	£	D.F (0.4)	£
0	-25	1.000	-25	1	-25	1	-25	1	-25
1	0	0.909	0	0.833	0	0.769	0	0.714	0
2	5	0.826	4.13	0.694	3.47	0.592	2.96	0.510	2.55
3	10	0.751	7.51	0.579	5.79	0.455	4.55	0.364	3.64
4	30	0.683	20.49	0.482	14.46	0.350	10.5	0.260	7.8
			7.13		-1.28		-6.99		-11.01

Tutorial note: The discount factors for 10% and 20% can be read directly from the PV tables, e.g. Project A at a discount rate of 10% has a PV of $-25 + (3.170 \times 10) = 6.70$. For 30% and 40% the factors must be calculated from first principles, e.g. Project B at a discount rate of 30% has a PV of $-25 + \frac{5}{(1.3)^2} + \frac{10}{(1.3)^3} + \frac{30}{(1.3)^4} = -6.99$. You may have some rounding differences in your answer.

(b)

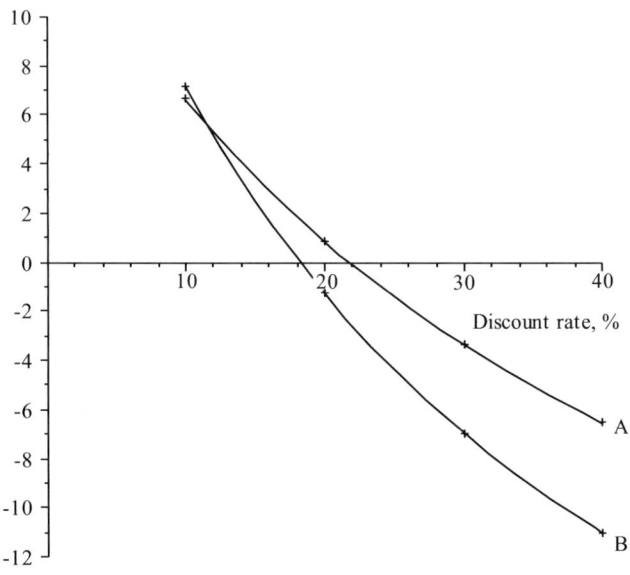

(c) The internal rate of return is the point on the graph where the curve cuts the horizontal axis. For Project A this is approximately 22%, and for Project B approximately 18%.

To obtain these values, graph paper must be used.

Note: for practice, students may wish to calculate the approximate IRR by interpolation:

$$\text{IRR} \approx A + (B - A) \times \left(\frac{N_A}{N_A - N_B} \right)$$

Project A (using 20% & 30%)

$20\% + (30\% - 20\%) \times \dfrac{0.89}{(0.89 - (-3.34))}$

Project B (using 10% & 20%)

$10\% + (20\% - 10\%) \times \dfrac{7.13}{(7.13 - (-1.28))}$

$= 20\% + 10\% \times 0.210$

$= 22.1\%$

$= 10\% + 10\% \times 0.847$

$= 18.5\%$

The differences are due to the fact that the interpolation method assumes a straight line relationship between NPV and discount rate and also because it is difficult to plot and read the graph accurately.

Chapter 6

ADDITIONAL QUESTION

Data and information

(a) **Data and information**

Data consists of numbers, letters, symbols, raw facts, events and transactions which have been recorded but not yet processed into information for use in a decision-making situation.

Information is data that has been interpreted and understood by the recipient. It reduces uncertainty, and has surprise value, i.e. is not already known.

Data on its own is not generally useful, information is.

(b) **Qualities of good information**

Good information should be:

(i) **relevant** to the problem being considered, and should not cloud understanding with irrelevant content

(ii) **sufficiently accurate** for it to be relied upon by the manager and for its intended purpose

(iii) **sufficiently complete** for its purpose

(iv) from a source in which the manager has **confidence**

(v) communicated to the **right person** and via an **appropriate channel of communication** e.g. letter, telephone call, fax

(vi) communicated to its intended user in **good time**, and be as up-to-date as possible

(vii) **sufficient**, but not too detailed

(viii) **understood** by the recipient; understanding is what transforms data into information.

Chapter 7

PRACTICE QUESTIONS

1 A

In a histogram you are not comparing the height of the bar, but the area represented by each bar. If the class intervals are different then the frequencies must be adjusted, otherwise the histogram will show a distorted picture.

In this example, the histogram class interval is one and a half times as large as the others, so the frequency must be divided by 1½. Assuming a frequency of one:

$$\frac{1}{1½} = 0.67$$

So the frequency must be multiplied by 0.67.

2 B

$$\text{Wages} = \frac{89}{360} \times 550{,}000 = 0.2472 \times 550{,}000 = 135{,}972$$

3 A

The sales of the second pie chart are double the sales of the first pie chart.

The area of the second pie chart must therefore be twice the area of the first pie chart.

This is achieved by making the radius of the second pie chart a ratio of $\sqrt{2}$ times the radius of the first pie charts.

$\sqrt{2} = 1.41$ (to two decimal places)

4 D

ADDITIONAL QUESTION 1

Pie charts and bar charts

(a) **Pie charts**

Calculation of angles of sections:

	20X8 Sales	20X8 Angles (degrees)	20X7 Sales	20X7 Angles (degrees)
UK	35.0	70.2	31.5	86.5
EC	47.4	95.1	33.2	91.2
NA	78.9	158.2	40.3	110.7
Aus	18.2	36.5	26.1	71.6
	179.5	360.0	131.1	360.0

Note:

The angles are calculated as $\dfrac{\text{Sales value}}{\text{Total sales}} \times 360$ degrees.

Thus the angle for UK in 20X8 is $\dfrac{35.0}{179.5} \times 360$

= 70.2°

Calculation of radii of circles.

The radii for 20X7 and 20X8 must be in the ratio:

$$\sqrt{131.1} : \sqrt{179.5}$$

$$= 11.4 : 13.4$$

Thus if the radius for 20X7 is 3cm, the radius for 20X8 must be:

$$3 \times \frac{13.4}{11.4} = 3.5 \text{cm}.$$

Annual Sales 20X7 & 20X8

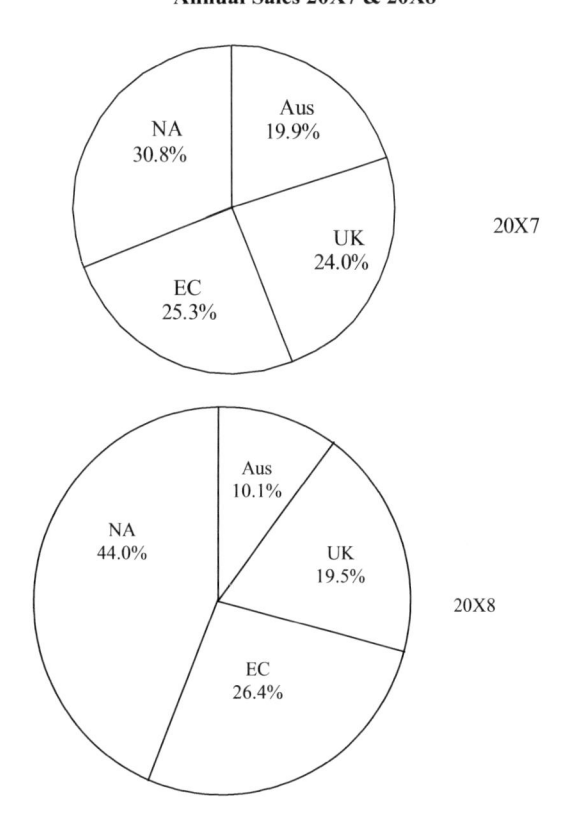

20X7

- NA 30.8%
- Aus 19.9%
- UK 24.0%
- EC 25.3%

20X8

- NA 44.0%
- Aus 10.1%
- UK 19.5%
- EC 26.4%

Note: time would have been saved by entering actual sales data rather than percentages.

(b) **Component bar charts**

Annual Sales 20X7 & 20X8

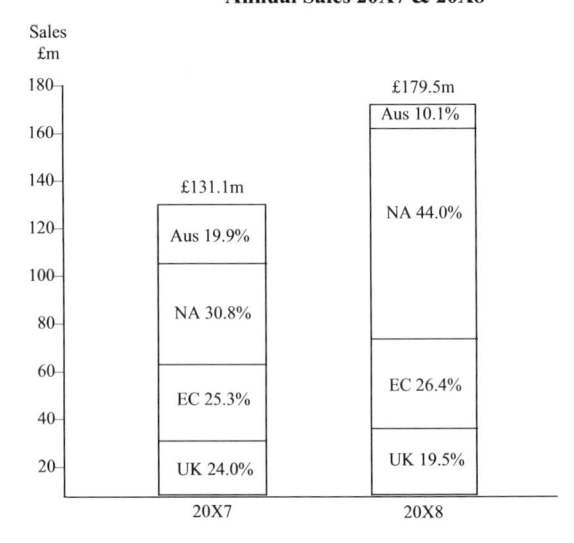

Sales £m

20X7: £131.1m
- Aus 19.9%
- NA 30.8%
- EC 25.3%
- UK 24.0%

20X8: £179.5m
- Aus 10.1%
- NA 44.0%
- EC 26.4%
- UK 19.5%

Notes:

(i) Once the chart has been completed the left hand scale could be erased.

(ii) Neatness is essential in any chart, but do not go to great artistic lengths, whether working by hand or playing with Excel graphics.

(iii) If there is no room to write the details in each section, shading and a key should be used.

Comparison of pie charts and bar charts

The pie chart can be made to look more attractive, for example by exploding one or more sectors or by drawing it in 3 dimensions, but it is very difficult to make comparisons between areas of sectors. It is easier to compare the heights of rectangles in a bar chart, which also shows the total for each year.

ANSWERS TO END OF CHAPTER QUESTIONS 279

ADDITIONAL QUESTION 2

Students' statistics

(a) & (b)   **Histogram and frequency polygon**

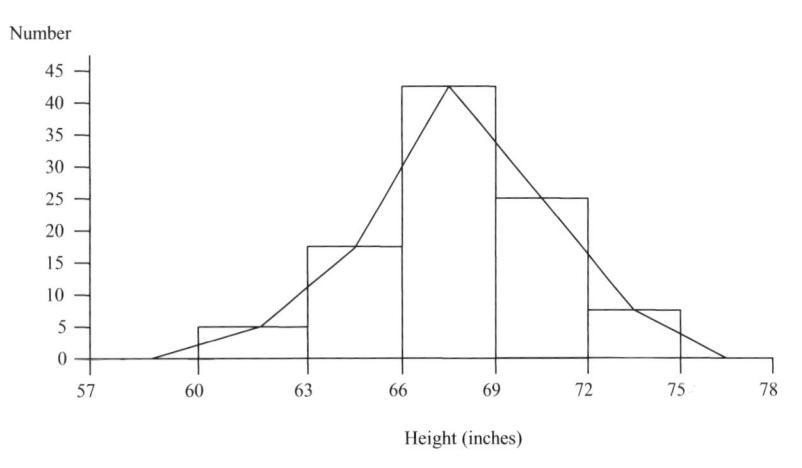

Note: the frequency polygon is achieved by joining up the mid-points of the histogram. Note the correct treatment of the two ends of the polygon.

(c)   **Ogive**

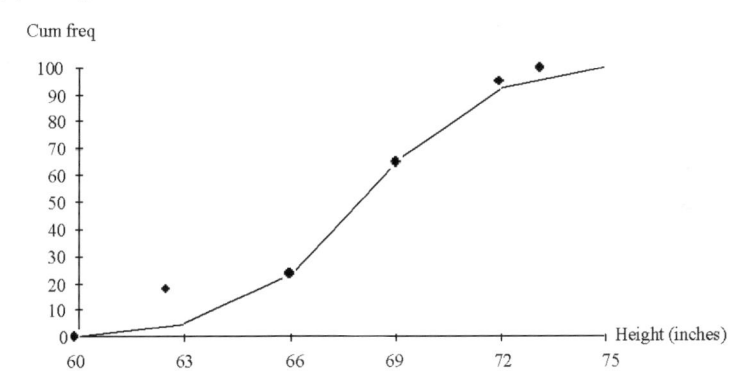

Note: the cumulative frequency is plotted against the upper class limit.

Chapter 8

PRACTICE QUESTIONS

1   B

10	units of X cost 10 × £1	=	£10
20	units of Y cost 20 × £2	=	£40
30	units of Z cost 30 × £3	=	£90
60	units in total cost		£140

So the average overall cost per unit is $\dfrac{£140}{60} = £2.33$

280 BUSINESS MATHS

2 B

The trader buys 90 units costing £10 each
75 units costing £12 each
50 units costing £18 each
45 units costing £20 each

Altogether they have spent 4 × £900 = £3,600 to buy 260 units.

The average price paid is $\frac{£3,600}{260}$ = £13.85

3 C

$$\frac{X+15+22+14+21+15+20+18+27+X}{10} = 20$$

$$\frac{2X+152}{10} = 20$$

$$2X + 152 = 200$$

$$X = 24$$

4 B

Department	Mean wage £	Number of employees £				Total wage
W	50	20	50 × 20 =	1,000
X	100	5	100 × 5 =	500
Y	70	10	70 × 10 =	700
Z	80	5	80 × 5 =	400
				40	2,600

Mean wage per employee = $\frac{2,600}{40}$ = £65.00

5 A

Arrange the scores in ascending order:

9, 12, 23, 24, 28, 34, 43, 56, 78, 87

The 'middle' term falls half way between 28 and 34, i.e. 31

ADDITIONAL QUESTION 1

Automatic filling machines

Arrange in numerical order:

501, 502, 503, 504, 504, 504, 505, 505, 506, 506, 507, 508

(a) (i) The median weight is $\frac{504+505}{2}$ = 504.5 kg.

(ii) The modal weight is 504 kg (it occurs three times).

(iii) To make calculating the arithmetic mean easier you can subtract 500.

$$\text{Mean} = 500 + \frac{1+2+3+4+4+4+5+5+6+6+7+8}{12}$$

$$= 500 + \frac{55}{12}$$

$$= 504.58 \text{ kg}$$

(b) Median becomes 504 kg. (The additional item appears at the beginning of the sequence.)

Mode remains as 504 kg.

Arithmetic mean:

The mean becomes $500 + \dfrac{55-5}{13} = 503.84$ kg.

ADDITIONAL QUESTION 2

Frequency distributions II

(a) Highest value = 469, Lowest value = 347, Range = 122.

Hence for 5 groups (122 ÷ 5 = 24.4), a class interval of 25 will be satisfactory

Production (units)	Tally	Frequency	Cumulative frequency
345 and less than 370	ﬀﬀ ﬀﬀ ﬀﬀ I	16	16
370 and less than 395	ﬀﬀ III	8	24
395 and less than 420	IIII	4	28
420 and less than 445	I	1	29
445 and less than 470	ﬀﬀ ﬀﬀ I	11	40
	Total	40	

(b) **'Less than' ogive of weekly production**

(c) The median as read from the graph is 380 items.

(d) The mean uses all the data and is therefore representative of all the data. It is easy to understand and calculate; it can be used in more advanced statistical theory.

It has the disadvantage that it can be unduly affected by a few extreme values, and it may not correspond to an actual value in the set if the set is discrete.

The median is also easy to understand. It is unaffected by extreme values, it can exist even if the items cannot be quantified, provided they can be ranked. It is a useful compromise between the mean and the mode.

As it does not use all the data, it may not be representative. Data has to be arranged in order of magnitude. It is not suitable for more advanced statistical theory.

Chapter 9

PRACTICE QUESTIONS

1 A

$$\text{Coefficient of variation (\%)} = \frac{\text{Standard deviation}}{\text{Mean}} \times 100$$

Process

W	$10/100$	×	100	=	10
X	$5/40$	×	100	=	12.5
Y	$8/80$	×	100	=	10
Z	$12/150$	×	100	=	8

2 C

The co-efficient of variation is calculated as $\frac{sd}{\bar{x}}$ and measures the relative dispersion of the given data.

3 B

This is the definition of inter-quartile range.

ADDITIONAL QUESTION 1

Dispersion of sales values

Note: the standard deviation is unaffected by subtracting a constant. Hence the data can be simplified by subtracting 200. This will not affect the spread of the data.

Calculations:

x	x − 200 (=d)	d^2
225	25	625
227	27	729
222	22	484
227	27	729
224	24	576
225	25	625
223	23	529
220	20	400
219	19	361
221	21	441
225	25	625
228	28	784
	286	6,908

Standard deviation $= \sqrt{\dfrac{\Sigma d^2}{n} - \left(\dfrac{\Sigma d}{n}\right)^2}$

$= \sqrt{\dfrac{6{,}908}{12} - \left(\dfrac{286}{12}\right)^2}$

$= 2.76\ (\pounds000)$

ADDITIONAL QUESTION 2

Manco plc

(a) The smallest value in the distribution is 105, the largest value in the distribution is 142.

The range to be spanned is 142 – 105, i.e. 37. Class intervals should be of the order of 37 ÷ 8 = 4.625; 5 is recommended. The following grouping is a suggestion.

The classes should be of equal width.

Share price	Tally	Frequency
105 but less than 110	||	2
110 but less than 115	++++	5
115 but less than 120	||||	4
120 but less than 125	++++ |||	8
125 but less than 130	++++ ++++	10
130 but less than 135	++++	5
135 but less than 140	||||	4
140 but less than 145	||	2

(b) To construct the ogive it is first necessary to calculate the cumulative frequency:

Share price	Frequency	Cumulative
105 but less than 110	2	2
110 but less than 115	5	7
115 but less than 120	4	11
120 but less than 125	8	19
125 but less than 130	10	29
130 but less than 135	5	34
135 but less than 140	4	38
140 but less than 145	2	40

Ogive – The price of ordinary 25p shares of Manco plc

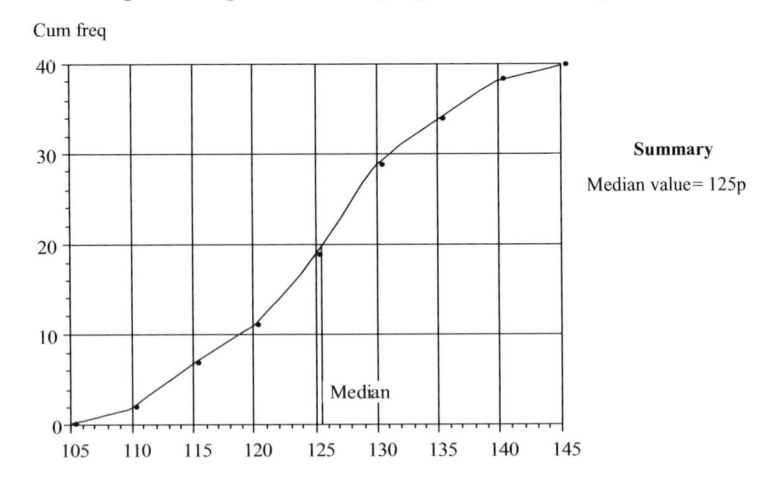

Cum freq

Summary
Median value = 125p

(c)

Share price	Mid point x	f	fx	fx²
105–110	107.5	2	215.0	23,112.50
110–115	112.5	5	562.5	63,281.25
115–120	117.5	4	470.0	55,225.00
120–125	122.5	8	980.0	120,050.00
125–130	127.5	10	1,275.0	162,562.50
130–135	132.5	5	662.5	87,781.25
135–140	137.5	4	550.0	75,625.00
140–145	142.5	2	285.0	40,612.50
		40	5,000.0	628,250.00
		$=\Sigma f$	$=\Sigma fx$	$=\Sigma fx^2$

$$\text{Arithmetic mean} = \frac{\Sigma fx}{\Sigma f} = \frac{5{,}000}{40}$$

$$= 125p$$

$$\text{Standard deviation} = \sqrt{\frac{\Sigma fx^2}{\Sigma f} - \left(\frac{\Sigma fx}{\Sigma f}\right)^2}$$

$$= \sqrt{\frac{628{,}250}{40} - \left(\frac{5{,}000}{40}\right)^2}$$

$$= 9.01$$

(d) This distribution is very nearly symmetrical and so consequently the mean, at 125, and the median, at just over 125, are close to one another.

Chapter 10

PRACTICE QUESTIONS

1 B

$$£10{,}000 \times \frac{142.0}{135.6} = £10{,}472$$

2 B

$$£55.35 \times \frac{100}{135} = £41$$

3 B

$$\frac{109}{100} \times \frac{126}{100} = \frac{13{,}734}{10{,}000} = \frac{137.34}{100}$$

ADDITIONAL QUESTION

Salaries of systems analysts

(a) The purpose of an index number is to show the changes in prices, quantities, wages, etc. over a period of time. Many items can be included in the index, combining them as a weighted average. By expressing this as a percentage of the weighted average in the base year, the index becomes independent of units, so that different items with different units can be compared. For example, prices (£) can be compared with quantities which are not in monetary units.

(b)

	\multicolumn{4}{c}{Comparison with previous years}
	Average salary		Published index	
Year	Increase	%	Increase	%
20X0	–	–	–	–
20X1	1,350	14.2	5.4	6.1
20X2	2,290	21.1	3.2	3.4
20X3	1,160	8.8	4.1	4.2
20X4	630	4.4	5.0	4.9
20X5	650	4.4	8.3	7.8
20X6	620	4.0	10.9	9.5
20X7	600	3.7	7.4	5.9
20X8	700	4.2	5.0	3.7

(c) To convert the salary for year n into the equivalent salary in year 20X8, multiply by I_{20X8}/I_n.

Year	Average salary at 20X8 values
20X0	14,751
20X1	15,885
20X2	18,608
20X3	19,436
20X4	19,343
20X5	18,731
20X6	17,793
20X7	17,429
20X8	17,500

Note:

The value for 20X0 is $\dfrac{9{,}500 \times 138.5}{89.2}$

The value for 20X1 is $\dfrac{10{,}850 \times 138.5}{94.6}$ and so on.

(d) In real terms, based on 20X8 prices, the average salary has steadily decreased from a maximum of £19,436 in 20X3 to £17,500 in 20X8. Comparison of the % increase columns in section (b) shows that this effective decrease is because in every year since 20X4, the published index has increased at a greater rate than the average wage. In the first three years, from 20X0 to 20X3, the reverse was the case, and salaries increased in real terms.

Chapter 11

PRACTICE QUESTIONS

1 C

	Ratio		% defective		
Machine 1 =	6	×	5	=	30
Machine 2 =	3	×	20	=	60
Machine 3 =	$\dfrac{1}{10}$	×	10	=	$\dfrac{10}{100}$

Percentage defects $= \dfrac{100}{10} = 10$

2 D

	Vaccination	No vaccination	Total
Flu	0.05	0.15	0.2
No flu	0.45	0.35	0.8
	0.5	0.5	1

$$P(\text{vaccination/flu}) = \dfrac{P(\text{vaccination and flu})}{P(\text{flu})}$$

$$= \dfrac{0.05}{0.20}$$

$$= 0.25$$

3 D

This is simply the total of 0.23 and 0.21.

4 A

	Large	Small	Total
Fast payer	20	10	30
Slow payer	40	30	70
Total	60	40	100

$P(\text{fast paying small co}) = \dfrac{10}{100} = 0.10$

5   C

P(serious or minor)

= P(serious) + P(minor) [assuming each invoice contains only one type of error]

= 0.06 + 0.12 = 0.18

ADDITIONAL QUESTION

Red, blue and yellow beads

Notes:

1. At the start, there are 4 reds and 7 beads, hence P(red) = 4/7 If the first is red, there will only be 3 reds left out of 6 beads. Hence in this case P(red) = 3/6 As there is only 1 blue bead, it cannot be selected more than once; similarly yellow cannot be selected more than twice.

2. The probability of traversing a path is the product of all the probabilities along it, the 'joint probability'.

   (a) There are six outcomes that give one of each colour (all those except that marked * below), each having the probability $\frac{(4 \times 2 \times 1)}{(7 \times 6 \times 5)}$.

   Hence probability of one of each colour $= 6 \times \frac{4 \times 2 \times 1}{7 \times 6 \times 5}$

   $= \frac{8}{35} = 0.23$

   (b) There is only one colour that can be selected three times, red, see (1) above.

   $P(3 \text{ reds}) = \frac{4}{7} \times \frac{3}{6} \times \frac{2}{5}$

   $= \frac{4}{35} = 0.11$

First bead   *Second bead*   *Third bead*   *Probability*

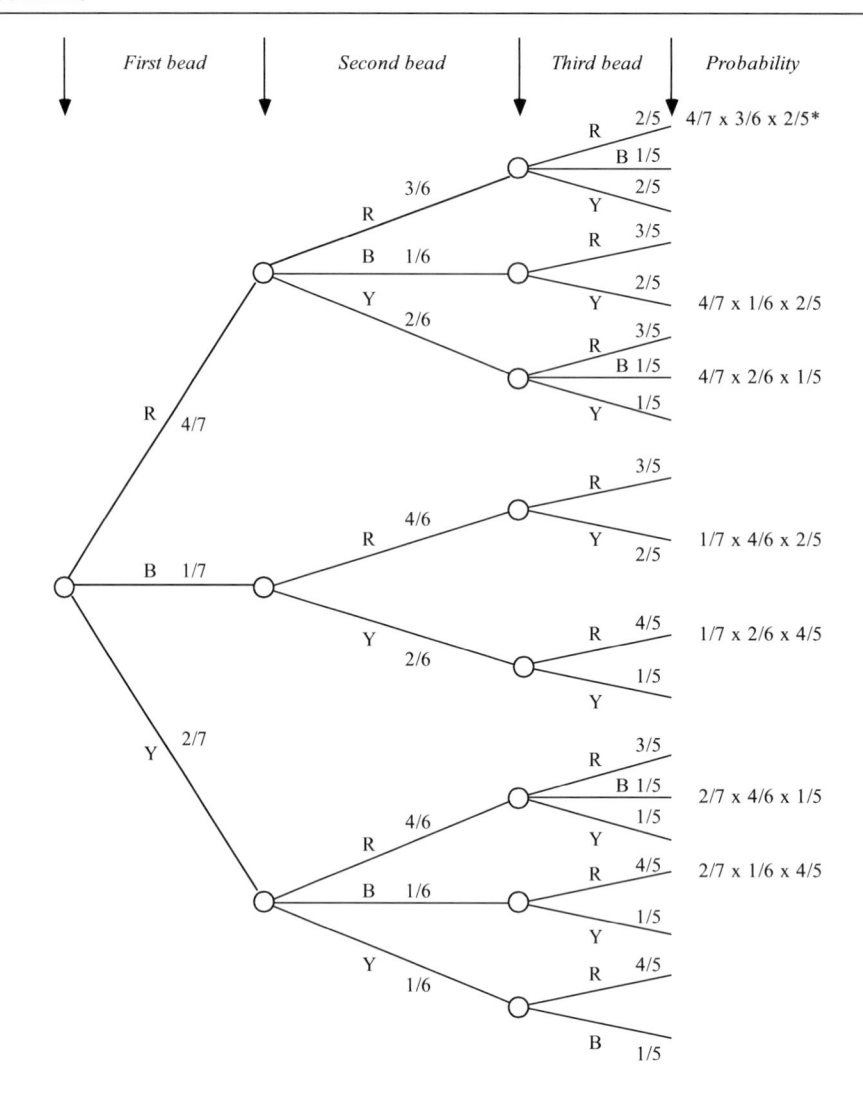

```
                              R  2/5   4/7 x 3/6 x 2/5*
                  R 3/6       B  1/5
                              Y  2/5
                              R  3/5
                  B 1/6       Y  2/5   4/7 x 1/6 x 2/5
       R 4/7      Y 2/6       R  3/5
                              B  1/5   4/7 x 2/6 x 1/5
                              Y  1/5
                              R  3/5
                  R 4/6       Y  2/5   1/7 x 4/6 x 2/5
       B 1/7                  R  4/5   1/7 x 2/6 x 4/5
                  Y 2/6       Y  1/5
                              R  3/5
                  R 4/6       B  1/5   2/7 x 4/6 x 1/5
                              Y  1/5
       Y 2/7                  R  4/5   2/7 x 1/6 x 4/5
                  B 1/6       Y  1/5
                  Y 1/6       R  4/5
                              B  1/5
```

Chapter 12

PRACTICE QUESTIONS

1 **A**

Expected profits:

For W = £30,000

For X = £15,000

For Y = £26,000

For Z = £27,000

ANSWERS TO END OF CHAPTER QUESTIONS 289

2 D

Expected sales

J	0.3 × 10,000	=	3,000
	0.5 × 20,000	=	10,000
	0.2 × 30,000	=	6,000
			19,000
K	0.3 × 10,000	=	3,000
	0.4 × 20,000	=	8,000
	0.3 × 30,000	=	9,000
			20,000
L	0.2 × 10,000	=	2,000
	0.6 × 20,000	=	12,000
	0.2 × 30,000	=	6,000
			20,000

3 B

$p(X) = 0.5$ $p(Y) = \frac{1}{3}$ $p(Z) = \frac{1}{5}$

Contract	Probability p	Profits £x (000)	Expected value of profits £px
X	0.5	50	25
Y	$\frac{1}{3}$	90	30
Z	$\frac{1}{5}$	100	20
			75

Chapter 13

PRACTICE QUESTIONS

1 D

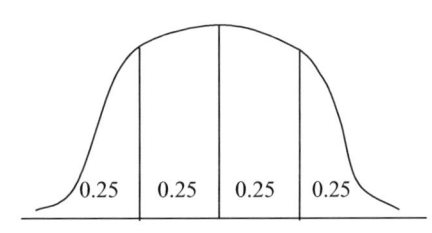

From tables, the Z value required is halfway between $Z = 0.67$ and $Z = 0.68$.

2 D

It is helpful to draw a sketch graph of the situation

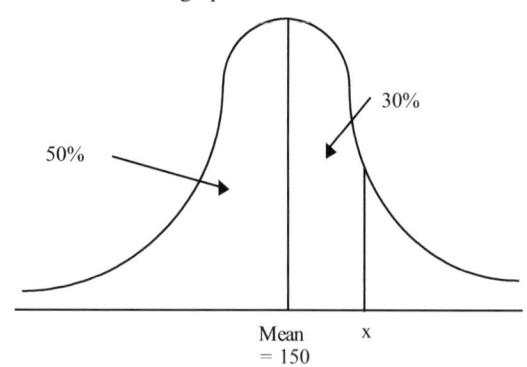

From the normal distribution tables 30% of a distribution lies between the mean and 0.84 standard deviations above the mean. (Find the value in the body of the table nearest to 0.3. This corresponds with the 0.8 row and the 0.04 column.)

Therefore

x   =   150 + (0.84 × 20)

      =   166.8

ADDITIONAL QUESTION

Workers' weekly wages

Note: it is always advisable to draw sketch diagrams for this type of problem. They need not be to scale.

(a)

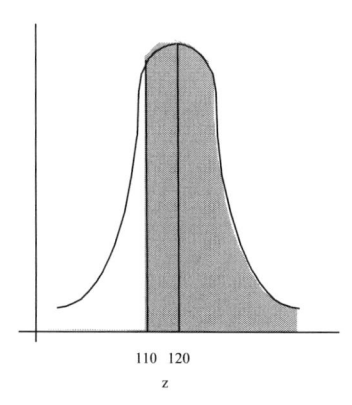

Standardise 110 to give $z = \left(\dfrac{110 - 120}{15}\right)$ = −0.67

From tables, area from 110 to 120 = 0.2486

(The negative value of z means that the area is to the left of the mean.)

P(> 110)   =   0.2486 + 0.5

              =   0.7486

(b)

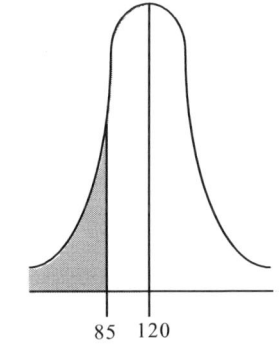

$$z = \frac{85-120}{15}$$

$$= -2.33$$

From tables, the area from 85 to 120 is 0.4901

P(< 85) = 0.5 − 0.4901

= 0.0099

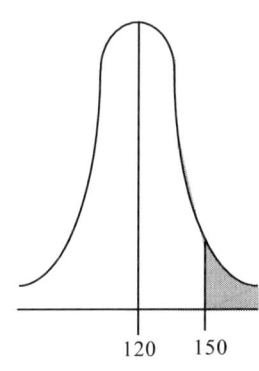

(c)

$$z = \frac{150-120}{15}$$

$$= 2.0$$

From tables, the area from 120 to 150 is 0.4772

P(> 150) = 0.5 − 0.4772

= 0.0228

(d)

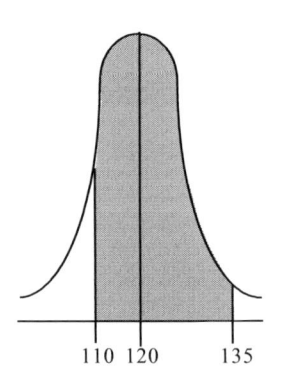

[Normal distribution curve shaded from 110 to 135, marked at 110, 120, 135]

The area from 110 to 120 has already been found (0.2486)

For 135, $\quad z = \dfrac{135-120}{15}$

$\qquad\qquad\quad = 1.0$

Area from 120 to 135 is 0.3413

Hence P(> 110 and < 135) $= 0.2486 + 0.3413$

$\qquad\qquad\qquad\qquad\qquad = 0.5899$

(e)

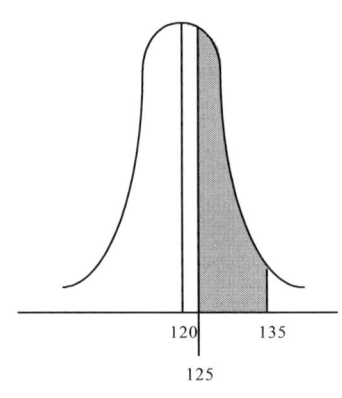

[Normal distribution curve shaded from 125 to 135, marked at 120, 125, 135]

The required area = area from 120 to 135 (= 0.3413) minus the area from 120 to 125.

For 125, $\quad z = \dfrac{125-120}{15}$

$\qquad\qquad\quad = 0.33$

Area from 120 to 125 is 0.1293

Hence P(125 to 135) $= 0.3413 - 0.1293$

$\qquad\qquad\qquad\qquad = 0.212$

(f)

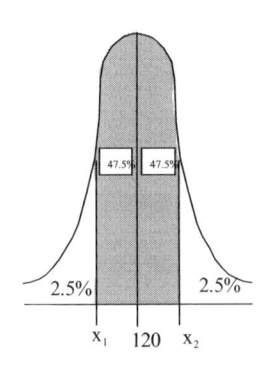

[Normal distribution diagram showing 47.5% on each side of 120, with 2.5% in each tail, and x_1, x_2 as the boundaries]

To find this, the tables must be used in the opposite way, i.e. work outwards from the area found in the body of the table to find the value of z.

For an area of 0.475, z = 1.96

$$\frac{x_2 - 120}{15} = 1.96$$

∴ $x_2 = 120 + 1.96 \times 15 = 149.4$

By symmetry, the lower limit is given by $\frac{x_1 - 120}{15} = -1.96$

∴ $x_1 = 120 - 1.96 \times 15 = 90.6$

Hence the middle 95% lies between £90.60 and £149.40

(g) For an area of 0.49, z = 2.33 (actual area = 0.4901)

∴ $\frac{x - 120}{15} = \pm 2.33$

$x = £120 \pm £15 \times 2.33$

$= £(120 \pm 34.95)$

Hence the middle 98% lies between £85.05 and £154.95

Chapter 14

PRACTICE QUESTIONS

1 C

C = 1,000 + 250P

Costs depend on production

Fixed costs = £1,000

Variable costs per unit = £250

2 A

y = 20 − 0.25x

When x = 12,   y = 20 − 0.25 × 12

y = 20 − 3

y = 17%

BUSINESS MATHS

3   C

$y = a + bx$

$491 = 234 + 20b$

$\therefore b = \dfrac{491 - 234}{20} = 12.85$

4   A

The variable to be predicted depends on some other variable (e.g. factory costs depend on the output achieved).

5   B

ADDITIONAL QUESTION

D & E Ltd

(a)   Scatter graph of electricity cost against production

Electricity costs
(£000)

[Scatter graph with Y-axis showing Electricity costs (£000) from 0 to 20, and X-axis showing Production (000 units) from 0 to 60. Data points plotted at approximately: (20, 5), (20, 10), (30, 10), (30, 15), (35, 10), (35, 10), (40, 14), (45, 17), (55, 20), (60, 18)]

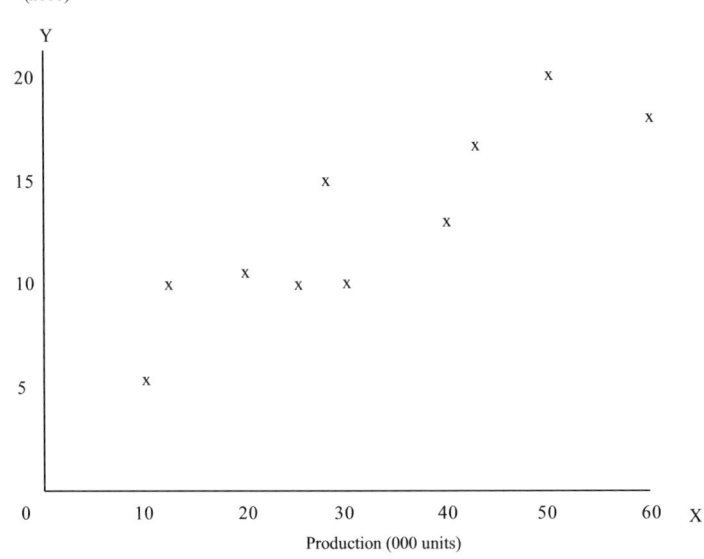

Notes:

(i)   Do not confuse this with a time series graph.

(ii) Choose the scales so that the graph fits the graph paper.

(iii) Do not attempt to draw a line through the scatter graph unless asked to do so.

(iv) Label the axes and state the units.

(b)   The regression line of Y on X is $Y = a + bX$ where

$$b = \dfrac{n\Sigma XY - \Sigma X \Sigma Y}{n\Sigma X^2 - (\Sigma X)^2} \quad \text{and} \quad a = \dfrac{\Sigma Y - b\Sigma X}{n}$$

$\Sigma X = 320$

$\Sigma Y = 130$

$n = 10$

$$b = \frac{10 \times 4{,}728 - 320 \times 130}{10 \times 12{,}614 - (320)^2} = \frac{5{,}680}{23{,}740}$$

$$= 0.2393$$

$$a = \frac{130 - 0.2393 \times 320}{10}$$

$$= 5.34$$

The least squares regression line of electricity costs (Y) on production (X) is therefore:

Y = 5.34 + 0.2393X

where Y is in £000 and X in 000 units.

Explanation

Assuming there is an approximately linear relationship between production and electricity costs, which is shown to be reasonable by the scatter graph, the electricity costs are made up of two parts, a fixed cost (independent of the volume of production) of £5,340 and a variable cost per unit of production of £239.30 per 1,000 units or 23.9p per unit).

(c) For quarter 11, X = 15, hence:

Y = 5.34 + 0.2393 × 15

= 8.93

The predicted electricity cost for quarter 11 is therefore £8,930.

For quarter 12, X = 55, hence:

Y = 5.34 + 0.2393 × 55

= 18.50

The predicted electricity cost for quarter 12 is therefore £18,500.

(d) There are two main sources of error in the forecasts:

(i) The assumed relationship between Y and X.

The scatter graph shows that there can be fairly wide variations in Y for a given X. Also the forecast assumes that the same conditions will prevail over the next two quarters as in the last ten quarters.

(ii) The predicted production for quarters 11 and 12.

No indication is given as to how these planned production values were arrived at, so that it is not possible to assess how reliable they are. If they are based on extrapolation of a time series for production over the past ten quarters, they will be subject to the errors inherent in such extrapolations.

Provided conditions remain similar to the past ten quarters, it can be concluded that the forecasts would be fairly reliable but subject to some variation.

Note: methods for calculation of confidence limits for forecasts are available.

Chapter 15

PRACTICE QUESTIONS

1 B

Multiplicative model: forecast = T × S

Sales last quarter = 240 (Q_2)

Seasonality for Q_2 = +50%, ∴ S = 150

$$\text{Trend} = \frac{\text{data}}{\text{seasonality}}$$

$$\text{Trend} = \frac{240}{150} \times 100 = 160$$

Assuming a constant trend, T = 160 for Q_3

Seasonality = -50% ∴ S = 50

$$\text{Forecast} = 160 \times \frac{50}{100} = 80$$

2 A

x = 16, trend value = 345.12 − 1.35 × 16 = 323.52

Seasonally adjusted = 323.52 − 23.62 = **300 in whole units**

3 B

Trend y = 7.112 + 3.949x

Seasonal variation 1.12 × trend

So for month 19 y = (7.112 + 3.949 × 19) × 1.12

y = 92

ADDITIONAL QUESTION

Report on sales

Quarterly sales of brands A, B and C

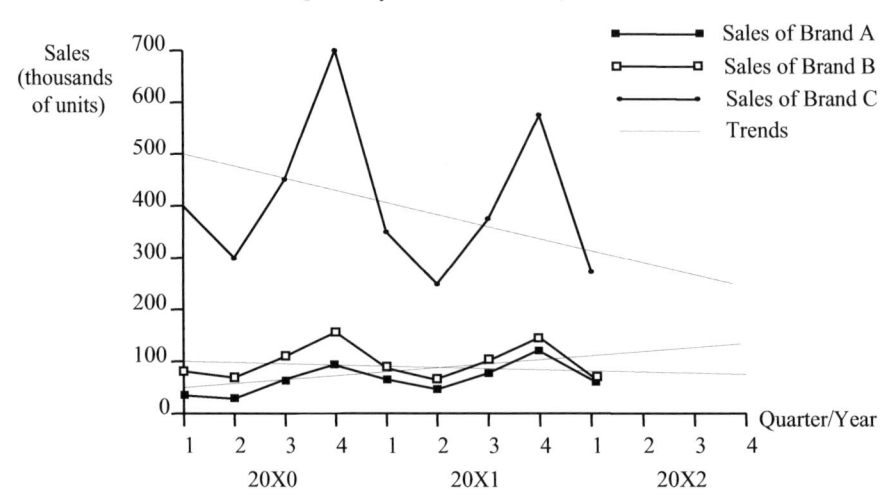

Summary table

	A			B			C			Total		
	20X0	20X1	20X2*	20X0	20X1	20X2*	20X0	20X1	20X2*	20X0	20X1	20X2*
Annual sales (000 units)	237	317	397	400	400	400	1,850	1,530	1,210			
Annual contribution (£000)	23.7	31.7	39.7	40	40	40	185	153	121	248.7	224.7	200.7
% of total for group	9.5	14.1	19.8	16.1	17.8	19.9	74.4	68.1	60.3			

* Estimated

Tutorial note: detailed time series analysis was not required. The values for 20X2 were therefore predicted by the crude method of assuming the same difference in the annual values from 20X1 to 20X2 as there was from 20X0 to 20X1.

The fact that the first quarter sales for 20X2 show the same trend as the previous first quarters for each brand (this can be seen from the graph) indicate that this is a reasonable assumption.

Points to note (at least five are required)

(a) Each brand has a strong seasonal variation.

(b) The seasonal variation occurs at the same time for each brand, being lowest in Q_2 and highest in Q_4.

(c) Brand A has an increasing trend of approximately 80,000 units per year.

(d) Brand B has a constant trend (i.e. no increase or decrease).

(e) Brand C has a decreasing trend of approximately 320,000 units per year.

(f) The total market is decreasing by approximately £24,000 per year.

(g) Brand C at present has the largest share of the market, but this is decreasing.

(h) Brands A and B have an increasing share of a decreasing market.

(i) Sales of Brand A will probably overtake those of Brand B in 20X2.

(j) The forecasts of performance for 20X2, as given in the summary table.

Chapter 16

PRACTICE QUESTIONS

1

=(6*D13-B13*C13)/(((6*E13-B13^2)*(6*F13-C13^2))^0.5

2

The formula for NPV assumes that the first cash flow is at t=1, not t=0 as is the case here. Thus the formula needs to be amended to

=NPV(0.10,C4:F4)+B4

Index

A
A priori probability, 173
Accuracy, 35
Addition, 2
Addition law, 175
Additive model, 239
Algebra, 42
Algebraic expression, 42
Amortisation, 86
Annual percentage rate (APR), 78
Annuities, 83
Annuity tables, 85
Antilog tables, 14
Applications, 208
Approximation, 42
Arithmetic mean, 132
Arithmetic mean of combined data, 135
Arithmetical progressions, 72
At least one event occurs, 180
Averages, 132

B
BANANA mnemonic (IRR), 90
Base year, 160
Basic mathematics, 2
BEDMAS mnemonic (order of operations), 3
Brackets, 4, 43

C
Calculator, 14, 31, 228
Calculator - and fractions, 179
Causal forecasting, 230
Certainty, 195
Chain base index numbers, 164
Class intervals, 111
Class limits, 111
Classification of data, 109
Coefficient, 42
Coefficient of correlation, 226
Coefficient of determination (r^2), 227
Coefficient of variation, 151
Combined normal distributions, 210
Common difference, 72
Common ratio, 73
Communication, 105
Complement, 180
Complementary probabilities, 180
Compound depreciation, 79
Compound interest, 76
Conditional probability, 184
Constant, 50
Contingency tables, 184
Continuous variables, 42, 133
Correlation, 216, 224, 226
Correlation coefficient, 226
Cumulative frequency graph (ogive), 136
Cumulative present value tables, 85
Cyclical variations, 237, 243

D
Data analysis, 127
Data and information, 104
Decimal equivalents, 31
Decimal places, 40
Decision analysis, 195
Decision criteria, 199
Decisions made under uncertainty, 195
Deflating a monetary series, 167
Denominator, 5
Dependent events, 179
Dependent variable, 44, 216
Diagrams and graphs, 116
Discount rate, 91
Discounting, 82
Discounts, 28
Discrete variables, 42, 133
Dispersion, 146
Division, 3

E
Empirical probability, 173
Equations, 44
Equation of a straight line, 50, 218
Exceptions, 128
Expanding brackets, 4
Expected frequencies, 210
Expected value (EV), 194
Exponent, 3, 7
Extrapolation, 224, 225

F
Factorisation, 52, 54
Forecasting using correlation and regression, 230
Forecasting using time series, 250
Formulae, 42
Fractional exponents, 9
Fractions, 5, 44
Frequency, 109
Frequency curves, 124
Frequency distributions, 109, 133
Frequency polygons, 124

G
Geometrical progressions, 73, 77
Good information, 104
Gradient, 50, 51

Graphical solution of simultaneous equations, 58
Graphing linear equations, 49
Graphs, 49
Graphs and diagrams, 116
Graphs of the quadratic function, 56
Grouped data, 133
Grouped frequency distribution, 109

H
Histograms, 122, 139

I
Independent events, 178
Independent variable, 44, 216
Index, 7
Index numbers, 159, 160
Infinite geometrical progression, 74
Inflation, 160
Information, 104
Information – cost of, 107
Information – qualities, 104
Information – value of, 106
Information requirements, 104
Integer, 42
Intercept, 50, 51
Internal rate of return, 89, 90
Interpolation, 224
Investment decisions, 90

L
Laws of probability, 175
Least squares linear regression, 220
Like terms, 42
Limitations of expected values, 198
Line of best fit, 218
Linear correlation, 218
Linear equations, 46, 49
Loans, mortgages and amortisation, 86
Log tables, 12

Logarithms, 11
Long-term trends, 237
Lowest common denominator, 6

M
Maximisation of expected value, 196
Mean, 132, 205
Mean for grouped data, 133
Measures of dispersion, 146
Median, 135
Mode, 137
Models, 127
Mortgages, 86
Moving averages, 240, 241
Multi-item indices, 162
Multiple bar chart, 118
Multiplication, 3
Multiplication law, 178, 179
Multiplicative model, 239

N
Negative exponents, 9
Negative numbers, 2
Negatively skewed distribution, 153
Net present value (NPV), 88, 90
Non-linear correlation, 217
Non-mutually exclusive events, 177
Normal curve - features of, 205
Normal distribution, 152, 204
Normal distribution table, 205
Numerator, 5

O
Ogive, 125, 136
Open ended class intervals, 111
Operators, 2
Order of operations, 3

P
Pay-off table, 197
Pearson's correlation coefficient (r), 226
Percentage component bar chart, 118

Percentage increase, 27
Percentage relatives, 160
Percentages, 26
Perpetuities, 87
Pictograms, 116
Pie charts, 119
Positive correlation, 217
Powers, 7, 10
Power of a product, 8
Powers and roots, 3
Precision, 41
Present value, 82
Price relative index, 160
Principal, 75
Probability, 172
Probability trees, 187
Project appraisal, 92
Proportions, 30
PV tables, 83

Q
Quadratic equations, 52
Quadratic function, 56
Quadratics - solution by formula, 54
Quality control, 210
Quantity relative index, 160

R
RC Cactus mnemonic (good information), 107
Random variations, 237
Range, 146
Ratios, 29
Rebasing an index, 166
Regression, 218, 224
Regression line of x on y, 223
Relax mnemonic for x axis, 49
Repeated trials, 173, 188
Replay button on calculators, 16
Residual variations, 237
Retail Price Index (RPI), 162, 165, 166
Risk, 195
Roots, 7, 10

Roots of a quadratic equation, 52
Rounding, 36

S

Scatter diagrams, 216
Scientific calculator, 14
Seasonal variation, 237, 245
Seasonally adjusted figures, 249
Sequences and series, 72
Sigma, 132
Significant digits, 40
Significant figures, 40
Simple bar chart, 117
Simple indices, 160
Simple interest, 75
Simultaneous equations, 46
Sinking fund, 81
Skewed distribution, 152
Skewness, 152, 153
Speculative risk, 195
Spreadsheets, 121
Spurious correlation, 227
Standard deviation, 147, 205
Standardised variables, 205
Subjective probability, 173
Subtraction, 3
Sum of the means, 150
Sum of the variances, 150
Symbols, 2
Symmetry, 152, 153

T

Tabulation of data, 108
Terms, 42
Time series, 236
Time series - additive model, 239
Time series - multiplicative model, 239
Time series graph, 238
Trend, 240
Trend extrapolation, 231
Trend lines, 218
Two possible outcomes, 180

U

Uncertainty, 195
Unequal class intervals, 122
Ungrouped data, 109, 132

V

Variables, 44
Variance, 150, 211

W

Weighted average, 133
Weighted indices, 162

Z

Z variables, 205
Zero exponent, 9